S

MADAME VESTRIS AND HER TIMES

Yours

Eliza Mathews

MADAME VESTRIS
AND HER TIMES

BY

CHARLES E. PEARCE

BENJAMIN BLOM   New York/London

Reissued 1969 by
Benjamin Blom, Inc., Bronx, New York 10452
and 56 Doughty Street, London, W.C. 1

Library of Congress Catalog Card Number 70-77975

Printed in U.S.A. by
NOBLE OFFSET PRINTERS, INC.
NEW YORK 3, N. Y.

INTRODUCTION

THROUGHOUT the adventurous life of Madame Vestris one fact is prominent : the publicity which accompanied every step of her career from her debut at the King's Theatre in 1815 to her final appearance on the stage at the Lyceum in 1854. It would be difficult to find another actress who so stamped her personality on the public mind. One may well assume that her admirers did not think so much of the characters she impersonated—no matter what they were—as of Vestris herself, her lovely voice, her irresistible smile, her magnetic gaiety, the perfection of her figure, the grace of her movements, and the indefinable charm with which she invested every part she undertook. Even those who looked askance at the stage and all who belonged to it could not escape the fascination of her name. She was the favourite theme of conversation with all ranks, her frailties were regarded with indulgence, she was an *enfant gâtée* to be pardoned rather than reproved. Both on and off the stage her doings provided excellent " copy " for the journalist, and a diligent perusal of the newspapers of the period supplies ample material for the biographer. Of this material I have fully availed myself, justification, I hope, being found in the endeavour to picture the characteristics of a fascinating and remarkable woman and in the desire to do justice to her one-and-twenty years' influence on dramatic art as the first woman theatrical manager.

I have to acknowledge my indebtedness to Mr. Guy Tracey Watts, of Lincoln's Inn, barrister-at-

3

law, for the use of much valuable matter collected for a biography of Madame Vestris which he contemplated, but which for various reasons he was compelled to abandon. Some of the illustrations, it is to be noted, are reproductions from the collection of the late A. M. Broadley, and were placed at my disposal by Mr. Broadley at the time of the projection of the book. The portrait of Isaac Nathan is from an engraving in the possession of his grandson, Mr. Douglas M. Gane, to whom I tender my thanks.

CHARLES E. PEARCE.

CONTENTS

CHAPTER I

THE DEBUT OF LUCIA ELIZABETTA

First appearance of Madame Vestris. The King's Theatre in 1815. Its interior. The "Omnibus" box and its privileges. "Fops' Alley." Lighted by lamps. Madame Vestris at eighteen. Her beauty and fascination. Appears in the opera *Il Ratto di Proserpina*. Favourable surroundings attend her debut. A pleasure-loving period. Chequered history of the King's Theatre. Mr. Taylor the eccentric and improvident proprietor. Perpetual litigation. Taylor "manages" the theatre from the inside of the King's Bench Prison. War between Taylor and the proprietors. A merry party in the King's Bench Prison. Lady Ladd's method of curing inebriety

CHAPTER II

THE BARTOLOZZIS' FAMILY HISTORY

Madame Vestris's good luck. Her chances in Italian opera. The King's Theatre green-room. Its bad reputation. "Omnibus-box" admirers of singers and dancers. Madame Vestris's family history. The mysterious Captain Best. His fatal duel with Lord Camelford. Vestris's dissolute husband, Armand Vestris, an unprepossessing person .   .

CHAPTER III

VESTRIS IN ITALIAN OPERA

Von Winter's *Il Ratto di Proserpina*. Grassini and Billington's curious arrangement. Their dispute. Michael Kelly's ruse to reconcile them. Vestris's success in the opera. A fashionable audience of 1815. Gentlemen's dress for the opera *de rigueur*. "Calls" before the curtain—their origin. Princess Charlotte of Wales enthusiastic over Vestris's voice and acting. Her charm of expression. Her husband, Armand Vestris, arrested for debt. A doubtful story of an intrigue with the Prince Regent. Scurrilous scribblers. *Il Ratto di Proserpina* with Elizabetta Vestris, repeated in 1816. Curious reason for the postponement of the opening performance. Furore over Braham's singing in Mozart's *Clemenza di Tito*. Armand Vestris's ballet. Elizabetta as Susanna in *Le Nozze di Figaro* .   .   .   .

CHAPTER IV

VESTRIS AND ELLISTON

The parting of Madame Vestris and her husband. She sings at the Paris Italian Opera and is the life of a "certain sort of society." Her alleged association with Windham Anstruther. The association dissolved. Madame Vestris introduced to Elliston, the manager of Drury Lane Theatre. Her first appearance at Drury Lane. Elliston and his eccentricities. His production of the *Coronation*. Poses as George IV. Vestris makes a hit in *The Siege of Belgrade*. Her success in *Artaxerxes*. Braham's extravagant style

5

CONTENTS

CHAPTER V

" GIOVANNI IN LONDON "

CHAPTER VI

MADAME THE TALK OF THE TOWN

CHAPTER VII

THE MONTAGU GORE AFFAIR

CHAPTER VIII

THE WAYS OF PRIMA DONNAS

CHAPTER IX

SQUABBLES AT THE KING'S THEATRE

CHAPTER X

THE MARIA FOOTE SCANDAL

CHAPTER XI

VESTRIS AND " CHERRY RIPE "

CHAPTER XII

MADAME'S MORALS CENSURED

CHAPTER XIII

MADAME AND HER ADMIRERS

CONTENTS

CHAPTER XVIII

THE CLIMAX OF EMBARRASSMENTS

CHAPTER XIX

MADAME'S MARRIAGE. THE AMERICAN TOUR

CHAPTER XX

FROM THE OLYMPIC TO COVENT GARDEN

CHAPTER XXI

DIFFICULTIES OF THEATRICAL MANAGEMENT

CHAPTER XXII

VESTRIS REVOLUTIONISES THEATRICAL ART

CONTENTS

CHAPTER XXIII

VESTRIS *VERSUS* MACREADY

CHAPTER XXIV

A STORMY TIME AT DRURY LANE

CHAPTER XXV

THE END OF A GREAT CAREER

LIST OF ILLUSTRATIONS

MADAME VESTRIS AND HER TIMES

CHAPTER I

THE DEBUT OF LUCIA ELIZABETTA

First appearance of Madame Vestris. The King's Theatre in 1815. Its interior. The "Omnibus" box and its privileges. "Fops' Alley." Lighted by lamps. Madame Vestris at eighteen. Her beauty and fascination. Appears in the opera *Il Ratto di Proserpina*. Favourable surroundings attend her debut. A pleasure-loving period. Chequered history of the King's Theatre. Mr. Taylor the eccentric and improvident proprietor. Perpetual litigation. Taylor "manages" the theatre from the inside of the King's Bench Prison. War between Taylor and the proprietors. A merry party in the King's Bench Prison. Lady Ladd's method of curing inebriety.

" King's Theatre. Monsieur Armund [*sic*] Vestris, Ballet Master, has the honour to inform the Nobility, Subscribers to the Opera, and the Public, that his Benefit is fixed for this Evening [the 20th of July], on which occasion will be produced, for that night only, the celebrated Opera, composed by Winter, entitled Il Ratto di Proserpina, in which Madame Vestris, late Miss Bartolozzi, will make her first appearance on any stage, in the part of Proserpina."

The above advertisement appeared in the London daily papers for 1815 on the day in question. Other attractions were also announced, but they do not concern us. It is sufficient to say that the mention of " Madame Vestris, late Miss Bartolozzi " was bound to excite the interest of the patrons of the opera, a large proportion of whom were members of the aristocracy.

The opera of those days was the " preserve " of the upper ten. The original King's Theatre, burnt down in 1789, was rebuilt in 1792 and constructed mainly to suit the requirements of its noble patrons. It was re-christened Her Majesty's when Queen Victoria ascended the throne and was again consumed by fire in 1867.

The exterior in 1815 was very like other play-houses of by-gone days, plain and unpretentious ; the colonnade, which gave it the distinctive character which many Londoners will remember, being added in 1820 by Nash, the architect who laid out Regent Street and who much favoured this type of architectural adornment. The principal feature of the interior—not forgotten, one may venture to surmise, by those septuagenarians who in their early days were opera-goers—was the number of boxes which, curving in horseshoe form, rose tier upon tier to the gallery and overlooked a pit of considerable area. There was no dress circle, and stalls were additions of later years —in 1829 to be precise—to the great disgust of the pittites, who hissed heartily but went no further, as they might have done twenty years before in the O.P. rioting days.

Of the boxes, sixty-eight were the private property of the holders, and the object of this unusual arrangement was to raise the money for rebuilding the theatre after its destruction in 1789—a method adopted by the projectors of the Albert Hall, many of the boxes and stalls in which are still held by the original purchasers as their personal property. The trust deed held by Mr. Taylor, the lessee, enabled him to dispose of forty-one boxes (known as property boxes) at one thousand pounds each for various terms, all of which expired in 1824 or 1825. As time went on these property boxes increased until they reached the number already mentioned. After 1825 many of the boxes were hired for the season and were paid for, occupied or not. The owner of the box for the time being had the right of giving it to his friends (each box held six persons) or of letting either for a period or for the whole season. The opera admissions were " bones," an ivory disc a little larger than a penny, and had on one side " Opera for " whatever the year might be, and on the other the name of the lessee of the box. When anything particularly attractive—usually a ballet was the "draw" —was on, the boxes would be filled by representatives of the fashionable world together with a considerable sprinkling of rich persons of humble birth desirous of rubbing shoulders with the aristocracy and of partaking in their exotic pleasures. The pit, sometimes called the " general boxes," was patronised by the middle classes; the gallery, known, oddly enough, as the " pit," was chiefly occupied by the servants of the occupants of the boxes.

Certain peculiarities attached to the boxes. Those at the back of the pit and on a level with it were at first called " resurrection " boxes, for what reason it is hard now to say, the name subsequently dying out. A permanent distinction was the " omnibus " box, a compartment of ample accommodation at each end of the stage and below its level. The renters of the " omnibus " box were permitted to go behind the scenes, where they flirted and philandered with the stars of the opera and ballet without let or hindrance.

A description of the interior of the theatre would not be complete without mention of " Fops' Alley," a feature of almost historic interest. " Fops' Alley" was the favourite lounge of the dandies, partly to see the performance, but chiefly, we suspect, to be admired by the ladies in the boxes and to ogle them when opportunity served. Lumley, in his *Reminiscences of the Opera*, thus describes it : " From an entrance occupying the centre of the lowest tier of boxes a few steps descended to the back of the pit, down

the centre of which a broad space was left un-
encumbered to within a few feet of the orchestra.
This formed the renowned ' Fops' Alley.' "

Although gas had been tried as an experiment in
the Lyceum Theatre in 1803, its use in 1815 was confined to a few of the public streets. The lighting of
the King's Theatre was probably the plan introduced
by Garrick from the Continent when the six heavy chan-
deliers, each containing twelve candles suspended over
the stage, were done away with and the stage was lit
by lamps not visible to the audience. " Taking away
the candle rings and lighting from behind," said a
writer in a contemporary newspaper contemptuously,
" the only advantage we have discovered from Mr.
Garrick's tour abroad." There were footlights—of a
sort—in addition.

The imperfect lighting of the theatre would favour
the interchange of amorous glances. Such a thing
would be very difficult in these days of brilliancy and
opera-glasses—at least without remark. Decorum
in places of public resort is now strictly insisted upon
and for the most part strictly observed, but a century
or so ago considerable latitude was the rule. The
days of candles and candle-snuffers were over and the
lamps no doubt gave a better light—when they did
not smoke and smell. It may be that the belles in
the boxes did not find the dimness a disadvantage.
Defects in complexion, or feature, if not concealed,
were softened thereby.

Young Madame Vestris, who, it is not to be questioned, was quite conscious of her charms, might have
preferred some better illumination to show them to
advantage. On the other hand, her artistic temperament and pardonable desire to make the best of herself
probably told her that she looked better—as every
woman does—in a soft, subdued light than in a glaring
one. Hazlitt, writing in 1820 of the opening of the
Lyceum by Arnold under the name of the New English
Opera-house, said as much from another point of

ARMAND VESTRIS,
First Husband of Madame Vestris.

view : " We like a play," he declared, " when we do not see the faces of the actors too near. We do not want to be informed, as at the Little Theatre in the Haymarket, that part of the rich humour of Mr. Liston's face arises from his having lost a tooth in front nor to see Mr. Jones's eyes roll more meteorous than ever. At the larger theatres we only discover that the ladies paint red ; at the smaller ones we can distinguish when they paint white. We see defects enough at a distance, and we can always get near enough (in the pit) to see the beauties. Those who go to the boxes do not go to see the play but to make a figure and be thought something of themselves (so far they probably succeed, at least in their own opinion) and if the gods cannot see they can make themselves heard."

Lucia Elizabetta Vestris—to give her her full name ; when she became famous no one thought of her as " Lucia "—commenced her career with powerful allies. She had youth, good looks, and luck on her side. Though she had been two years a wife, she was but eighteen. Without claims to satisfy the exacting connoisseur to whom regularity of features is everything, she had what was infinitely preferable, eyes which could be languishing or sparkling as occasion demanded, ripe lips, mobile and delightfully shaped, a firm, round chin, and an enchanting smile. Add to this a melodious voice, the seductive lusciousness of which would stir the heart of an anchorite, and a figure a model of womanly grace. The full perfection of that figure was, however, not developed at eighteen years of age, and had it been the decorous dress of Proserpina would not have revealed it. The culmination of her attractions was some six years later, when in the daring *Giovanni in London* and as Captain Macheath she took the town by storm. But as she was in 1815 she was as well equipped for conquest as any woman, who was burning to see the world at her feet, could desire ; for apart from her physical endowments, she had courage and plenty of will-power, she was intelligent, she was as shrewd as she was witty, and—no common gift in those days—she could tolerate nothing that was inartistic.

The time of her advent was propitious. The victory of Waterloo was little more than a month old. The stress and strain of a long war had passed away. The dread of " Boney," of an invasion of our shores, of the press-gang and excessive taxation, was over. There perhaps was not so much rejoicing at the prospect of peace as a feeling of relief that an intolerable burden and menace no longer existed. People gave themselves up to pleasure according to their various tastes. The "fashionables" revelled in festivities at their own houses. The *Morning Post* duly recorded how this or that nobleman and lady leader of fashion gave " an elegant ball and supper "—" a large rout " —" a card party "—" a splendid rout "—" a grand rout "—" a fashionable party "—" a large assembly " —" entertained a large party of fashionables " : the Court journalist must have been at his wit's ends to find appropriate adjectives for the innumerable society functions. Lords and ladies with money to spend and nothing to do hailed the announcement of a new aspirant for operatic honours with gratitude as a relief from *ennui*, for the time being the fashionable ailment.

The sudden cessation of war's alarms was not the only thing in Elizabetta's favour. For nearly seven years the affairs of the King's Theatre had been in a state of apparently inextricable confusion, and only in 1815 had the management subsided into something approaching settlement and business-like order. The curious circumstances attending the transition period of the King's Theatre are such as belonged peculiarly to the times, and for this reason the story is worth relating, especially as the peaceful end synchronised with the stepping-stones trodden by Elizabetta Vestris towards fame and popularity.

When the theatre was burnt down in 1789, a Mr. Taylor was the proprietor, and in 1803 he sold to

Mr. Francis Goold one-third of the new building. Goold was to have the entire management of the theatre during their joint lives, and it was to devolve, on the decease of either of them, on the survivor. Taylor, who, says Ebers, " had all Sheridan's deficiency of financial management without that extraordinary man's resources," got into difficulties and mortgaged the rest of his interest in the theatre to Goold. In course of time Goold died, and then commenced interminable litigation between Mr. Waters, Goold's acting executor, and Taylor. Waters entered upon a suit in Chancery against Taylor to have a manager appointed in his place, but no change took place before 1813 when the Lord Chancellor made his decree, ordering that the partnership between Taylor and Waters should be dissolved, accounts taken between them, and the house sold. But matters were by no means settled, for the Chancellor, having no ear for music nor sympathy with the subscribers and owners of the boxes, refused to appoint a manager and the house was shut up.

In April 1814, however, the house opened under the management of Waters, and the new régime was inaugurated with what was remarkably like a free fight. On Waters's agents presenting themselves at the theatre, Taylor's people, who were still there, refused to admit the newcomers. The latter were the stronger party and turned out the possessors. The triumph was but short-lived, for the Taylorites, having gathered reinforcements, returned at night and retook the contested edifice. Hostilities were eventually put an end to by the Lord Chancellor, and the season commenced in 1815 and proved highly successful, for, it being the year of the peace, various foreign princes and ambassadors were in London and not a night passed without several of these distinguished persons being present. The Prince Regent was also fairly constant in his attendance.

The odd thing was, and it is very characteristic

of that happy-go-lucky period incident to the rule
of the "First Gentleman in Europe," that for years
previous to the trouble with Waters Taylor had
never lived out of the rules of the King's Bench. Ebers,
who afterwards ran the opera for several seasons, did
his best to finance the improvident manager (it was
the interest of Ebers to do so, as he had the letting of
the boxes in his hands) and was in a state of constant
worry. "How can you conduct the management of the
King's Theatre," said Ebers to Taylor one day, " per-
petually in durance as you are ? " " My dear fellow,"
was the Sheridanesque reply, " how could I possibly
conduct it if I were at liberty ? I should be eaten
up, sir—devoured. Here comes a dancer—' Mr.
Taylor, I want such a dress ' ; another, ' I want such-
and-such ornaments.' One singer demands to sing in
a part not allotted to him ; another to have an addition
to his appointment. No—let *me* be shut up and
they go to Masterson (Taylor's secretary) ; he, they
are aware, cannot go beyond his line ; but if they get
at *me*, pshaw ! no man at large can manage that
theatre, and in faith," he added, " no man that under-
takes it *ought* to go at large ! "

Shut up though he was, Taylor contrived to set
everyone by the ears—to his own great satisfaction.
As a protest against his raising the rate of subscription,
a number of the subscribers combined and the Panthéon in Oxford Street, celebrated in the eighteenth
century for its masquerades, being disengaged, Caldas,
a Portuguese wine merchant, undertook the management under a licence to Colonel Greville (an enterprising man about town and sportsman to whom the
early- and mid-Victorian bloods owed that place of
gaiety the Argyll Rooms, and who was the originator
of " picnics ") for the performance of concerts, burlettas, and such other musical entertainments as could
be performed without infringing the exclusive licence
of the King's Theatre.

The effect of the opposition was to reduce the

receipts of the older house, and the opinion was expressed that could the Panthéon have been licensed as an opera-house the other theatre had inevitably been ruined. The litigious Taylor cared little for this, and when the Panthéon closed he had a project of taking it and turning it against the opera-house, as it had formerly been turned against himself. But this project he was never able to bring about. Ebers says, " It was impossible to do anything effectually for Taylor. It seemed his delight to involve himself and, as much as it was possible, to perplex others. He quarrelled with everybody, ridiculed everybody, and hoaxed everybody." He was a fellow of infinite merriment, and his manner was so persuasive that Ebers found it difficult to refuse his requests for money.

Taylor was as disregardful of the rules of the King's Bench as he was of the rights of Waters and of the box owners. Whenever inclined to indulge in his favourite amusement of fishing, he would somehow manage to escape and live in perfect tranquillity in some obscure village, until recaptured. It was a mystery how, utterly impecunious, as he was believed to be, he contrived to obtain the money for his mad freaks. On one occasion he bought an estate in the country and " here he lived and ate, drank and fished, till at the end of two or three months the officers of the law hooked him." On another occasion he actually went down to Hull and put up as a candidate for Parliament. Needless to say he was not returned.

The man seems to have been more at home inside the King's Bench Prison than anywhere else. Here he entertained his friends, and some of his parties must have been exceedingly free and easy. Ebers mentions one of these Bohemian gatherings at which Sir John Ladd, Lady Ladd, and Nelson's Lady Hamilton were among the guests, and Taylor having drunk too much wine, Lady Ladd thought fit by way of correction to pour the contents of a boiling kettle upon him !

Others times, other manners. This Sir John Ladd (or Lade) had been the manager of the royal stables, and having married a very pretty wife, formerly a cookmaid in the royal kitchen, received a knighthood from the Prince Regent in consequence. He was an illiterate fellow, and was happier in his groom's dress than in the high collar and stiff cravat of fashion. He was probably as much entitled to his knighthood as hosts of others who had received the same dignity during the Regency. As for Lady Ladd, the manners of the kitchen came more naturally to her than those of the drawing-room. Her method of administering a rebuke certainly belonged to the first.

CHAPTER II

Madame Vestris's good luck. Her chances in Italian opera. The King's Theatre green-room. Its bad reputation. " Omnibus-box " admirers of singers and dancers. Madame Vestris's family history. The mysterious Captain Best. His fatal duel with Lord Camelford. Vestris's dissolute husband, Armand Vestris, an unprepossessing person.

WHEN Madame Vestris made her debut there was, so far as the operatic stage was concerned, no rival of any consequence against whom she could be pitted. No great Italian star was in the ascendant. Madame Grassini's glories had faded and she had left London, never to return. Catalani was in retirement in Paris. Mrs. Billington, who was able to sing higher than any of her compeers, and excelled all in the abundant elaboration of her roulades which she introduced in season and out of season, was past her zenith and had quitted the operatic world ; Miss Paton, a charming singer and an accomplished vocalist but with very little imagination, was too young for public life ; and the only operatic artist of any importance was Miss Stephens. But where Eliza Vestris was concerned, Kitty Stephens hardly counted ; she never essayed Italian opera and was contented with British musical plays, in the ballads of which she was acknowledged to be the most delightful warbler who had ever appeared on the stage.

Madame Vestris consequently had every chance of making a name in Italian opera. Writing of her last appearance at the King's Theatre in 1827, Mr.

H. F. Chorley said: "There, if she had possessed musical patience and energy, she might have queened it, because she possessed (half Italian by birth) one of the most luscious of low voices—found, since Hero's time, excellent in women—great personal beauty, an almost faultless figure, which she knew how to adorn with consummate art, and no common stage address. But a less arduous theatrical career pleased her better; and so she, too, could not—one might perhaps say because she *would* not—remain on the Italian stage."

Of a truth she had the ball at her foot, but when she appeared at the King's Theatre she did not know her capabilities and maybe also she did not know her own mind. Then there were the attractions of the green-room. She was adventurous. She loved to fascinate, and young as she was she had a past, if the vague stories which have been written concerning her are to be trusted. She could dance as well as she could sing, and this accomplishment added to her attractions, for in 1815 the "fashionables" were dancing mad. Scottish reels and country dances which up to 1813 were the vogue, two years later came to be regarded as antiquated; and quadrilles and the waltz—the last-named looked upon with horror by Mrs. Grundy and Byron—imported from Germany, were the rage. The new dances had to be taught and Madame's husband, Armand Vestris, was much sought after. He had a weakness for drinking, gambling, and gallantry, and his young wife was left to take care of herself.

It was hardly likely that she, still in her 'teens, with her warm southern blood, her exuberant vitality, and her impetuous temperament, would tamely submit to neglect. She was not without resources, with the theatre, its Bohemian surroundings, and the unrestrained gaiety of the green-room or what passed as such in the King's Theatre. "Arthur Griffinhoofe," one of the chroniclers (or inventors) of scandalous gossip appertaining to Madame Vestris and other stage ladies, averred that " of all the places for intrigue, downright lasciviousness, and intemperate intrigue there is nothing to equal the King's Theatre." Griffinhoofe was writing of the King's Theatre as it was some ten years later, but in 1815 it was possibly not free from reproach. "Arthur Griffinhoofe," it has been asserted, was the pen-name of George Colman the younger, who, a boon companion of the " First Gentleman in Europe," got himself appointed Censor of Plays, and is credited with a propensity for cutting out the *double entendres* and oaths he met with in the manuscripts sent in for inspection for use in his own conversation. It is doubtful whether " Griffinhoofe " was really Colman, as the latter had been dead three years when his *Memoirs of Madame Vestris* was published.

Mr. T. H. Duncombe, in his biography of his father, Thomas Slingsby Duncombe (who as M.P. for Finsbury is not forgotten by political students and whose name was closely associated with that of Madame Vestris), to some extent confirms Griffinhoofe. " It was not unusual for the dilettanti among them (the ' omnibus-box ' renters) to cultivate rather intimate relations with the ' reigning favourite.' It passed for admiration of genius. The ' protector ' of the beautiful cantatrice or danseuse was certain of exciting the envy of his less fortunate associates till the lady left him for a more liberal admirer. This was so expensive a luxury that only an opera-goer with a handsome income could venture to indulge in it, but it was so fashionable that married men and even elderly men were proud of the distinction. Highly respectable grandfathers established themselves as patrons of the prima donna, while grave and reverend seigneurs competed with beardless ensigns for the smiles of the coryphée. This was particularly the case when the clever and fascinating granddaughter of Bartolozzi the engraver joined the Italian opera

company. Few actresses enjoyed such celebrity.
Later when on the English boards performing Don
Giovanni (i.e. *Giovanni in London*) she was so much
the rage that a modeller made a capital speculation by
selling plaster casts of *la jambe* Vestris."

Mr. Duncombe is here somewhat involved in his
chronology. *Giovanni in London*, in which Vestris
made her name as one of the most fascinating of
male impersonators of her or any other time, was
not produced until 1821, and when she " joined the
Italian opera company " there was only an apology
for a green-room. Ebers in 1820 was the creator of
this most desirable adjunct to the King's Theatre,
much to the delight of the wealthy habitués. Thomas
Duncombe probably did not become acquainted with
Madame prior to 1819, as he was up to that time
occupied with his military duties abroad.

Whatever the green-room experiences of the debutante may have been in 1815, it is presumable that
she had the advantages of a circle of aristocratic
male admirers and possibly of the curiosity of ladies
of fashion. The age was one of tittle-tattle, and it
may be hazarded that the wife of the butterfly
Armand Vestris did not escape the attention of society
gossipers. Moreover, she was not a nobody sprung
from nowhere. She was the granddaughter of a
man who occupied a unique position in the world of
art—Francisco Bartolozzi. It is hardly an exaggeration to assert that though a hundred years ago the
name of Vestris was better known than that of Bartolozzi—save among art connoisseurs—the reverse is
the case to-day. Bartolozzi's granddaughter in the
twenties and thirties of the nineteenth century was
the most-talked-of woman in London, and her fame
rested as much upon her reputation as a Circe whom
few men could resist as upon her powers as an actress,
great as they were. It is probable that the man in
the street of to-day regards her more as a " gay lady "
rather than as one who had a never-tiring devotion

to stage-craft, to lighting, colour, grouping, and appropriate scenery and costume.

Mr. A. W. Tuer has told all there is to tell concerning the Bartolozzis, and a summary of the family history is alone necessary here. Francisco, the father of the family, the son of a goldsmith and artificer in filigree work, was born in Florence on September 21st, 1727, and was trained as an artist and engraver. After his marriage he removed to Rome, where his son Gaetano was born. Apparently Francisco's talent was not recognised in the Papal city, and he went to Venice and subsequently came to England, where he was " discovered " by Mr. Dalton, the royal librarian, and by him introduced to George III. A description of this introduction, which took place about six months after his arrival, may be given in Bartolozzi's own words :

" I was shaving myself in the morning," he says, " when a thundering rapping at the door announced the glad tidings, and I cut myself in my hurry to go to Buckingham House, where I was told His Majesty was waiting for me in the library. When I arrived, I found the King on his hands and knees on the floor, cleaning a large picture with a wet sponge, and Mr. Dalton, Mr. Barnard, the librarian, and another person standing by. The subject of the picture was the ' Murder of the Innocents,' said to be by Paul Veronese, and I was sent for to give my opinion of its originality. Mr. Dalton named me to the King as a proper judge, as I had so lately come from Venice ; and I suppose he intended to give me some previous instructions; but when delay was proposed, the King said, ' No, send for Mr. Bartolozzi now, and I will wait here till he comes.' On my entering the room, the King asked me whether the picture was an undoubted original by Paul Veronese, to which I gave a gentle shrug, without saying a single word. The King seemed to understand the full force of what I meant to convey, without requiring any further

comment, asked me how I liked England, and if I
found the climate agree with me, and then walked
out at the window which led into the garden and
left Mr. Dalton to roll up his picture ; and here
ended the consultation.   The picture was an infamous
copy, and offered to the King for the moderate price
of one thousand guineas."

The result of this interview was Bartolozzi's appointment as " Engraver to His Majesty."   He remained
thirty-five years in England, during thirty of which
he was an exhibitor at the Royal Academy.   At first
he lived with Cipriani, once a fellow-student, in
Warwick Street, Golden Square, and about 1780 he
removed to North End, Fulham.   When he was
seventy-five he was invited by the Prince Regent
of Portugal to reside in that country.   Despite his
age, he accepted the invitation, was created a knight
by the Prince, and resided in Portugal until he died at
the advanced age of eighty-eight.

In England Francisco is said to have lived " a
tolerably gay life."   He entertained freely ; he lavished
money on those needing it, especially Italians ;   and
he seems to have been a bon-vivant without any
serious vices.   Meanwhile his wife with their son
Gaetano remained in Italy and never rejoined her
husband.   Gaetano married Theresa Janssen, the
daughter of a dancing-master at Aix-la-Chapelle,
an accomplished musician and a pupil of Clementi,
and brought her to England.   His father set him up
as a print-seller in Great Titchfield Street, but he was
more attached to music than to business or to engraving,
for which he had been trained, and he was indolent
withal.   In 1797, a few months after the birth of his
first child, Elizabetta, he became insolvent, and he
went to Paris, where he opened an academy for dancing
and fencing.   Gaetano did very well at first, but
soon fell into his old careless ways and, like father,
like son, he quarrelled with his wife and they separated.
Probably there were faults on both sides, Madame

Bartolozzi having the reputation of being vain, inordinately fond of bright colours in dress, and prodigiously proud of her small feet and ankles.

All these domestic differences could not but have had a disturbing effect on their children. Elizabetta and her sister Josephine must have longed for the day when they could shake themselves free from family shackles and face life in their own way. Meanwhile their mother, after leaving her husband in Paris, brought her children to England and supported them by giving music lessons. Whatever faults Madame Bartolozzi may have had, neglect of her children was not one of them. Elizabetta received her scholastic training at Manor Hall, Fulham Road, and studied music under Dr. Jay and Domenico Corri, the progenitor of numerous Corris all more or less connected with the musical profession. Mr. T. P. Grinsted, in his obituary notice of Madame Vestris in *Bentley's Miscellany* in 1856, says of her at this period : " In the course of a liberal education she evinced an early talent for music as well as a most retentive memory ; she soon became mistress of the French and Italian languages, and, we are pleased to add, had not forgotten the purity of her own. At the age of fourteen she was a visitant at the principal places of resort in the metropolis—her brilliant eyes attracting towards her considerable notice. With the symmetry of youth and the grace of mien there were blended in her—

' The glance that wins us and the life that throws
A spell that will not let our looks repose,
But turn to gaze again and find anew
Some charm that well rewards another view.' "

Another version of the early history of this most elusive lady is given in John Coleman's *Players and Playwrights I Have Known*, the authority being a Madame Mariotti, a servant of the Bartolozzi family. Madame Mariotti says that Elizabetta was born at Marylebone in 1800, and that " at that period it was customary at all the foreign schools in London to have a play performed by the pupils in French or Italian every Saturday in the presence of their parents and guardians," and thus the girl's proficiency in these two languages is explained. The same informant tells us that at fourteen she entered the school of Her Majesty's Theatre and danced in the ballet there for the season. She then went to the Académie of Paris for the winter, and on her return to London became a pupil of Armand Vestris, who kept her hard at work for twelve months before bringing her out.

Mrs. Baron-Wilson, a lady journalist of the thirties, who writes in the semi-sprightly, semi-sentimental style of the *Keepsake* and *Book of Beauty* days, provides us a further variation in *Our Actresses* for the bewildered biographer to ponder over. She remarks : " Her parents denied her none of the amusements of the metropolis, and her interesting and brilliant features might have been seen at opera, concerts, balls, etc., during the winter of 1811. At this period, it has been observed that she played the piano pleasingly, but her singing was wild and rather uncultivated. She had been from her infancy very impatient of control, and as she was not intended for the stage little pains were bestowed upon her vocal powers."

Mrs. Baron-Wilson makes mention of a Captain Best who was said to have been " much interested in the education of the brilliant-eyed little Eliza," which one can well believe, though the nature of this " interest " may be left in doubt. At any rate, the elements of a love-affair were present. Elizabetta was precocity personified. Though but fifteen, she was a woman in everything but years. Captain Best (of whom it may be remarked that he was destined in after-years to pass mysteriously in and out of her life, but why or wherefore is not to be explained) was greatly her senior ; a man of fashion, neither better nor worse than the rest of his class, most of whom in those frivolous and self-indulgent days lived only for intrigue. Some seven years previous to his association with Elizabetta, Best had the doubtful honour of fighting a duel with the notorious Lord Camelford.

The quarrel arose out of the usual cause—a woman. The lady in question had lived with Captain Best, but they had quarrelled and parted. Subsequently she met Best at the opera and wanted to make up their differences. He refused, upon which she declared she would " set Lord Camelford upon him." Lord Camelford was a professed duellist, the hero of number-less disturbances at theatres and elsewhere, and always ready to pick a quarrel and fight on the slightest pretext. Apparently he thought of nothing else and a portion of his drawing-room must have been designed with that object, as according to Horace Smith (of *Rejected Addresses* fame), over the fireplace, " a long thick bludgeon lay horizontally supported by two brass hooks. Above this was placed parallel one of lesser dimensions, until a pyramid of weapons gradu-ally rose tapering to a horse-whip."

On being told by the irate lady that Best had spoken disrespectfully of him, Camelford, meeting the Captain at the Prince of Wales's coffee-house in Conduit Street, challenged him, and as the pugnacious nobleman would accept no denial, Best was compelled to fight. Men no longer wore swords, when a quarrel could be settled there and then at the rapier's point, but the duelling spirit was as strong as in the days of Sir Lucius O'Trig-ger. It was typical of the duellist that Camelford, while convinced that he had wronged Best, should persist in fighting ; the real reason, however, was that Best was a skilled marksman and this was an affront not to be smoothed over. They met, and Best killed his man. Public opinion easily found an excuse for duelling, and though there was no doubt who was Camelford's antagonist, a coroner's jury returned a verdict of " wilful murder against some person un-known."

Elizabetta was but fifteen when by an unlucky stroke

of fate she made the acquaintance of Armand Vestris, the grandson of the famous Vestris whom the enthusiastic Parisians termed "*Le Dieu de la Danse*." Beyond his dancing there was little that was attractive about Armand Vestris. According to Mrs. Baron-Wilson, " he was rather of a clumsy make and by no means the man that a casual observer would fix upon to put in training either for a dancer or an Adonis. His visage was chubby and inexpressive, and his eye had an expression of dissipation that was displeasing. It was the gloating of passion without its fire." Elsewhere Mrs. Baron-Wilson says : " He was just two-and-twenty, but was fast sinking into old age from his dissipated course of life." Evidently when he was on the light fantastic toe one forgot his face and figure. His dancing in a Spanish fandango with the celebrated Madame Angiolini turned the heads of half the women in the audience. But off the stage he could not have had much to recommend him, and how Lucia Elizabetta came to fall in love with a young man of such doubtful reputation and unpleasant appearance is a puzzle. However, married they were, after a very brief courtship, on January 28th, 1813, at St. Martin-in-the-Fields, the church in which lies buried another actress of fascination equal to that of Madame Vestris, if not of equal ability—Nell Gwynne.

The marriage had not long been celebrated when Armand Vestris, who did not know what economy was, discovered that matrimony brought with it extra expenses. He was heavily in debt, the fashionable circle amid which he moved involved constant demands upon his purse, and accustomed all his life to the theatre he saw in his young wife the makings of a clever actress. Madame had not the slightest objection to a theatrical life, and after some preliminary training, for she knew nothing of stage-craft, she stepped upon the boards of the King's Theatre.

LORD HARRINGTON,
The husband of Maria Foote.
(From the collection of the late A. M. Broadley.)

CHAPTER III

THE opera selected for Madame Vestris's debut on July 20th, 1815—Peter von Winter's *Il Ratto di Proserpina*—was a happy choice. Von Winter was not a genius and his music at best is but a mixture of Mozart and water, but this did not trouble the audience, who were quite satisfied with the general prettiness of the melodies. The Handelian operas had long since been out of date. Mozart was beginning to be popular and Rossini, Weber, and Meyerbeer had yet to come. *Proserpina* had been a great success when produced at the King's Theatre some eleven years before and many of the airs were familiar to the 1815 audience. Winter composed the opera for Madame Grassini and Mrs. Billington, the first taking the title-rôle and the second the part of Ceres, Proserpina's mother.

Michael Kelly says that *Proserpina* (which was written in three weeks) was the only opera in which these two celebrated cantatrices appeared together.

33

He describes a curious arrangement by which the two ladies were to appear on alternate Tuesdays and Saturdays, so far as operas other than *Proserpina* were concerned, and it happened that on one particular Tuesday Mrs. Billington was attacked by a cold which brought on so severe a hoarseness that she could not sing a note nor indeed leave her bed. Grassini was entreated by Mr. Goold, one of the lessees of the King's Theatre, to sing in her stead, but she declared that no power on earth should induce her to do so, as Saturday was her night and not Tuesday. Kelly tried to persuade her to oblige, but in vain. Kelly, however, knew the ways of prima donnas and was equal to the occasion. After apparently coinciding with the lady's views, he was leaving the room when he suddenly turned and said, " To be sure, it is rather unlucky you do not sing to-night, for this morning a message came from the Lord Chamberlain's office to announce the Queen's intention to come incog., accompanied by the Princess, purposely to see you perform, and a *loge grillée* is actually ordered to be prepared for them, where they can perfectly see and hear without being seen by the audience ; but of course I'll step myself to the Lord Chamberlain's office and state that you are confined to your bed and express your mortification at disappointing the Royal party." " Stop, Kelly ! " said she. " What you now say alters the case ; if Her Majesty Queen Charlotte wishes to hear me, I am bound to obey Her Majesty's commands. Go thou to Goold and tell him I will sing."

Grassini accordingly did sing, but during the evening, the Queen not having arrived, she suspected a trick, taxed Kelly with it, and he confessed. It is to her credit that she forgave the astute manager. She was, according to all accounts, an amiable soul. Some prima donnas would have gone into a passion, after the fashion of one of the most celebrated queens of song of modern times, who, according to Mr. Mapleson, when a rival singer received more applause than she, went into hysterics, threw herself down, and beat a tattoo on the stage with her heels!

There was nothing in Winter's music with which even an immature vocalist could not grapple successfully. Elizabetta, it is pretty certain, did not show any nervousness when she faced her audience. She had ever unbounded confidence in herself. The audience probably interested her far more than the opera, which to-day would be pronounced decidedly dull. A brilliant sight must have met her eye. Extravagance in dress was then at its height. Women of fashion vied with each other in the daring cut of the short-waisted corsage and in the display of jewels. For all that the costume of the period was a very charming one, as the fashion plates in the *Ladies' Magazine* for 1815 show. It was simple and classical, especially as to the hair, which was arranged naturally and without adornment, save perhaps a flower at the side. The ugly turban and prodigious feathers were monstrosities of a later date.

No sumptuary laws governed the dress of the ladies at the opera, but it was otherwise with the gentlemen. We read that the costume *de rigueur* for admission to the opera " consisted of a long-tailed coat with ruffles at the wrists ; white cravat with stand-up shirt collar, small clothes with gold or diamond buckles ; silk stockings, shoes, a waistcoat open to show the shirt front or frill, and white kid gloves. A cocked hat called a *chapeau bras*, because usually carried under the arm, and a sword at the side, completed the costume, while the hair was always carefully dressed."

The new operatic star was rapturously applauded, and had she appeared a few years later she would have been called before the curtain. But in 1815 this method of showing appreciation had not come into vogue. "Calls," Parke, the oboe player, records in his *Musical Memoirs*, were introduced during the opera-season of 1824, when Rossini was director and composer to the King's Theatre. Madame Catalani was the first recipient of the unusual compliment. Pasta, who was a member of the same company, " also had a call when the curtain fell and was brought back to receive the reward due to her distinguished talents." The fashion caught on, and Parke, two seasons later, speaking again of Pasta, says : " At the end of the opera [Rossini's *Otello*] by desire of the audience she came forward once more to receive that reward which is becoming so common that it will shortly cease to be a mark of distinction." It is hardly necessary to add that in modern days the observance has been carried to excess, and in some cases where an actor or actress insists upon a " call," whether the audience asks for it or not, fashion degenerates into a nuisance.

The newspapers did not commit themselves concerning this first performance. The *Times* and the *Morning Chronicle* were silent. The *Morning Post* was contented with the following brief paragraph : " M. A. Vestris gave an exquisite treat last night at his Benefit, but we have no room at present for particulars. Madame Vestris (pupil to Mr. Corri) made her debut on this occasion ; and her performance was such as leaves no doubt of her becoming a splendid acquisition to this theatre."

The debutante was, however, much talked about at clubs and dinner-tables, and when the opera was again presented the house was crowded, and the *Post* was moved to give one of the gushing notices in which it excelled : " Madame Vestris's second appearance in *Proserpina*," wrote the critic, " received the most extraordinary marks of approbation ; in fact her reception was almost beyond all precedent. Her voice is a contr'alto, and from its compass capable of all the most touching and delicious influences of music ; her skill seems sufficiently practised ; time may be required and her youth has much to give for the perfect development of her powers ; but even in their present state they are attractive in the extreme. The

Princess Charlotte, who came to the opera at an early hour, seemed uncommonly delighted with the whole of her performance.   In the trio between Madames Sessi and Vestris and Signor Graam the attention of Her Royal Highness was excited to such a degree that she actually got up from her seat and joined in the general plaudits so profusely bestowed on this exquisite composition. . . . The house was crowded in every part.   Among the fashionables we perceived " —well, it does not matter much now who were perceived.   One is quite contented to know that there were dukes and duchesses, marquesses and marchionesses, the Romish and Spanish Ambassadors, and a host of smaller fry.   The enumeration of titled " fashionables " was a task dear to the heart of the journalist whose duty it was to provide material for the column headed " Fashionable World."

Equally laudatory was the *Theatrical Inquisitor*, and the praise is the more noticeable because later on the magazine changed its tone, and its criticisms were carping, and when fault could not be found, approval was given grudgingly.   In its first notice, however, it was enthusiastic enough.   It remarked of Madame Vestris : " Her voice is a perfect *contr'alto* possessing a peculiar sweetness accompanied by a correct harmonious articulation which imparts to each note a mellowness creating delight rather than astonishment.   She appears about eighteen, is elegant in her person, and has a countenance expressive rather of modest loveliness than of any marked passion.   There is a chasteness in her acting which seldom fails to please, yet we know no representation so little calculated for a display of an actress's powers as that of an opera, no situation so embarrassing as that of patiently awaiting the conclusion of another's song. Yet we scarcely ever remember to have seen so much ease and simplicity evinced on a first appearance. . . . It appears extraordinary that the managers should not have brought this lady forward at an earlier period of

the season; it would undoubtedly have been more to
their advantage. . . . Madame Vestris has only been
announced as appearing for the benefit of her husband,
but we presume she is permanently engaged."

The opera continued to the end of the season, which
terminated in August, and was shown, in all, seven
times.   The final performance is thus noticed by the
Inquisitor : " The revival of the beautiful opera of
Proserpina has been attended with deserved success
and reflects credit on the taste of the manager.   Much
of its attraction, however, has doubtless been owing
to the exquisite performance of the debutante ; it
introduced to public notice, Madame Vestris, of whom
we spoke in such high terms of admiration on her first
appearance. . . . We consider this lady as by far the
most valuable acquisition which the strength of this
company has received for a length of time. . . . That
she is already a perfect mistress of her art we do not
assert, but whatever ' trifling errors ' the critic may
discern, we may truly say with the poet :

'Look at her face and you'll forget them all.'"

The weak, vain head of Armand Vestris was turned
by the triumph of his young wife—a triumph which
augured well for the future of the debutante.   Her
husband indulged in golden visions and on the strength
of them plunged into extravagances.   Maybe Madame
helped him.   She was certainly entitled to some
reward.   Armand increased his already heavy debts ;
but whether he was arrested and sent to a debtors'
prison at this period, as reported, is not so certain,
though such an episode in the life of a man of fashion
was common enough in 1815.   The anonymous writer
of a scurrilous production privately printed (for very
good reasons) and published in 1830 without any
printer's name, purporting to be a life of Madame
Vestris, makes the assertion, but there is reason to
believe that this arrest took place at the end of Elizabetta's second engagement at the King's Theatre.

The object of the author of the book in question (an edition of which considerably Bowdlerised appeared in 1839 under the auspices of the notorious Molloy Westmacott, editor of the *Age*, and best known to fame as an associate of the disreputable Captain Garth and as the persistent maligner of Harriot Mellon after she became Mrs. Coutts and subsequently Duchess of St. Albans) in fixing the arrest between the two seasons of 1815 and 1816 was to give him the framework of a scandalous story and to provide a fitting *dénouement*. All that it is necessary to say of this farrago is that it represents Madame while walking in the Park with a girl-friend during the incarceration of her husband making the acquaintance of a couple of beaux. An intrigue follows in the manner of Boccaccio, told without the Italian's grace. After the release of her husband Madame happens to be in the green-room of the King's Theatre when she perceives the aforesaid two beaux and discovers, to her consternation, by the deference paid them, that one is the Marquis of Hertford and the other the Prince Regent ! !

Whatever may have been Elizabetta Vestris's adventurous proclivities and however fond she may have been of pleasure, she was no fool and was not likely to indulge in promiscuous escapades of this nature. The narrative, like others in the book, may be dismissed as a gross concoction intended to gratify the vicious taste of those who patronised this kind of literary garbage. An ample supply of the stuff was to be had in the Regency days, and the mystery is that the perpetrators were allowed to go scot-free. But the hunger for scandal was so intense—even respectable journals did not scruple to publish paragraphic innuendoes concerning well-known personages, and especially ladies of the stage—that it was probably thought that more harm than good would result from a prosecution. The papers might not report the action in full, but publishers of the Stockdale and Duncombe class were always ready with the muck-rake and before long a " verbatim account " would be on sale. Eighteenth-century shorthand writers, in fact, derived a good part of their income from the taking of notes of *crim. con.* cases *in extenso*, not for the newspapers, which could not in decency print them, but for certain unscrupulous booksellers. Volumes of unsavoury records are still in existence, as may be seen by the occasional appearance of some of them in the book-auction rooms of to-day.

Of the interval between August 1815 and February of the following year nothing can be said of the doings of either Armand Vestris or his wife, since nothing is recorded. It may be imagined, however, from what is known of the temperament and tastes of the couple, that their domestic happiness did not increase. Mrs. Baron-Wilson says : " The husband spoke of the wife's temper and the wife of the husband's indifference." In all probability they went their own way. Armand Vestris certainly had more than a *penchant* for Made-moiselle Mori, a *figurante*, and it is scarcely likely that Madame looked upon his faithlessness with equanimity. But professionally all seemed well.

In the beginning of 1816 Armand Vestris resumed his post as ballet master at the King's Theatre, and *Il Ratto di Proserpina* was announced to open the season with an accomplished vocalist—Madame Fodor —as Ceres to Elizabetta's Proserpina. The first per-formance was advertised for January 31st, but was postponed for what in these days would be deemed a very inadequate and even ludicrous reason. On January 30th appeared the following advertisement : " In consequence of the day on which the Martyrdom of King Charles the First took place falling on the Tuesday, one of the usual nights of performances at this theatre, the Opera Divertissement which we announced for to-morrow will, at the request of many subscribers to the opera, be postponed until Saturday, when Madame Fodor will make her appear-ance in Winter's celebrated opera of *Proserpina* with

Madame Vestris, her first appearance this season." Apart from the cause, it is difficult to understand why the opera should have been postponed, since the date at first fixed was that of the day *after* the monarch's martyrdom. But the ways of theatrical managers are past finding out.

So far as the performance was concerned, the *Post*, after praising the newcomer, added : " Madame Vestris as Proserpina justified the favourable reception she met with last year. . . . Her countenance is pleasing and her skill will enable her to make progress with time." A few nights later, however, the critic was in the mood to admonish. " Madame Vestris," he wrote, " with a fine natural talent sometimes loses its advantages by languor; she should learn that sweetness is not incompatible with spirit and that monotony is fatal to the finest tones." If the truth were known, it might be that the vivacious Elizabetta was becoming wearied of Winter's prettiness, and that she felt that the absence of inspiration in the conventional posings belonging to the operas of Winter's school was foreign to her dramatic temperament.

Following *Proserpina* came *Zaira*, also by Winter, and of her performance the *Post* said : " She looked better and sang better than we expected even from her handsome person and captivating voice." The organ of the upper ten for some reason was not disposed to be enthusiastic. In one notice, where nothing was said of the opera, it was explained that only space could be found for the names of the " fashionables."

The great feature of the season was the appearance of Braham and Madame Fodor in Mozart's *Clemenza di Tito*. The great tenor's reception was overwhelming, and we read that " it was half-past twelve before the performance was ended, and the throng was so immense that though the greatest order and decorum were preserved, it was with great difficulty that the company could retire. The house could not have been cleared before two in the morning." One is tempted to ask that if it occupied so much time in getting the audience out, how long did it take to get them in ?

Meanwhile, " the grandest ballet ever produced at the King's Theatre," to quote the advertisements, was in preparation. This was *Gonsalves di Cordova*, arranged by Armand Vestris. Several times the date for its production was announced, but postponement followed, once on account of the indisposition of M. Vestris, and at others without any explanation. The cause, however, to those who knew the ballet master's propensities was no doubt intelligible. Eventually the ballet was produced and proved a success. It kept its place in the bill until the end of the season. Besides the operas already mentioned, the *Cosa Rara* of Vicente Martin y Solar (generally known as Martini), Mozart's *Così fan tutte*, and lastly *Figaro* were given. At the first performance of *Cosa Rara* the Princess Charlotte and Prince Leopold were present, and Braham, Fodor, and Vestris sang " God Save the King " with an additional verse in honour of the royal visitors, which so pleased them that, not contented with hearing the anthem at the beginning of the opera, they insisted upon a repetition of it at the end !

CHAPTER IV

VESTRIS AND ELLISTON

The parting of Madame Vestris and her husband. She sings at the Paris Italian Opera and is the life of a "certain sort of society." Her alleged association with Windham Anstruther. The association dissolved. Madame Vestris introduced to Elliston, the manager of Drury Lane Theatre. Her first appearance at Drury Lane. Elliston and his eccentricities. His production of the *Coronation*. Poses as George IV. Vestris makes a hit in *The Siege of Belgrade*. Her success in *Artaxerxes*. Braham's extravagant style.

DISASTER followed Armand Vestris after the closing of the King's Theatre. He was arrested for debt, cleared himself by bankruptcy, and went to Paris with his wife and also, says one of the unreliable biographers, with Mademoiselle Mori, his favourite dancer. Paris seems to have been the undoing of both husband and wife, certainly of the first, though judging by his past there was not very much to undo. It is asserted that Armand, having secured for himself and Mademoiselle Mori an engagement at Naples, set out for Italy and left his wife without any means of support.

As for the latter, Mr. T. P. Grinsted, who seems to have given much time and attention to theatrical history, writes : " Whilst in this gay city she found herself neglected by her liege lord with but little inclination to pine in solitude. The licentious metropolis beckoned her with its smiles, and for a time she revelled in its giddy maze. She had constant thoughts, however, of the profession to which she had been introduced, and being a perfect mistress of the language, frequently played at the French theatres both in tragedy and drama."

43

According to the *Dictionary of National Biography* she obtained engagements at the Italian Opera, where she played Proserpina in a revival of Winter's opera, with Mrs. Dickons, a favourite English singer, as Ceres; at the Théâtre Français, where she played Camille to the Horace of Talma, and at other theatres. Mrs. Baron-Wilson says: " Her appearances at the Italian Theatre were not very frequent, but she was the life of a certain sort of society."

The story goes that at the Odéon she met a well-to-do Englishman, one Windham Anstruther, " who paid her every attention " and so far insinuated himself into her good graces as to draw from her the avowal of a wish that she had met with him at an earlier period while both her hand and heart were disengaged. Anstruther, fervently believing that he himself was the first and only man who had succeeded in making an impression on her heart, endeavoured to convince her of the folly of remaining constant to a husband who had so cruelly deserted her, but all in vain. " So excellent an actress was she, that, believing her virtue was impregnable, he pretended to have discovered a flaw in her marriage articles by which in England the union would be declared null and void. He even assured her that he had sufficient influence to procure the passing of a Bill which would release her from her vows, when he would instantly make her his wife. By arguments such as these she finally suffered herself to be persuaded and accepted his protection."

This circumstantial story reads very plausibly, but its truth is considerably discounted by the impression the writer (the anonymous author previously alluded to) was under that Madame was married to Armand Vestris in Paris, apparently not knowing that the marriage took place in London. The " flaw in the marriage " (and maybe the whole story) was therefore purely imaginary.

According to this doubtful authority, the couple came to England, at what date does not appear (Mr.

Grinsted says she returned in 1819, but he makes no mention of Anstruther), and took apartments at Mrs. Harrison's, the New Hummums Tavern in Covent Garden. Here Anstruther became on bad terms with Mrs. Bartolozzi, his wife's mother, over some financial transaction in which he behaved shabbily. Anstruther's " sole dependence at this time," we are told, " was on an allowance from his mother and on the liberality of his elder brother, which being very inadequate to support him in the extravagant style in which he was living with Madame at the Hummums, he found himself in a short time greatly involved in debt and in consequence he was arrested and conveyed to the King's Bench. He afterwards " took the rules " and removed to a lodging within the limits of Melina Place, Lambeth. Monetary difficulties leading to wrangles, the couple parted, and Madame took apartments for herself and mother and Josephine her sister in Brydges Street, Covent Garden.

Brydges Street, Covent Garden, is an unknown thoroughfare to the Londoner of to-day. It has long been absorbed by Catherine Street, of which it is a continuation. In 1819 Drury Lane Theatre was at the corner of Brydges Street, and in 1824, Poole, the author of *Paul Pry*, who had had a long-standing dispute with Robert Elliston, the lessee of Drury Lane, in the preface to his comedy of *Married and Single*, setting forth his grievances, alludes to the house as the " Theatre Royal Elliston, at the corner of Brydges Street near Catherine Street, in the Strand." If Madame Vestris was residing in Brydges Street in 1819 it was a most natural thing that she, already launched in the theatrical world, should become acquainted with Elliston. It is certain she was no stranger to him by reputation.

Lord William Lennox, who married Miss Paton (and a very unhappy marriage it was), claims credit for the introduction of Madame Vestris to the Drury Lane autocrat. " One evening," he says in his

Plays, Players, and Playhouses, " when I was leaving the private-box entrance at Drury Lane, I saw two ladies, evidently waiting for their carriage. It was a dark, stormy, windy night ; hackney-coaches were scarce, four-wheelers and hansom-cabs were not then in prospective existence, and there seemed little prospect of getting one of the above-mentioned vehicles.

" Addressing the ladies, I said that if their carriage did not come, they were welcome to have the hackney-coach I had sent the link-boy to procure for me, and that, in the meantime, I advised them to return to their box, which was on the pit tier. This they did, and in course of conversation I discovered that one of the ladies was Madame Vestris, who was most anxious to be introduced to the great Robert William Elliston. While expressing my willingness to take an early opportunity of forwarding Madame Vestris's views, no less a personage than the lessee himself came down from the back of the stage towards the footlights, which were nearly extinguished.

" ' Firemen,' he exclaimed, in a loud, pompous tone, ' see all lights put out ! I hear some voices in that box.'

" ' Yes, Mr. Elliston,' I replied. ' I am here with a lady who is most anxious to be presented to you. You've not forgotten me, Lord William Lennox ? '

" ' Delighted, my lord, to see you.'

" He came into the box, seemed delighted at Madame Vestris's looks, and there and then engaged her."

She appeared in February 1820 as Lilla in Cobb's *Siege of Belgrade,* a poor play with songs inserted, the kind of thing which in those days did duty for English opera. Braham, who played in it, was of course the attraction.

Elliston was a strange combination of a talent which at times amounted to genius and an impulsive eccentricity that was not far removed from insanity. He was, when he chose to be, an admirable actor, and there were few characters in his own particular line that he could not play better than anyone else. His readiness of resource and his instinct for advertisement were never wanting, and his self-possession under all manner of difficulties was perfect. One of his most daring assumptions was the impersonation of George IV in his production at Drury Lane of the Coronation of that monarch. The preliminaries to this extraordinary pageant were highly amusing, but are too long to detail here. The show itself is pronounced by Elliston's biographer, George Raymond, " as a piece of theatrical effect—perhaps the most complete ever represented on the English stage," and " it attracted the attention and admiration of the whole town."

Raymond significantly adds of Elliston himself : " There is no doubt that the extraordinary success of the piece, the crowded assembly, the heated atmosphere, and his own highly rectified temperament, not unfrequently qualified by more material alcohol, produced the transmutation of his wits or perhaps drove him completely out of them. That there were moments in which he verily believed himself not the shadow but the substance of monarch there can be no question. . . . But when, amid the acclamations of hot-pressed Drury threading his way through the ' upturned, wondering eyes ' of all London in the pit, he exclaimed, ' Bless you my people,' he believed himself no less than ' the Lord's anointed.' " Actually a Coronation medal was struck and specimens presented for several nights to the first two hundred persons who entered the theatre.

With so autocratic and self-willed a personage as Robert Elliston it would not have been surprising had his relations with the tempestuous Madame Vestris been marked by friction, and no doubt they had their differences. Elliston's sense of humour, however, and his whimsicalities saved him from any quarrel which

could not be made up. His manner, unlike that of
Macready, with whom Vestris was destined to have
many a deadly passage of arms, was never overbearing,
and he had too much affection for and too much admiration of the fair sex to be rude to so charming a representative as Eliza Vestris.

Small as the chance Cobb's inane ballad-play (produced on January 19th, 1820) gave Vestris to show
her accomplishments, she made a hit. The *Times*
wrote : " This theatre has made a splendid addition to
its company of vocal performers in the person of
Madame Vestris, who made her first appearance on
an English stage on Saturday evening, in the character
of Lilla in the *Siege of Belgrade*. . . . If we must
hesitate to place her in the first rank of the profession,
it is because her command of its mechanical difficulties
is less complete than is required, her shake failing sometimes in brilliancy and her execution in distinction,
but in all that constitutes the soul of the art, in grace,
pathos, and just intonation, we may associate her with
the greatest names of the day." The *Morning Post*
was laudatory in much the same terms and mentioned
in the most flowery language at its command her
introduction of a song by Clare the " peasant poet,"
which she " understood with the most happy effect."

A much more ambitious effort was that of Arne's
opera *Artaxerxes*. The cast was a strong one. Braham
was Arbaces ; Incledon, Artabanes ; Miss Carew,
Mandane ; and Madame Vestris, Artaxerxes. " At
no other theatre," said the *Post*, " could such talents
be united in the same opera ; the taste, the brilliancy, the pathos of Braham, the power, the richness,
the volume of Incledon, the execution and science
of Miss Carew, the clearness and the intelligence of
Madame Vestris. The character of Artaxerxes, though
it gives its name to the opera, is a part of second-rate
importance and much below the level of Madame

Madame Vestris.

Engraved from an original Painting by R. E. Drummond

MADAME VESTRIS,
At the age of 30.

Vestris's talent. But talents can give a prominence to parts of inferior importance."

The *Times* was more discriminating and more critical. Of Arne's experiment of writing an English opera in the grand Italian operatic style it remarked : " The piece is now compressed into two acts, a licence that deserves indulgence as all the best songs have been retained and the construction of the opera in continued recitative, a solitary imitation of the Italian manner, has never been understood or relished by an English audience. It has pleased solely as a musical composition ; as a drama it is unintelligible and therefore tedious." Whether this compression was successful is extremely doubtful.

The character of Artaxerxes was originally written for a soprano, but for some reason had been appropriated by a male voice. Madame Vestris restored it to its original intention. " The song of ' In Infancy our Hopes and Fears,' " said the *Times*, " as given by her was chaste and touching and may almost be adduced as a specimen of the true style of simple singing. The experience in recitative acquired by Madame Vestris in the Italian style gave her great advantage over the other performers."

Braham the writer reproved, and not without reason, because of his tendency to over-ornament. It was pointed out that " in the song of ' Water Parted from the Sea,' by labouring too much at expression he injured its character. It should have been given with far more lightness and tenderness and wholly without ornamentation, a sacrifice Braham may make without danger to his reputation, as his power is too well known to require its display on every occasion." Braham had a voice of the finest quality, and when he chose he could use it with the greatest effect—in oratorio especially. But in opera or in the concert-room he played to the gallery and " frilled and frittered in the Italian manner " till a simple ballad was turned into a piece of embroidered vulgarity.

He could be, as Lord Mount-Edgcumbe, who must have heard him in all his styles, has pointed out, "two distinct singers according to the audience before whom he performs."

The best description of Braham's singing when the control within him asserted itself is give by a Mr. Heywood in the *Cornhill Magazine* (December 1865). Writing of a performance of *Israel in Egypt*, Mr. Heywood says : " A little thick-set man with a light brown wig all over his eyes, a generally common appearance, and a most unmistakably Jewish aspect got up to sing one single line of recitative. He stood with his head well on one side, held his music also on one side and far out before him, gave a funny little stamp with his foot, and then proceeded to lay in his provision of breath with such a tremendous shrug of his shoulders and swelling of his chest that I very nearly burst out laughing. He said, ' But the children of Israel went on dry land,' and then paused ; and every sound was hushed throughout that great space, and then as if carried out upon the solid stillness came those three little words ' through the sea.' And our breath failed and our pulses ceased to beat and we bent our heads as all the wonder of the miracle seemed to pass over us with these accents—awful, resonant, triumphant. He sat down while the whole house thundered its applause."

He was a very poor actor, but he did not think so, or he would not have attempted to act the Bay of Biscay as well as sing it. On one occasion his histrionic effort made him surprisingly ridiculous. It was at one of the provincial musical festivals. The orchestral platform had an exceedingly high front and Braham's lack of stature hardly enabled him to show more than half his body, but when he came to the last verse in which he cries, " A sail—a sail—a sail ! " and he went down on one knee, which he always did as if in thankfulness, he disappeared altogether. The audience, puzzled at first and alarmed, thinking he had vanished through some mysterious trap-door, roared with laughter when they saw the little man, with his unmistakably Israelitish countenance and his brown wig, reappear safe and sound.

In addition to the pieces mentioned, an old concoction, *Shakespeare versus Harlequin*, was revived, in which Madame Vestris played Dolly Snip in so sprightly a fashion that it was soon seen she would be a very valuable acquisition by reason of her versatility. *Shakespeare versus Harlequin* merits a passing note. It was produced under the name of *Harlequin's Invasion* by Garrick, who adapted it from an older piece in which he himself played at the Goodman's Fields Theatre. It was described as a " Christmas gambol in the manner of the Italian comedy," and represented Harlequin invading the region of poesy and the kingdom of Shakespeare and, after various and comical adventures, being expelled. Though ostensibly a pantomime, all the characters had " speaking" parts. The original Dolly Snip was Miss Pope, one of the best comedy actresses of the Garrick period. So far as Dolly Snip is concerned, Miss Pope had a worthy successor in Madame Vestris. " Madame Vestris . . . evinced a spirit and a naïveté in Dolly Snip," writes Mrs. Baron-Wilson, " which was highly captivating, and if cultivated with zealous attention will render her one of the most pleasing actresses it has ever been our honest enjoyment to applaud."

Applauded as she was in everything she undertook, it was not until the end of May that the real Vestris in all her sparkle and charming audacity burst upon the town in Moncrieff's burlesque of Mozart's *Don Giovanni* entitled *Giovanni in London*. Irrepressible gaiety, beauty of face and figure, the voice of a siren, combined to form a living picture the like of which London had never seen before.

CHAPTER V

"GIOVANNI IN LONDON"

Vestris as Captain Macheath. Her stupendous success in *Giovanni in London*. A severe condemnation. Madame's charms described in verse. The plot of *Giovanni*. The music, and Vestris's vivacity and daring costume, its attraction. "Joe Gould," the first impersonator of the Don at the Olympic Pavilion. Played for one night only. Elliston's style of advertising. Tom Moore delighted with Vestris in *Giovanni*.

THE BEGGAR'S OPERA paved the way for *Giovanni in London*. Gay's perennial piece of satire, humour, and the sweetest of music was revived at the Haymarket on July 22nd, 1820, for the express purpose of exploiting Vestris as Captain Macheath. She was not the first woman to personate the rollicking captain. Sprightly Anne Catley, the very soul of audacity, played the character at Smock Alley Theatre, Dublin, then run by Mossop, in 1764. Anne had crept into the hearts of the Irish play-going public, and as a counter-attraction, Barry, Mossop's rival at Crow Street, put on *The Beggar's Opera* with himself as Macheath, Mrs. Dancer as Polly, and Mrs. Abington as Lucy. The revival was so successful that Mossop determined to go one better. Anne Catley's Polly was familiar enough to the Smock Alley audience, as the opera had been running some time, and when it was announced that she would appear as Macheath the house was packed and the novelty was the rage for some time. Thirteen years or so later Mrs. Kennedy, an Irishwoman with a remarkable contralto voice, made a hit in the part at Covent Garden; and in 1780 Mrs. Cargill was the Macheath in Colman's travesty of the opera, when all the parts were reversed. Catley, somewhat piqued at Mrs. Cargill's success, once more essayed Macheath, though by this time her powers were failing, and the rival female Macheaths were the talk of the town.

In 1820 the opera had not been performed for seven years. With Vestris as Macheath it came as a refreshing surprise—a surprise all the greater as the costume revealed the exquisite form of one of the most beautifully proportioned women who had ever appeared upon the English stage. It is not a little singular that, coarse and vulgar as was the taste of the day, some people professed to see impropriety in an actress in a " breeches " part. However, the *Theatrical Inquisitor*, which afterwards denounced *Giovanni in London* for its indecorum, was fain to admit that " though our sentiments of this lady's appearance in Macheath are not precisely such as will blazon her merit or confirm her success, . . . we are half inclined to instance this momentous effort as the most amusing personation in which we have hitherto beheld her. The muses, according to Gay's ' Beggar,' pay no attention to dress, . . . but Madame Vestris in her scarlet frock and blue cravat, . . . her dapper appearance, high spirits and unflagging activity, were apparent in every branch of her impersonation and rendered her Captain Macheath . . . one of the prettiest rattles for overgrown children with which the stage can at present supply them." The opera ran for ten consecutive nights, Vestris's salary being sixty guineas.

The *Inquisitor* a few months later relapsed into its habitual somewhat dour mood. Elliston, immensely taken with the " dapper " Macheath, produced the opera at Drury Lane on November 4th. There is no reason to believe that Vestris's performance in this revival was at all inferior to her Haymarket impersonation ; the *Inquisitor*, however, pronounced it a " disaster," and asserted that " money was lost every night she repeated it," and, sinking to a low depth of pessimism, remarked that " if the public will go farther than at present they seem prepared to do, the total abandonment of this singer and her flimsy prettiness will *in every point of view* do credit to their taste and feelings." Greatly to the censor's disgust, the public *did* go farther, and in a fashion which annoyed the prudish magazine and those who thought with it.

The records of the English stage contain no exact parallel to the furore which *Giovanni in London* and Vestris as the rakish Don created. The elements of attraction were totally different from those of *The Beggar's Opera*. When Gay's masterpiece was produced, the wit and satire of the play, the delightful old ballads, and the sweet voice and modest demeanour of Lavinia Fenton drew the town. *Giovanni in London* had no wit ; such humour as it had appertained to coarseness ; and the music for the most part was taken from the contemporary songs popular at the moment and very inferior to the old English ballads. The sole fascination was provided by Madame Vestris in a " breeches " part !

Female physical beauty strongly appealed to the public of that day, not, it is to be feared, from appreciation of it in an artistic sense. No Greek statue could have been more harmonious in its proportions than the graceful actress upon whom hundreds of eyes gazed entranced, but it is certain that the possessors of those eyes had no thought of Greek statues. Their senses were pleased and this was all that mattered. It was then the fashion for the devotees of feminine beauty to burst into verse over the divinity who happened for the moment to be the toast of the town. The charms of Vestris in *Giovanni in London* called forth the following poetic effusion in her praise, couched with the freedom characteristic of the times :

"What a breast—what an eye ! What a foot, leg, and thigh !
    What wonderful things she has shown us ;
  Round hips, swelling sides, masculine strides—
    Proclaim her an English Adonis !

" In Macheath how she leers, and unprincipled appears,
      And tips off the bumpers so jolly ;
  And then, oh ! so blest, on two bosoms to rest,
      And change from a Lucy to Polly.

" Her very air and style could corrupt with a smile—
      Let a virgin resist if she can ;
  Her ambrosial kisses seem heavenly blisses—
      What a pity she is not a man.

" Then in Don Giovanni, she puts life into many,
      And delights with her glass and her catches ;
  Her best friend, at will, she can gracefully kill,
      And the wife of his bosom debauches.

" The profligate youth she depicts with such truth,
      All admire the villain and liar,
  In bed-chamber scenes, when you see through the screens,
      No rake in the town can come nigh her.

" Her example so gay, leads the youth all astray,
      And the old lick their lips as they grin ;
  And think, ' if she would,' why, mayhap, they still could !
      Have the pleasure and the power to sin.

" How alluring is beauty when ankle and shoe-tie
      Peep out like a bird from the nest ;
  They're like heralds of delight, and morn, noon, and night,
      Fond fancy can point out the rest.

" There be breeches, on they go, give me the ' fur-below '
      Which appears with such grace upon many ;
  But Vestris to please, must her lovely limbs squeeze
      Into the pantaloons of Don Giovanni."

As these verses appeared in the *Inquisitor*, which
was not disposed to be friendly towards Madame
Vestris, it may be they were intended to be spiteful.
The public, however, did not regard them in this
light and were inclined to look upon them as complimentary. What Madame thought cannot be conjectured. She was a veritable sphinx in her silence
respecting herself and her doings. No woman appears

to have been better able to hold her tongue and keep
her own secrets. Another versified effort was this :

" *To Vestris Turned Don*

" When first in petticoats you trod the stage,
  Our sex with love you fired—your own with rage ;
  In trousers next—so well you play'd the cheat,
  The ' pretty fellow,' and the rake complete ;
  Each sex were then with different passions moved,
  The men grew envious, and the women loved ! "

Frivolous as *Giovanni in London* reads, it really
contains little or nothing approaching indecorum.
It is packed with lively verse wedded to popular tunes,
from the charming air from *Midas*, " Pray, Goody "
to " Here's a Health to all Good Lasses." At the
same time, while the words of some of the songs as
they stand are fairly harmless, yet with the assistance
of a nod and a wink and the art of the comedian one
can easily understand that they could be made somewhat suggestive. But no equivocal lines are to be found
in the songs of the fascinating Don. The *Theatrical
Inquisitor*, in continuation of its ill-temper towards
Vestris, was constrained to be virtuously indignant.
" This extravaganza," it wrote, " as it is properly
termed, has been transplanted from the Olympic
Pavilion, a soil in which its dulness and obscenity were
of indigenous growth. We are unwilling to tax Mr.
Elliston with the very worst motive by which he
could have been actuated, but *Giovanni in London*
appears to have been introduced at Drury Lane
Theatre for the sole purpose of making money by the
sacrifice of every feeling which ought to be devoted
to the respectability of that establishment."
Describing the plot, the *Inquisitor* says : " The
Don is involved in a variety of adventures which the
dramatist has not troubled himself to explain or connect,
and though the auspices under which this farrago was
originally produced might warrant the utmost frivolity, something of a better cast was due to the natural

stage upon which it has been represented. We shall overlook the extreme indecency which runs through every vein of this stupid composition and confine our censure to the want of probability by which it is pervaded. Giovanni obtains access to a fashionable party without an invitation ; seduces a married lady in ten minutes after he has first accosted her ; is brought to trial in Westminster Hall and defended by a female ; gets out of the King's Bench by the insolvent act just after he gets into it ; and is finally married to a foolish young woman who knows nothing about him but the enormous vices by which his character to the very last is degraded. . . . We pity Madame Vestris from every consideration by which her performance of Don Giovanni has been attended. The disgusting woman who undertook this libertinic character at its outset, prepared us very fully for the only result that can ever be drawn, in the nicest hands, from its loathsome repetition ; and we, there-fore, feel bound to treat it as a part which no female should assume till she has discarded every delicate scruple by which her mind or her person can be dis-tinguished," and much more to the same effect.

The " disgusting woman " who so outraged the *Inquisitor's* susceptibilities was a " Mrs. Gould (late Miss Burrell)," as Elliston's advertisement of the piece when it came out at the Olympic Pavilion puts it. How Mrs. Gould came to achieve notoriety is of no consequence. It may suffice to say that the lady was of such masculine habits that she was known as " Joe Gould " throughout the country. *Giovanni in London*, when produced at the Olympic, attracted no attention and was unnoticed by the newspapers. But there was a reason for this. It had only been performed once when Queen Charlotte died ; the theatres were closed for a few days and no more was heard of the " Don." Elliston's grandiose announce-ment of the piece may, however, be quoted as a good specimen of his style of advertising : " To conclude with the Broad Comic Extravaganza Entertainment in two Acts, comprising a grand moral, satirical, magical, comical, operatical, melodramatical, pantomimical, critical, infernal, terrestrial, celestial, Gallymaufrical-ollapod, ridacle, Burletta, spectacle, y'clept *Giovanni in London*."

Another of Elliston's notices is also worth reproducing, showing that a practice in vogue before Garrick's time had not died out. It runs thus : " The Box-keeper most respectfully solicits the nobility and gentry who send servants to keep Places to give particular directions that they may be at the theatre at six o'clock precisely. According to the etiquette of other theatres, the seats taken will be preserved until the end of the first Act." The practice has been revived at the present day but in a mutilated form. The substitute cannot get beyond a place in the queue.

The result of the *Inquisitor's* attack was what might be expected. It drew the town to Drury Lane. The house was packed nightly and the fame of Madame was established. The " second house " alone, when the admission price was halved, brought in £100 every evening. It may be that Madame Vestris was as much surprised as gratified by her success, for it is said that she was very reluctant to assume a " breeches " part, whether because the Don was associated with the notorious lady at the Olympic or because of the daring costume is not recorded. Most probably it was for the first reason, as she had already made a hit as Macheath, besides wearing a masculine dress as Artaxerxes. As Arne's opera was a " serious " one, doubtless the dress was prim and proper. So far as *Giovanni in London* was concerned, it received no advantage from the brief notices in the daily papers. But in those days space was limited— the *Times* had but four comparatively small pages and two of these were filled with advertisements—and a play succeeded nor not according to the amount of talk it created. Audiences, if they disapproved, preferred to do their own " damning " on the first night, without waiting for the critics. There were no half measures. If the play was a poor one or did not take, the patrons of the theatre—who were a class by themselves—stayed away and something else was tried. But when regular playgoers were pleased, the unanimity in front of the stage as well as *on* the the stage was wonderful. Before a week was out the only topic in gossiping circles, whether of the " fashionables " or of the " mob," was Madame Vestris, as the daring, the seductive Don.

In one respect—but at a distance—the effect of *Giovanni in London* on its admirers resembled that of *The Beggar's Opera* at its first production. In the latter case fans, screens, and other articles ornamented with scenes from the opera, with, of course, the portrait of the " all-conquering Polly," were sold in large quantities. Popular admiration of Madame Vestris went a step further. She was so much the rage that, as Mr. T. H. Duncombe has already told us, a modeller made a capital speculation by selling plaster casts of what he asserted was *la jambe de Vestris*. *Inter alia*, the opinion of Thomas Moore may be quoted, though he did not see the play until 1822. A note in his " diary " under date of April 18th says : " Dined at the George and went to Drury Lane. Elliston (whom I had called upon in the morning, but who was ill in bed) had a private box prepared for me. Saw Madame Vestris in *Don Juan*, and was delighted with her."

The " run " of a play at this time was as a rule brief. Regular playgoers were limited in numbers and constant change was indispensable to attract them. But *Giovanni in London* did not pall by repetition nor " custom stale its infinite variety." It ran night after night from May 30th to July 8th, when the season ended.

CHAPTER VI

MADAME THE TALK OF THE TOWN

Vestris's success in the provinces. Her alleged escapades and gallantries. The " Giovanni " fever renewed in London. Drawbacks to her career as a concert singer. She appears in Italian opera at the King's Theatre and in ballad opera at Drury Lane. Elliston's pageant of the *Coronation*. Extraordinary scene at the real Coronation. Production of *Giovanni in Ireland*, and failure both in London and Dublin.

THE winter season of 1820–21 at Drury Lane did not begin until October 30th, and between this date and July 8th the blank so far as Madame's movements are concerned is difficult to fill. With her extravagant habits, the indulgence of her whims, and her love for everything that made her attractive, no matter what it cost, her mode of living could hardly be supported on what she had saved—if such a thing as saving can be imagined of one who had suddenly become the idol of the public—out of her salary at Drury Lane. The admirers of pretty and fascinating dancers did not mind what they spent to gratify the caprices of their divinities, and it can be safely asserted that at this period of " resting " Vestris did not want for money.

If we may believe the *Gossip of the Century*, her old flame Captain Best had not deserted her. The writer's words are : " After her separation from her husband, Captain Best persuaded her to let him manage her affairs and also advised her to leave London and accept an engagement at Manchester, where she gave seven nights for £100, making a most favourable impression. In fact her fame had preceded her thither, so that before she arrived the house was taken and applicants were eagerly demanding places at increased prices. The receipts amounted to £400 that night—a sum never before realised on a single night in that theatre. The manager was so delighted with the lady's efforts that he went to her dressing-room to present her with a bouquet of roses, out of which dropped a purse containing thirty guineas.

" The delicate generosity of this proceeding so profoundly touched the clever actress that she sent him a note—laconic and expressive—as follows :

" ' DEAR SIR,—I will play Cowslip to-night (in the *Agreeable Surprise*), and to-morrow will take Don Giovanni. You are a queer fellow—I wish to oblige you.—VESTRIS.' "

Accepting this statement, Madame's visit to Manchester was *after* her success in *Giovanni in London*, but we need not say that stories of this most ubiquitous lady which cannot be verified and to which no dates are attached must be received with caution. The anonymous author of the 1830 *Memoirs* at all events had no hesitation in reproducing the words of the *Gossip of the Century*, and proceeded to enlarge upon them in his own peculiar fashion.

According to this imaginative biographer, Captain Best at Manchester abandoned his protégée, and went off to London with " Lady Bennet—a lady whose husband has of late become notorious." For a time Madame Vestris was despondent, but was roused from her depression of spirits by a present of £50 from Lord Derby. She reappeared at the theatre, and a Major Brookes appears upon the scene and was " her Cicisbeo for several months," until he was shot in a duel which the biographer is good enough to say " Madame Vestris had nothing to do with." From Manchester she went to Liverpool, where she came forth as Macheath. " She was placarded on every wall and her likeness stuck in every window of every print-shop. The town rang with her praises and for twenty-seven nights Macheath was received with cheers by a Liverpool audience. . . . Her performance at the theatre delighted all, and she had a benefit which produced her £500."

Then followed a "slight altercation with Lord Derby," of whom the scribbler remarks : "Lord Derby was a rum fellow ; he married an actress" (Miss Farren), "and had all his life been acting. But it is no matter, I have nothing to do with him and must push on in my old way "—which way may be described as mendacity and muddle. Of the second a good sample is his assertion that in Liverpool Vestris was Cowslip in the *Agreeable Surprise* as " breeches were not then in her contemplation." Yet a few weeks later she appears in *Giovanni* and " electrified the town," the writer apparently not being aware that she had played the Don for two months previous to her provincial tour and had previously made a hit in the " breeches " part of Captain Macheath. To attempt to set the muddles right, or even to understand them would be an impossible task, and one can only fall back on the author's mendacity and pronounce the whole business a concoction of falsehoods.

Appearing at Drury Lane in November Vestris revived her popularity. The *Giovanni* fever ran as high as ever, continued through the winter months, and showed little sign of abatement in the following year. During the spring Madame Vestris divided honours with Braham : and *Artaxerxes, The Lord of the Manor, The English Fleet,* were now and again interposed with *Giovanni.* In all these so-called English operas Madame Vestris had a part. Indeed had she chosen to devote herself to ballad singing, she might have excelled in this direction as she did in others.

But there were considerable obstacles in the way of a concert career. She had a powerful rival in Kitty

Stephens, and Kitty, at the very time when Vestris was revelling in her delightful impertinences in *Giovanni*, was the despair of musical critics, who could not find " sufficient compliments to shower upon her." Of Miss Stephens's singing in *Rob Roy* at Covent Garden, in which she appeared after a long time in Ireland, one of the daily papers said : " Her voice, which is one of the finest nature ever formed, possesses even more strength, clearness, and purity than before. Some of the notes have a power truly electric, and we never witnessed her triumph more complete." Probably she was not much of an actress, but her vocal powers sufficed to give her a higher position among the staider section of the " fashionables " than Vestris could ever have hoped to attain, even had her voice been comparable to that of Kitty Stephens.

On other grounds Vestris could not look for advancement purely as a ballad singer. A very considerable portion of a vocalist's income was derived from concerts given in private houses of rich people. Mrs. Coutts (formerly Harriot Mellon and subsequently the Duchess of St. Albans) and Sir George Warrender, a patron of musicians, vied with each other in the programmes they put before their friends. Mr. T. H. Duncombe quotes a statement that Madame Catalini was once invited to Stowe and asked to sing. " On quitting, she charged the Marquis of Buckingham £1,700 for the pleasure she had afforded his guests." The story may be a *ben trovato*, but it is a certainty that Madame was naturally avaricious and found an admirable supporter in her husband, who did his utmost to spend what she earned. It is on record that she received as much as two hundred guineas for singing " God Save the King " and " Rule Britannia." Be this as it may, the rich paid large sums for artists to sing at their houses, and Vestris could scarcely hope for engagements from this source. Her reputation, and *Giovanni*, were against her. The Lady

Jerseys, the Lady Castlereaghs, the Lady Cowpers, and other select leaders of the *beau monde* would hardly allow her within their doors, though no doubt she would have received a warm welcome from the men of the family.

Yet apart from what Mrs. Grundy might say, Madame Vestris had every claim to be considered a lady in manners and speech. The age permitted considerable freedom, but Madame Vestris never followed the fashion in this respect. She was the very antithesis of the Countess Aldborough, who was not only not ashamed, says Gronow, of the irregularities of her early life, but whose language was " plain and unvarnished, and many hardened men of the world have been known to blush and look aghast when this free-spoken old lady has attacked them at her dinner-table with sundry searching questions respecting their tastes and habits, in the presence perhaps of their wives and daughters." In addition, " she did not possess the French art of wrapping up a joke of doubtful propriety." But what may be tolerated in a countess is not to be endured in an actress. There was no fear of Vestris shocking the proprieties in the Aldborough fashion, but she was outside the pale of the exclusives and was never invited to sing at their concerts.

Vestris was truly a delightful creature of infinite variety, and, as Mr. Chorley subsequently wrote, she could have made a name for herself in Italian opera had she chosen. But she was not desirous of succeeding in any one groove to the exclusion of others which she might fancy. She was a woman of strong will, and doubtless felt that she was made to command and not to serve. Maybe she had ambitions which she was able to gratify when she grasped the reins of government at the Olympic Theatre some ten years later, and, the first woman to manage a theatre, showed her unsuspected business capacity. But in 1821 she had to content herself

MADAME VESTRIS,
As Giovanni in *Giovanni in London.*

MADAME VESTRIS,
As Don Felix in *The Wonder.*

with *Giovanni in London* and—a strange contrast—
Italian opera !

Ebers had taken the King's Theatre and was very
anxious to obtain the best talent available. He had
his eye on Madame Vestris as an attractive and useful
member of his company, but Elliston and his contract
with the lady had to be overcome and, says he (*Seven
Years of the King's Theatre*), " a great deal of trouble
was bestowed to obtain permission from Elliston for
her to appear at the King's Theatre on the two weekly
nights of performance. The difficulty was, however,
overcome, and Madame was engaged at twenty-five
pounds a night." What part she took in Rossini's
La Gazza Ladra, with which the operatic season
opened on March 10th, neither the advertisements
nor the notices tell us. It was probably Pippo.

The opera to-day is forgotten save the spirited
overture, which might well be played more often
than it is, but it was very popular a century ago. The
plot is based on the simple story of the " Maid of the
Magpie," not altogether unlike the Ingoldsby legend
of " The Jackdaw of Rheims," which for reasons best
known to himself Rossini chose to treat in melodramatic
fashion and invest with a martial spirit. Madame
Camporese was the prima donna, and the production
was received enthusiastically, the *Morning Post* remarking that " the walls of this theatre have not contained so numerous an audience as that on Saturday
night for many years." The *Post*, whose duty it
was to keep an eye on the " fashionables," congratulates
" our fair countrywomen upon the substitution of
wax lights for gas, which in the principal tiers for
several seasons has been permitted to carry on open
warfare against bright eyes and fair complexions."
This may well have been so ; the gas of those days
was not particularly pure and the burners very primi-
tive, and the illumination must have been strongly
tinged with yellow. At what date gas was introduced
into the King's Theatre does not appear. If in 1818

candles were in use—judging from a print in Acker-
man's *Microcosm of London*—the " several seasons "
would seem to be an exaggeration.

Of notices of Madame Vestris only that in the
Times need be quoted. " We have seen Madame
Vestris," it wrote, " when in better voice and spirits,
but there was still much left to admire. No singer
of the age surpasses her in the purity of her intonation
or in passages of simple pathos and sensibility, though
languor and want of exertion sometimes impeded their
full success. The cause may be in part the transition
to a larger theatre, but the Italian stage, where she
was first nationalised, is her true sphere, and the interest
of her reputation with the gratification of the public
will be best consulted by her never again quitting it."
It is interesting to note in coming to this conclusion
the *Times* anticipating Mr. Chorley that the Italian
opera was the real *métier* of Vestris. But evidently
she did not think so herself. She was apparently not
disposed to exert her powers. Maybe she did not
have the necessary stimulus, since her part was subordinate to that taken by Madame Camporese. In
Giovanni in London she was paramount—the one
striking figure that everybody went to see. She had
no share in any opera save *La Gazza Ladra*, and in a
little-known work of Rossini, *Ricciardo e Zoraide*.
Tancredi and Paer's *Agnese*, which were also produced,
did not contain a part suitable for her.

Her performances at Drury Lane during the operatic
season and afterwards were not confined to *Giovanni*.
For her benefit on June 29th she played in the *Lord of
the Manor*, in July she was seen in *Rob Roy*, doubtless
making an effective and picturesque Di Vernon, and
in the same month undertook Effie Deans in the
Heart of Midlothian—a part which one would imagine
was hardly in her line, but the *Post* found that she
" imparted infinite pathos to the character and in
the Scotch airs which fell to her lot sang most deli-
ciously." No doubt the singing of the ballads was

her strong point. Other productions were *The Kind Impostor*, a ballad play, the music arranged by C. E. Horn, the composer of " Cherry Ripe " and " I've been roaming," two among his many songs not yet forgotten. Drury Lane appears to have been kept open all through 1821, the great feature being the revival of the pageant of the *Coronation*, in which Elliston as George IV was the central personage and which ran for eighty-eight nights.

The Coronation was undoubtedly the outstanding feature of 1821. The actual Coronation does not need a place in these pages except in one aspect— the scene which took place in Westminster Hall. As a sidelight on the manners of the times in which Madame Vestris moved and lived, a newspaper description of this scene deserves quoting. "As soon," we read, " as his Majesty retired . . . a rush was made by hundreds of ladies and gentlemen and persons of greater dignity to *plunder* the royal table on which, O dire omen, the Throne was overturned ! When this tumult had subsided, the hungry spectators, who had swarmed down from the galleries into the area of the Hall, began to occupy the tables which the guests had left, and the remainder of the dinner and dessert quickly disappeared. After an attack by the chorister boys upon the table ornaments, the instinct became universal. Ladies were seen in every part beseeching the gentlemen to assist their fair endeavours to procure some memorial of the Coronation spoils. . . . At the Barons' table a gorgeous dame took possession of a golden statue of Britannia and her lion too stupendous for her to carry, but doating on her magnificent acquisition, she waited in patience for assistance to help her home with it." The odd thing about this is that no one was surprised and still less shocked at what to-day we should call ill-breeding and rowdyism.

In consequence of the great success of *Giovanni in London*, Elliston conceived the idea of a sequel to be called *Giovanni in Ireland*. The Irish version was announced for December 11th, but postponed until December 22nd. The house was packed, but, like most sequels, it proved a disappointment. An extract from the notice in the *Morning Post* will suffice to indicate its character. " Saturday last," it recorded, " proved the great, the important day, big with the fate of *Giovanni in Ireland*. From the ' stunning whispers ' which had been abroad for some time this was looked forward to as a most portentous birth, . . . and although speaking of this production singly as a drama disappointment may have been experienced, still as a vehicle of the most delectable Irish melodies . . . and presenting as it does a series of the most beautiful scenery, we consider it on the whole as a piece entitled to public patronage and respect."

This reads remarkably like damning with faint praise. The audience went further and showed signs of a desire to damn it without any praise at all. A tumult after the fashion playgoers revelled in when they desired to show their disapproval arose, and " when the curtain fell, Mr. Russell came forward to announce the second performance, it was impossible to hear what he said for the uproar." The farce began, but the actors were assailed with cries of " Off, off ! " Mr. Russell again presented himself. A new storm interrupted him, but he succeeded in saying that " if accidents inseparable from a first performance had given offence, the most strenuous efforts would be made to guard against their recurrence, and he trusted it would afford greater satisfaction on its next performance."

The malcontents permitted themselves to be pacified and on the whole showed great moderation and attempted nothing like the violence which was exhibited in the same theatre some two years before, when at a first-night performance indignation rose almost to rioting-point. No explanation or apology

then sufficed.   Stephen Kemble, whose rule at Drury
Lane was a series of disasters, dared not face the tumult,
and the audience, in default of entertainment on the
stage, proceeded to amuse themselves in other ways
and refused to leave the theatre.   The attendants,
to show that everything was over, let down the canvas
in front of the boxes, upon which the stuff was seized
and torn into shreds.   A lady from one of the boxes
spouted Shakespeare to pass away the time, and it
looked as if the pittites intended to spend the night
in the theatre, when the happy idea was hit upon of
pouring buckets of water upon them from the gallery,
and this had the desired effect !

Elliston's strong point was that he never knew when
he was beaten, and announcing that this first performance was simply a " public rehearsal," put the
extravaganza on again.   It was shortened and improved and was received with a little grumbling, but
" Madame Vestris soon succeeded in arresting general
attention and sang the house into perfectly good humour."   However, the piece ran only for five nights.

Elliston then conceived the notion of producing
the piece in Dublin.   The King contemplated visit-
ing the sister-isle, and, mindful of his brilliant production of the Coronation, Elliston hoped that the
presence of George IV would add to the attraction
of the venture.   The " gallimauphry " underwent a
thorough revision, presumably to suit an Irish audience,
and as during his visit the King took part in the
installation of the Knights of St. Patrick, Elliston
determined to embody in Giovanni a representation
of this imposing ceremony ; but the piece proved an
utter failure.

CHAPTER VII

THE MONTAGU GORE AFFAIR

The King's Theatre green-room. Lord Fife and his mania for
ballet dancers. His passion for Mlle Noblet. Court regulations
altered to suit her. Maria Mercandotti and Ball Hughes. The
" bucks " of the day and their fads. Fashionable gallantries. Madame
Vestris and Mr. Montagu Gore. Their correspondence. Harris
the useful " go-between." Gore's offer of £300 per annum rejected.
The affair broken off.

IN the twenties and thirties the " fashionables " went
mad over ballet dancers. Prima donnas had their
following, but in a lesser degree. It was to ogle the
première danseuse and her subordinate sisters and to
seek an opportunity to flirt with them that the young
bloods nightly haunted Fops' Alley. Ebers was a
shrewd man and he saw his way to a good thing when
he added a green-room to the attractions of the
King's Theatre. He says complacently : " This room
was certainly an advantage to the dancers, who could
now practise in it immediately before their entrance
on the stage," and no doubt to the delight of the
habitués who possessed a golden key by which directly
or indirectly they gained admission to the sanctum.
Paris was the great forcing house of stage dancing,
and the " stars " were tempted to London not only
by the high salaries offered, but by dreams of sumptuous
dinners, costly dresses, and sparkling diamonds—
dreams which were generally realised.

Lord Fife was the great patron and protector of
dancers. He passed his time in thinking how to lavish
money upon them. In 1821 and 1822 Mademoiselle
Noblet was the bright particular star of his adoration.

Ebers tells us " that the incense offered to Noblet's vanity must have been overwhelming. . . . She was run after, worshipped, everybody thought and spoke of her." The Earl provided a carriage for her during her stay in London, and every Sunday gave a dinner to her and other *figurantes* at the Pulteney Hotel. According to Captain Gronow, Lord Fife had known Mademoiselle Noblet in Paris, " where he made himself conspicuous in the foyer by his unremitting attentions. He never quitted her for an instant. He would carry her shawl, hold her fan, run after her with scent-bottle in his hand, admire the diamond necklace someone else had given her, or gaze in ecstasy on her pirouettes. On his return to London the old *roué* would amuse George IV with a minute description of the lady's legs and her skill in using them. . . . He from first to last spent nearly £80,000 on this fair daughter of Terpsichore."

His lordship was not the lady's only admirer. The heads of other men of fashion were turned by her perfect form and the sparkling vivacity of her black eyes. Her charms put money into the theatre treasury, thanks to Ebers's foresight in providing a green-room. Whenever a rehearsal was announced, Ebers was besieged by applications for admission, and a charge was made for the liberty of being present, as to a regular representation. Ladies were as eager as the men to see her. Noblet's wishes were always gratified, even to the extent of getting the court regulations on one occasion altered to suit her convenience. She had fixed her benefit on a certain day, but a prohibition for some reason was issued from the Lord Chamberlain's Office. The King's Theatre was at that time licensed not under a patent but by the Lord Chamberlain, and renewed annually. The Lord Chamberlain was the Marquis of Hertford, whose reputation for susceptibility to female charms, despite his age, was well known. Mademoiselle therefore did not despair. She first applied to Lord Ailesbury, the chairman of the Theatre Committee, who wrote to the Marquis. The latter's reply began thus :

" MY DEAR LORD,—

" I have this moment (eleven o'clock) received your letter, which I have sent to the Chamberlain's Office, . . . and as Mademoiselle Noblet is a very pretty woman, as I am told, I hope she will call there to assist in the solicitude which interests her so much."

Mademoiselle's charms were irresistible, and she gained her point. The anonymous author of the Vestris *Memoirs* had, of course, something venomous to say concerning the lady, remarking with an air of hypocritical propriety, " Madame Noblet was a virtuous woman [how did *he* know ?] till she breathed the air of this Paphian temple [the King's Theatre green-room], and then even an old cracked fife could set her dancing the Highland Fling." The punning allusion to his amorous lordship will not be overlooked.

Lord Fife did not confine his attentions to the fascinating Noblet. A charming little Spanish girl who came out as a dancer when she was but fifteen and at once had the world of Paris at her feet captured the susceptible nobleman, and was induced by him to come to the King's Theatre, where she was engaged for the season at a salary of £800. Maria Mercandotti produced the most tremendous sensation. The most experienced habitué of Fops' Alley could remember nothing like it. She was hotly pursued by the dandies, and Ebers was pestered to death by the frequenters of the green-room for introductions ; but he had the astuteness to refer the eager suitors to Lord Fife.

At the very zenith of Mercandotti's glory Ebers one day received the following note :

" MONSIEUR,—

" Ma santé étant extrêmement dérangée j'ai consulté mon médecin, qui m'a conseillé d'aller à la campagne pour passer quelque temps ; je m'empresse de vous en prévenir afin que vous puissiez donner mon rôle à une autre personne. J'ai l'honneur d'être, Monsieur,

" MARIA MERCANDOTTI."

Consternation reigned among the beaux when Ebers made his apologies (one may well believe that he did so with his tongue in his cheek ; no one was better acquainted with the pretty ways of *premières danseuses*) for the young lady's non-appearance, but in a very few days the truth oozed out. Maria had run away with Ball Hughes, one of the most popular gallants of the day ! Hughes carried her off to Banff, where they took advantage of the free-and-easy marriage law of Scotland. A *jeu d'esprit* which the affair evoked is not unworthy of quotation :

" Sir, being a-miss et ma santé dérangée
    Mon médecin declares qu'il y a quelque chose à changer.
    I suppose he means â la campagne je vais,
    So dispose of my rôle à quelque autre, I pray,
    But Mama ne veut pas que je sois paresseuse,
    Bids me go to a Ball and I cannot ref-Hughes !

The admired Mercandotti figures in a coloured cartoon of the period, one of many sprightly caricatures of the most-talked-of woman of the day, Mrs. Coutts, once the favourite actress Harriot Mellon, who married Coutts the banker and became the richest widow in Great Britain and eventually the Duchess of St. Albans. The caricature is entitled " A Visit to Court," and represents the Lord Chamberlain asking Mrs. Coutts and Mademoiselle Mercandotti for their cards. Mercandotti holds a card in one hand and a ball in the other and apparently is about to execute a pirouette on her right big toe.

Disraeli, writing from Spain, in a letter to his mother dated August 1830, thus refers to the charms of the all-conquering dancer : " At seventeen a Spanish beauty is poetical, tall, lithe, and clear, though sallow. But you have seen Mercandotti. As she advances, if she does not lose her shape, she resembles Juno rather than Venus. Majestic she ever is; and if her feet are less twinkling than in her first career, look on her hand and you'll forgive them all."[1]

"Ball" Hughes was a typical dandy. His name was originally Ball, but as his uncle, Admiral Hughes, left him a fortune which brought him in £40,000, he added "Hughes" to "Ball" and in consequence was nicknamed "The Golden Ball." He was good-looking, he dressed well—a most important qualification in the days of the dandies—and he gambled incessantly. Betting became second nature with him, and the object of the bet did not much matter. It is said that he and Lord Harrington once played at battledore and shuttlecock from evening till daylight with heavy wagers on each game. Lord William Lennox says of him: "Ball Hughes was a most delightful companion, good-natured, unaffected, and full of fun; I do not remember ever seeing him out of temper. One trifling annoyance he had, and that was that a gentleman known as Pea-green Hayne from the verdant colour of his coat and called 'The Silver Ball," was set up as a rival to the original 'Golden Ball.' Of Hayne I know little. He was conspicuous for having a black servant and a prize-fighter up in the rumble of his travelling carriage." Pea-green Hayne afterwards became notorious for his association with Maria Foote—and the story of his folly will find its place in these pages later on.

One of the fads of the moment was the craze of giving nicknames to prominent men of fashion. Besides "The Golden Ball," there was "The Silent Hare," "Kangaroo Cooke," "Red Herrings," otherwise Lord Yarmouth, so called partly because he had red hair and whiskers and had Yarmouth in his title, "Monk" Lewis (the author of *The Monk*, a novel

[1] *Life of Disraeli*, W. F. Monypenny.

which did him more harm than good because of its alleged immoral tendency, and of *The Castle Spectre*, a play immensely popular and entitled to be called the first of the melodramas), " King Allen " (Lord Allen, the greatest dandy in town), " Handsome Jack " (Jack Phillipson), " Poodle Byng," " Pea-green Hayne," and a host of others.

The aim of every buck was to be talked about, and the possessor of any marked peculiarity bestowed upon him by nature was envied, and those who were thus denied set their wits to work to invent some eccentricity. Hayne's negro servant and his prize-fighter were the outcome of this craze. These fads had to conform to certain rules laid down by the " fashionables." Mr. T. H. Duncombe says of his father, Thomas Slingsby Duncombe, that " he was expected to do as young men of family and fortune were reported to him as having invariably done. . . . He must be seen at Tattersall's as well as at Almack's ; be more frequent in attendance in the green-room of the theatre than at a levee in the palace ; show as much readiness to enter into a pigeon match at Battersea Red House as into a flirtation in May Fair ; distinguish himself in the hunting-field as much as at the dinner-table ; and make as effective an appearance in the Park as in the Senate ; in short, he must be everything—not by turns but all at once, sportsman, exquisite, gourmand, rake, senator, and at least a dozen other varieties of the man of fashion." Mr. Duncombe omits gambling and the prize-ring ; with these amusements added, one may admit the truth of Pierce Egan's *Life in London*, which, it may be noted, appeared in 1822 and instantly caught on, leading to the production of the popular drama *Tom and Jerry*, which was played in almost every theatre in the United Kingdom.

So far as gallantry was concerned there was not much to choose between the men and women of the West-end world. The influence of the flagrant profligacy of the Regency was continued into the Monarchy. Public opinion was so hardened to the spectacle of immorality in high places that the amatory follies of the rich formed the staple topic of conversation. Mr. Cyrus Redding remarks, " Whatever charges Lord Brougham may bring against the aristocracy, . . . they have still a respect, at least some of the female part of it, for what is due to morality and religion, if it be not exhibited beyond external conduct."

This is not saying very much in the defence of the ladies, and what with the scandals disclosed by the trial of Queen Caroline and with Lady Conyngham established as first favourite of the King and living with him at " The Cottage " near Windsor, it was not to be expected that dancers and actresses would pose before their betters as examples of decorum. In an age of reckless extravagance when pleasure must be had no matter what it cost, Madame Vestris, who had not been accustomed to deny herself anything, plunged into luxuries the money for which did not come from her purse. There is little to reproach her with in this. As already pointed out, it was the fashion. Young men who came into the possession of fortunes got rid of their money as fast as they could, and when all is said and done, more gold found its way into Crockford's coffers than was spent on ladies of the stage.

It may be safely assumed that in the green-rooms of the King's Theatre and Drury Lane the fascinating Vestris was greatly admired and sought after by the bucks. Whether she cared for any one of them beyond the rest cannot be positively asserted, but that in 1821 and 1822 she was closely associated with a Mr. Montagu Gore, a young man of good family and means, certain scraps of correspondence which came to light in the catalogue of a country auctioneer, who sold a bundle of letters from which he made brief extracts, fully show. Mr. Gore may have made her acquaintance in the green-room, but the inference to be drawn from some of Madame's letters is that he was not one of the favoured few who had the entrée.   Most probably he was a devotee of Drury Lane, and from the pit had succumbed to the charms of the shapely " Don." Had he been one of the green-room circle the goddess would not have had occasion to utilise the services of Mr. Harris.   Otherwise the two would have been constantly meeting and would most likely have made up their differences by word of mouth.

For there were differences, but from what cause the extracts do not disclose.   The lady's passion for poor Montagu (if she had had a passion, which may be doubted) may have cooled, or she may have favoured some other admirer, or she may have been bothered by monetary troubles for which the young gallant's means did not suffice.   Whatever it was, she sought the assistance of Harris, who wrote letters which she copied and sent to Gore.   It may be that at the delicate and disagreeable stage in which the " affair " had arrived she could not bring herself to deal with it in a businesslike spirit.   She might have dreaded losing her temper or was afraid of saying too much or too little.

One thing is clear, she was on terms of comradeship with Harris and sent him Gore's letters to be answered, and we have her writing him in this playful fashion : " Madame Troothy presents her compliments to Charlie Tidlams and requests he will come and fetch her to take a little drive as she has a little headache "— " Pray write answer to the enclosed."—" C—— is arrived, therefore I cannot have the pleasure of dining with you to-day."—" Pray let me know what you have said to the Maypole."   If by the " Maypole " the unhappy Montagu is meant—highly probable— one can fancy him tall and thin and melancholy with disappointed love.

Harris's letters sent via Madame seem to have had due effect.   Mr. Gore writes : " I pledge myself to settle on Madame Vestris the sum of £300 per annum for her life.   December 3rd, 1821."   Apparently this was meant as a kind of atonement for some offence he had committed, for in the same letter occurs this entreaty : " My dearest love, it will require no great exertion of strength to see the man who longs to ask your forgiveness."

But the divinity was not to be moved. Either her heart was not touched or the sum offered was too insignificant for her to consider. On the whole, it may be taken for granted that she was not prepared to give up her freedom of action for £300 per annum, if such a condition were hinted at. And indeed, in comparison with the huge sums which were being flung at the feet of the Noblets and Mercandottis it was a trifle. Vestris, at all events, remained silent, upon which the swain stood upon his dignity and delivered himself thus : " Mr. Montagu Gore presents his compliments to Madame Vestris, and having received no answer to his last note, begs to say that he considers the connection as *finally* and *irrecoverably* broke off. . . . She must have been aware that he expected to have met with a return for his kindness."

The lady seems to have relented so far as her silence was concerned. Further correspondence followed, and then it looked as if the secret was out. It is the eternal triangle—two men and one woman. " I have explained," writes Elizabetta (or Charles Harris for her), " that I was in possession of a settlement which nothing could take from me, but the very act I had in contemplation would bind me in honour to return that which I could not in honour retain."

Mr. Harris is slightly involved here ; anyhow, it is pretty clear why the £300 per annum did not appeal to Madame ; at the same time one wonders whether the conclusion of the letter was Harris pure and unadulterated or was amended by the lady. The extract is fragmentary and has a flavour of the senti-mental mood of the period. It starts with a burst of versified emotion : " No, Monti, no, I'll ne'er forsake the man, Who gives me all I want and all he can." Then follow a few more rhyming lines and it proceeds : " Were I to make one more and you recede, I am ruined."—" If my actions or my manner is to be governed by any particular rule unconnected with my own feelings, I must say millions could not tempt me to make such a sacrifice." On the whole, this effusion reads more like Harris than Vestris.

Here this interesting sidelight on Madame's private life ends. As it reads, there does not seem much romance in it. But how could there be—in a love-affair conducted by a deputy ? Who was the man whom the lady would ne'er forsake and what was the amount of his settlement which satisfied all her wants ? But the answer to the last question would settle no-thing. Vestris might be satisfied for a brief space, but soon would be wanting more. The demands of the world she lived in had to be met.

If Disraeli's opinion of Montagu Gore was correct— and so shrewd a judge of character did not often make a mistake—the gentleman could not boast of qualities likely to attract a woman who never allied herself seriously with mediocrity. Writing to his sister on February 13th, 1834, Disraeli says : " Montagu Gore has accepted the Chiltern Hundreds, and asked me to stand for Devizes, which I have refused. . . . Gore, according to his address, resigns for two reasons— his health, and also because he has recanted and turned Tory ! His health and head seem equally weak. He is an ass, who has terminated an asinine career with a very characteristic bray." [1] One is justified in assuming that Mr. Gore in 1822 was not in possession of more wisdom than he could claim in 1834. (Vestris's letters to Gore and others will be found in a subsequent chapter.)

[1] *Life of Disraeli* (W. F. Monypenny).

CHAPTER VIII

THE WAYS OF PRIMA DONNAS

Vestris in Italian opera. The Montagu Gore "affair" again. Josephine Bartolozzi and her admirers. Madame Vestris's alleged "victims." Vestris announced to sing in Rossini's "oratorio" Cyrus in Babylon. Vestris returns to the King's Theatre. The ways of prima donnas. An impresario and his troubles. The rules of dressing-rooms at the King's Theatre. Vestris insists upon more candles. A queer offer to Ebers. The beautiful Miss Chester. She is appointed reader to George IV.

THE year 1822 was not marked by any event of outstanding importance. Madame Vestris continued at Drury Lane, and *Don Giovanni in London* was put on at intervals throughout the year. She also played in *The Pirate*, a musical adaptation of Scott's novel, and in *The Beggar's Opera* on March 7th, the *Post* remarking that in the leading character she " bore away the palm from all other Macheaths of the day." In *The Duenna* she converted Don Carlos, hitherto always taken by a man, into a " breeches " part and the play ran for a few nights. *Artaxerxes* and *Paul and Virginia* (Vestris as Paul) also provided alternatives to *Giovanni*. In January she took part in the first of a series of concerts described as " Covent Garden Musical Performances " conducted by Bochsa, a well-known harp player in great request. He had not then distinguished (or extinguished) himself by running away with the wife of Henry Bishop, the composer. At this concert, Vestris sang her favourite song from *Artaxerxes*, " In Infancy."

Her connection with Italian opera was renewed in 1822, but she only sang once, taking the place of

Madame Caradori (afterwards Caradori Allen), who
found that her soprano voice did not suit the contralto
part of Pippo in Rossini's *La Gazza Ladra*.   During
the remainder of the season at Drury Lane she appeared
with Braham in *The Haunted Tower* and in the *Siege
of Belgrade*, and took the part of Julian in *The Peasant
Boy*, a musical play of no particular merit.   When the
season ended at the " Lane " she went to the Haymarket, which was then open only during the summer
months—a condition of its licence, so as not to interfere with the patent rights of Drury Lane and Covent
Garden Theatres.   At the Haymarket she sang in
The Beggar's Opera, and " by permission of the proprietor " of that theatre appeared as " Macheath "
in a performance of the opera at Covent Garden for
the benefit of Abbott, a member of the company.
On this occasion Polly was played by Miss Stephens,
" the most charming impersonation of the character
of that or any other period."

The name of Madame Vestris at this time and for
the next four or five years was not so well known to
the " man in the street " as it afterwards became.
Her engagement at the King's Theatre probably
gave her a *cachet* which lifted her above the common
gossip of the day.   She was talked of simply as a
delightful and enchanting singer and actress, but of
herself outside the theatre little had oozed out for
the scandalmongers to take hold of.   She managed
her amours skilfully and her tender affair with Montagu
Gore never became the property of the scurrilous
catchpenny writers for them to embellish in their
own peculiar style.   But some of her intimate circle
of friends were acquainted with the story.   One item
in the auction catalogue from which we have quoted
is very suggestive.   It runs thus : " 12 unsigned letters
to Harris apparently from a rejected lover of ' Madame's.' "   It is impossible to quote the more characteristic passages from these extremely free letters.
References are made to " Best," Josephine (Madame's

sister), Duncombe, and others.   Madame is constantly
referred to in the most outspoken manner ; she is
nicknamed " Plaguemidamnables."   Montagu, one
learns, is settling £700 a year on her—" gold becks her
on—she cannot coin you or me into it."

The dates of these letters are not given.   They
probably belong to different periods, as there is no
evidence to show that Mr. Duncombe was so closely
associated with Madame Vestris at the time of the
Montagu Gore episode as he was later on, when she
was contemplating taking the Olympic Theatre.

" Best " was of course the Captain Best who,
according to Mrs. Baron-Wilson, was interested in
furthering Vestris's education in her girlhood, and
who is represented by Madame's anonymous biographer
as having an interest in her of a totally different kind.
In later years, when the *Age* newspaper came into
being, he was lampooned under the name of " Kettle-
drum " Best.   Best's reputation does not incline one
to believe in his benevolent motives.   Rumour certainly connected his name with that of Josephine
Bartolozzi in a sense which in these days would not
redound to his credit, but which a hundred years
ago would surprise few.

Mr. Tuer, in *Bartolozzi and his Works*, gives a
description of a miniature in ivory of Josephine,
painted after her marriage with Anderson (a racing
man who subsequently figured discreditably in Vestris's
financial matters), which represents her as " a creature
of more than ordinary loveliness.   The features are
pleasing, but hardly sufficiently regular to be strictly
classical ; fine bust, very dark eyes with arched,
delicately pencilled eyebrows, a Roman nose perhaps
a trifle too long ; a mobile, smiling mouth sufficiently
open to disclose a suspicion of pearly teeth, a profusion
of auburn hair slightly shot with gold tucked behind
small shell-like ears and gathered into a simple knot,
and a skin of pearly fairness flushed with health "—
altogether an attractive beauty, and one can conceive

that she was as much run after by the beaux as her sister Elizabetta.   But she had not Elizabetta's cleverness.

The anonymous biographer asserts that Josephine was the object of Lord Petersham's pursuit and that to escape him she ran away, finding that her mother was on the side of his lordship.   "Captain Best had afforded her protection when she fled from her mother," says the biographer, " and it was said entirely on the score of humanity, which no one doubted, for he was nearly treble her age and had done many just and disinterested actions."   How this eulogium can be reconciled with statements in other parts of the book that " this Captain's connection with the two sisters does not do honour to his name," that he left Madame Vestris at Manchester for a Lady Bennet because she paid him better and he " wanted money and would have linked himself to the devil to have got it," and that he " was a man possessed of as little feeling as one of the houyhnhnms in *Gulliver's Travels*," it is impossible to say.   Going back to the catalogue, an item runs as follows : " Six letters to Harris from W. Duncombe (T. S. Duncombe ?)—mentioned in a letter in parcel 5 in connection with Josephine Bartolozzi—mainly relating to money difficulties."   Parcel 5 consists of the " 12 unsigned letters to Harris " already alluded to.

The description of Josephine given by Mr. Tuer justifies one in suspecting that she was of a nature born to love and be loved.   It can easily be imagined that she was a source of anxiety and expense to her elder sister.   Whatever faults Eliza Vestris had, she possessed the redeeming quality of being exceedingly generous.

Josephine's marriage was not a very happy one (it took place some years later than the period now dealt with).   Her husband attempted the stage, but he was a poor actor, and probably could not support his wife.   It will be seen what kind of character he was by what is told of him later on in these pages.

Madame Vestris was certain to help her sister as she helped her mother—later on she was allowing the latter £200 a year—and these burdens, added to her own lavish expenditure, accounted for her always being in want of money. But she was surrounded by a host of rich admirers, and she does not seem to have been particularly diffident in going to them when she was in difficulties. Mr. T. H. Duncombe must have had Madame in his mind when he wrote : " There was one popular actress who had the reputation of exhausting the resources of the wealthiest admirers. The Dives at the commencement of these intercourses invariably became a Lazarus at its conclusion ; at last she beggared him and she sought another dupe. The catalogue of her victims is a remarkable one and includes men of high social position." But an excuse may be made for Mr. Duncombe's bitterness. She certainly cost his father a pretty penny. Excuses are also due to Madame. She was mingling with the *beau monde* ; she had to keep up appearances, and money flowed through her fingers like water. On her assuming the reins of management at the Olympic demands for financial assistance became never-ceasing, and Mr. Duncombe probably stood her friend.

Don Giovanni in London, which had made Vestris famous, ceased to attract after 1822, and no novelty could be found to take its place. She had to some extent severed herself from such parts as would attract the pit and gallery. It looks as if at this time she had ambitions to shine in higher forms of dramatic art, but had not made up her mind in what direction. She was hovering between Italian opera and the " legitimate " drama. She renewed her engagement at the King's Theatre for the 1823 season and appeared in her old part of Pippo in *La Gazza Ladra,* as Malcolm in *La Donna del Lago* and in *Ricciardo e Zoraide.* Hitherto Mozart's music had held the sway, and *Don Giovanni, Figaro, La Clemenza di Tito* and *Così fan tutte,* were the favourite operas.

In 1823, however, a large section of the musical public went Rossini mad, and anything from his fertile brain was eagerly looked for. It is odd to find him talked of as having composed an oratorio; however, *Cyrus in Babylon*, produced at Drury Lane, is so described. A semi-public rehearsal conducted by Bochsa took place in March, when Braham, Mrs. Salmon (identified with oratorio singing), Miss Ellen Tree, and Madame Vestris were announced to sustain the principal parts; but when the first performance was given the " Oratorio " seems to have been " cut " and Madame Vestris did not appear—her name, at all events, is not among the soloists mentioned. The music is described as " adding to Rossini's reputation " —whether it did or not subsequent generations have had no chance of judging, as the work was promptly shelved and has not been heard since, at all events in England.

Public opinion, very tolerant in regard to morality or rather the absence of it, made up for its laxity in one direction by its strait-laced attitude in another. Rossini's *Mosè in Egitto*, touching as it did upon a Biblical subject, was not to be thought of as fit for the theatre, and it was produced at the King's Theatre transformed into *Peter the Hermit*. Probably the " fashionables " did not care two pins either way.

A characteristic instance of the way in which prima donnas love each other is recorded of one performance of *Peter*. One of the most beautiful airs in the opera is " Mi manca la voce " (My voice fails me). It was sung by Madame Camporese, and upon her pronouncing the words Madame Ronzi di Begnis (over whose surpassing beauty Ebers goes into a paroxysm of ecstasy) remarked audibly, " È vero " (Quite true). When the curtain fell, the encounter between the two ladies in its forcible language would not have disgraced a couple of Neapolitan lazzaroni. A more subtle display of antagonistic feminine feeling was that shown a half-century or so later when, as

Arditi relates, Madame Lablache was singing the part of Donna Anna in the famous trio in *Don Giovanni*. Brignoli, the tenor, had the unpleasant habit of expectorating constantly, and Madame, who knew this and who was wearing a very expensive dress, was in agony lest her gown should suffer. At last, unable to contain herself, she whispered to him, entreatingly, "*Voyons, mon cher ami, ne pourriez-vous pas, une fois par hasard, cracher sur la robe de Donna Elvina ?*"

Ebers pathetically records his troubles arising out of the jealousies, the fits of ill-temper, and caprice of operatic stars, male as well as female. The rehearsals were times of tribulation. The prima donna, not satisfied with her part, would demand certain alterations, and if they were refused she would walk out of the theatre. Should the manager prove obdurate, she promptly had an attack of illness. Whenever there was a squabble between the leading singers, the rest of the company took it up, all talking at once in three or four different languages, while the chorus vociferated their opinions pro and con. The orchestra, not interested in the quarrel, would go on playing without the voices, until the leader, tired out, put on his hat and departed and was speedily followed by the members of the band, leaving the distracted manager to tear his hair.

The method adopted by Harris, one of the best stage managers on record, the father of the late Sir Augustus Harris, to show his disgust when things went wrong, was equally effectual and original. Mr. Harris always wore a top-hat of extreme glossiness, which he appeared to regard as a sort of fetish. If the principals, the chorus, or the ballet were inclined to be rebellious and refused to yield to persuasion or reprimand, Harris would burst into a torrent of angry remonstrance, and having worked himself up to the proper pitch, he would switch the glossy hat from his head, throw it on the stage, and jump upon it with an emphatic " There ! " thus indicating that the end of the world had come.   The unruly crowd, struck with awe at the unparalleled sacrifice, generally recovered their senses.

The traditions attending the privileges of operatic stars in respect to their dressing-rooms were strictly adhered to in Ebers's time.   The prima donna was entitled to a separate room with a sofa and six wax candles.   The secunda had to put up with a room *without* a sofa and had to be satisfied (or more likely dissatisfied) with two candles only.   It goes without saying that no self-respecting *cantatrice* could possibly dress herself properly with so miserable a glimmer. At all events, Madame Vestris could not, and as the management dared not break the rules which from time immemorial had governed this important matter, she went her own way and provided herself with two additional candles at her own expense.   On one occasion when the resources of the establishment were exhausted and the extra candles were not forthcoming, her imperious spirit was roused, and taking her stand behind the curtain, she refused to dress for the part until the required number of lights was furnished, and she won the day !

In the midst of all these worries Ebers had now and again compensating experiences which lightened his burdens.   One of the most amusing of these experiences is that revealed in the indignation of a gentleman who, having presented himself for admission at the pit door in a pair of drab pantalons, was refused admission.   He wrote a letter of protest to Ebers, in the course of which he said : " I was dressed in a superfine blue coat with gold buttons, a white waist-coat, fashionable tight drab pantaloons, white silk stockings and dress shoes, *all worn but once a few days before at a dress concert at the Crown and Anchor Tavern !* I have mixed too much in genteel society not to know that black breeches or pantaloons with black silk stockings is a very prevailing full dress, and why is it so ?   Because it is convenient and economical, for

you *can wear a pair of white silk stockings but once*
without washing, and a pair of black is frequently worn
for weeks without ablution. P.S.—I have no objection
to submit an inspection of my dress of the evening
in question to you or any competent person you may
appoint." It does not appear that this offer was
accepted, which on the whole was a pity, as the opportunity for much fun was lost.

Vestris's work at the King's Theatre in 1823 could
hardly be called arduous, as operas were given on two
nights in the week only, and £700 for the season, which
she received, was a fairly liberal remuneration, especially as she still retained her engagements at Drury
Lane, where her old successes (excepting *Giovanni*)
were repeated again and again, involving no trouble,
no rehearsals, and no necessity for fresh study.

She also renewed her position at the Haymarket,
where the successful novelty was a musical play entitled
Sweethearts and Wives. Owing to the preposterous
restrictions of theatrical licences only *burletta* could
be given in theatres other than the patent ones, and
to add to the absurdity no one could define exactly
what a *burletta* really was. " Something with a little
music " was probably its nearest description. *Sweethearts and Wives* was a *burletta*, and as such it caught
on and retained its place in the bill throughout the
season. It owed its success to the powerful attraction
of the two ladies in the principal characters—Madame
Vestris and Miss Chester, the last-named one of the
most beautiful women on the stage. The two played
together in subsequent seasons, and Vestris's vivacity
and archness and Miss Chester's charm of face proved
a combination in which the audience revelled.

Sweethearts and Wives deserves more than a passing
notice. It was written by James Kenney, a prolific
dramatist of the sprightly order, and contained a song
which has come down to our time, figuring in number-
less editions of English popular ditties. This was
" Why are you wandering here, I pray ? " a simple

and charming ballad which when first sung by Vestris
was received with delight.   It became one of Madame's
favourites, and was never given without the reward
of an encore.   The composer, Isaac Nathan, was a
musician of considerable talent, in great request as
a teacher of singing, and occasionally acted as musical
director in the theatre.   He also wrote the music
for several operas, pantomimes and melodramas,
among them *Alcaid* and *The Illustrious Stranger*,
written for Liston by Kenney.   Nathan's claims for
recognition rest, however, upon his arrangement of
Hebrew melodies for which Lord Byron wrote his
well-known verses.

Miss Chester achieved great distinction by the
solace she afforded George IV in the last year of his
life, which he passed in the seclusion of " The Cottage,"
Virginia Water.   Huish, who records the circumstances,
may be left to tell the story in his own words.   " His
Majesty in his enforced retirement," he says, " being
prohibited fishing by the doctors, enjoyed the lighter
literature of the day, and the reading of the drama
was a favourite amusement.   The latter circumstance
led to the introduction of Miss Chester into his establishment as *reader* to His Majesty.   It was at the theatre
where the graces of the lively actress attracted the
notice of royalty, and he made his *penchant* known
through the means of Sir Thomas Lawrence, who
was at that time engaged in taking the portrait of
the lady as well as of His Majesty.   A meeting was
soon obtained, and a kind of excuse was invented to
have Miss Chester near his person ; the dexterous
one of appointing her ' female reader ' was adopted,
and a salary of £600 per annum allowed.   Thus was
Miss Chester placed in the royal establishment and
her name was emblazoned in the red book."   The
gobemouches were provided with a tit-bit of gossip
of which no doubt every use was made in the way of
embellishment.

CHAPTER IX

SQUABBLES AT THE KING'S THEATRE

Ebers transfers the King's Theatre to Benelli. Rossini appointed musical conductor. Rossini's lucrative private engagements. Madame Vestris in *The Barber of Seville*. Her " Rosina " not a success. Her engagement at Drury Lane. In Shakespeare at the Haymarket. *The Beggar's Opera* and incongruous costumes. Success of *Alcaid*. Vestris in a " breeches " part. Private Sunday concerts projected. A " misunderstanding " at the King's Theatre. Madame Vestris alleged to be in fault. Hostile reception of Vestris. She bursts into tears. The matter explained and Vestris held to be blameless. An angry scene at Covent Garden. Vestris infuriated.

By the time the operatic season of 1824 had commenced Ebers had had enough of the King's Theatre and its responsibilities and had transferred his interest to Signor Benelli for the sum of £10,000. The sale, however, was attended by certain liabilities, the consequences of which Ebers did not foresee ; and though Benelli paid the £10,000, he defaulted subsequently and Ebers again found himself in difficulties.

Benelli commenced with the usual flourish of trumpets inseparable from operatic management. The spirit of the " reformer " was shown in this intimation which accompanied his announcement of a redecoration of the interior of the theatre on a scale of unprecedented magnificence : " Anxious as well to avoid an overcrowd behind the scenes as not to refuse one gentleman while another is admitted, it is thought right to state that the admission behind the scenes will be strictly confined as it is at Paris to the annual subscribers." From this it may be assumed that Ebers's rule in respect to visitors had been somewhat elastic.

Benelli had a trump card in Rossini, who had been engaged as musical conductor, his wife, Madame Colbran, being prima donna for the season. Rossini could not have wished for a more enthusiastic reception. He was fêted everywhere, and when at Brighton he was received by the King, the latter ordered the band to play the overture to *Il Barbiere* out of compliment to his visitor, who, when asked by His Majesty to say what he would like to hear, suggested, as a tactful courtier, " God Save the King." The episode of Rossini's introduction to Henry Bishop indicates the famous composer's readiness and his desire to please. Rossini could speak no English, and in default hummed the opening bars of Bishop's haunting melody " When the Wind Blows " from *The Miller and his Men.*

Rossini had a melodious tenor voice and his emoluments from the many private parties to which he was invited were very considerable. Indeed, his pursuit of pleasure combined with profit was carried to an extent which aroused the wrath of the *London Magazine.* " *Il gran* Maestro Rossini," it wrote (July 1824) " is engaged to direct the music and to compose a new opera. He does neither the one nor the other. The Signor is disgusted at the outset by the failure of his wife and he leaves the orchestra pretty much to its fate ; when . . . finding that he could obtain fifty guineas per night . . . for conducting a private concert (our poor English conductors do the same thing for five) and that . . . this stipend was generally increased, often doubled, and once or twice more than doubled . . . the Signor allows the libretto of *Ugo Rè d'Italia* to lie untouched upon his table and the people of England to wait till next year for the greatest of his works which we have the assurance of Signor Benelli it was to have been." The *London Magazine* did not make allowance for Rossini's incorrigible indolence and his love of good living. As he was able to indulge both tastes and be well paid

into the bargain—it is said he made £7,000 out of his
private engagements—he could afford to be indifferent
to the comments of his censor.

The season opened with *Zelmira*, in which Madame
Vestris had a part. The house was packed, and
when Rossini made his appearance and took his seat
at the piano, the applause was overwhelming. There
is no record whether he used a baton. He probably
did not, as that method of conducting had not come
into general use. Spohr at the Philharmonic Concerts
in 1820 was the first to do so. Up to that date and
for some time afterwards the pianist had the score
before him not exactly to conduct from it, but to
read after and play in with the orchestra when he
thought it necessary. The real conductor was the
first violin. When Spohr drew a baton from his pocket
and gave the signal to begin, the worthy directors of
the Philharmonic Society were quite perturbed at
the innovation and were beginning to protest; but
Spohr begged them to let him have at least one trial.
They yielded, and he so convinced them of the advantage of the baton that they allowed him to have
his own way. Spohr's baton was shown at the Musical
Exhibition of 1891. It was a clumsy stick not quite
a foot long wrapped round with parchment.

It could hardly be said that Madame Colbran was
a success, either in *Zelmira* or in any other opera. She
had an imposing presence and possessed a powerful
voice, and she had great dramatic talent; but she was
past her prime and at times sang terribly out of tune.
Zelmira proved to be an uninteresting work, and it
was not extraordinary that Madame Vestris in the
minor part allotted her had no chance of distinction,
the *Post* remarking that " Madame seemed quite an
interloper in the business of the drama, but she sang
with much spirit."

Rossini was the fashion. With the exception of
Zingarelli's *Romeo e Giulietta* and Mozart's *Don
Giovanni* (on the last night of the season) no operas

save those of the popular composer were performed. Such was the excitement that we have the *Post* writing : " Rossini's genius acts with the force of an irresistible magnet at this magnificent theatre. It has effected a revolution in the habits of the fashionable world, and in spite of the rules of *Bon Ton* which forebad individuals claiming any connection with high life to appear at the opera before the second act was nearly over, it collects them in crowds at an early hour even before the opening of the doors. On Saturday evening this was particularly apparent, for the pit was suddenly filled and all its avenues overflowed." To modify the rigid etiquette of the " fashionables " was a triumph indeed.

Vestris had her chance when *The Barber of Seville* was put on. The beautiful Ronzi di Begnis was announced as Rosina, but the lady had one of those unaccountable indispositions to which all prima donnas are liable and Madame took her place. The part, as most operatic goers know, is as delightful as it is difficult. It demands the most perfect vocalisation, and every Rosina was expected to introduce some *tour de force* in the singing-lesson scene. It is therefore not surprising to read that " Madame Vestris was the Rosina and as the arrangements of the theatre forced her into the part we shall only compare her with herself. Everyone knows that the music requires greater power of voice and execution than she has ever aspired to, but we must do her the justice to say that if the attempt was not equal to the occasion it displayed better singing than we have ever heard or expected from her lips."

Zerlina was another character which did not show her to advantage. Ebers says she took her benefit in 1824 in *Don Giovanni*, but there is no record of this in any of the contemporary journals. However, she certainly was Zerlina when the opera was produced on the last night of the season, and her singing did not particularly please the critics. This is not surprising when it is remembered that the music for Zerlina, as in the case of Rosina, was written for a soprano, while Vestris's voice approached that of a contralto. She was far more at home when as Arsace in Rossini's *Sémiramide* she sang with Madame Pasta the effective duet " Giorno di orrore." The music here was entirely within her compass.

During the operatic season she continued her engagement at Drury Lane, and a musical piece, *Philandering, or The Rose Queen*, in which she appeared was quite a success. The meretricious attractions of *Giovanni in London* no longer appealed to her, and her wayward mind and her restless ambition craved for some more exalted attraction. She had succeeded in establishing up to a point a reputation as an Italian operatic singer, but she had probably discovered from experience that she could not go very far in this direction. She had not had the requisite training nor had she the voice. In Italian opera it was the soprano first and the rest nowhere. Composers did not write leading parts for contraltos. With the exception of Gluck's *Orfeo* hardly an opera can be named where a contralto is the leading lady. Vestris no doubt was fully aware of this, and maybe she was beginning to be tired of continually playing second fiddle.

But where could she shine ? In the legitimate drama ? Hardly. Tragedy and strong emotional parts were beyond her reach. Even in her own line as a comedienne she had rivals. Maria Foote, Mrs. Waylett, Mrs. Humby, Mrs. Orger ran her very close, but they had not her fascinating personality. Notwithstanding this advantage she may be said to have succeeded only when she could make use of her great powers as a ballad singer pure and simple. In 1824 she experimented with Shakespeare, but the range of characters open to her was limited. However, she made a fair success as Mrs. Ford, and *The Merry Wives of Windsor* was given several times at Drury

Lane in 1824 and at the Haymarket in 1825. Indeed, she selected this character for her benefit at Drury Lane.

Another Shakespearean venture in 1824 was Ariel —a somewhat mature sprite, it must be confessed, seeing that she was seven-and-twenty and her charms fully developed. But that she sang " Come unto these yellow sands," " Full fathom five," and " Where the bee sucks " delightfully one can well imagine. As for her Luciana in *The Comedy of Errors*, it is hard to form an opinion. The notices in the newspapers do not amount to criticisms. They were purely perfunctory. As, however, the Adriana, the companion part—Adriana and Luciana run in couples throughout the play—was Miss Stephens, it is pretty certain that songs for both were introduced. The idea of Kitty Stephens, the peerless English songster, and Eliza, unequalled in her own particular line, appearing on the stage without singing is inconceivable! That Shakespeare did not consider songs for either lady necessary was not of the slightest consequence. Managers in those days cared nothing for Shakespeare's plays save as things to be cut about to suit particular players or particular exigencies.

Macready was acting at Drury Lane in June of this year, and it is curious to find that *Giovanni in London* followed his tragedy on his benefit night. It would be interesting to know what the solemn tragedian thought of the naughtinesses of the extravaganza. In the autumn Vestris essayed Nell in *The Devil to Pay*, which the one and only Dora Jordan had made her own. What Madame Vestris made of it we are not told. Her partner in the little play was William Farren. *Rob Roy*, with Vestris as Diana Vernon, among other plays all of which are now forgotten, was given towards the end of the Drury Lane season.

During the Haymarket summer season Madame was fairly active. *The Beggar's Opera* was put on several times, and on one occasion both Macheath (Vestris) and Peachum came in for gentle censure for wearing costumes of the twenties. It had been the fashion for some years to dress the parts in haphazard style. Incledon played Macheath in a coat with a high roll collar and a voluminous cravat *à la* Brummell, and what the dress of Madame Vestris was like the illustration elsewhere shows very plainly. No doubt in the adaptation of the Georgian dandy costume to feminine requirements the dress was "fetching" enough, but it was absurd so far as the opera was concerned. The time came when Madame outlived this folly, and becoming conscious of the incongruities which had been perpetrated for generations, produced *The Beggar's Opera* with costumes of the period when it was written.

The principal novelty at the Haymarket was *Alcaid*, an opera with a Spanish plot and with Vestris in a "breeches" part moving the *London Magazine* to write : "Madame Vestris enacted Don Felix in a good loose dashing rakehelly fashion. She is the best bad young man about town, and can stamp a smart leg in white tights with the air of a fellow who has an easy heart and a good tailor. We remember once seeing Madame Vestris in female attire and thought her a very interesting young person in that solitary instance, but we presume that she herself inclines to pantaloons and prefers to contemplate the daring knee and boot to the neat and modest foot veiled below the ankle." The music was composed by Isaac Nathan. "It is pretty," said the *London Magazine*, " but Mr. Nathan is one of those composers that require poetry to inspire them." This may have been so ; at all events there was nothing in the *Alcaid* which caught the popular fancy like Nathan's " Why are you wandering here, I pray ? " Other plays at the Haymarket were *Intrigue* and *Sweethearts and Wives*, the season ending with *The Marriage of Figaro*, Madame Vestris being the Susanna, a part which suited her admirably.

MISS MARIA FOOTE.

(From a painting by G. Clint, A.R.A.)

It is pretty evident that the " fashionables " had come to regard music as a very desirable amusement. No dinner party was complete without the engagement of whatever singer might be in vogue, and selections by Mozart and Rossini figured in every programme. The extent to which the fashion was carried is significantly shown by the following announcement which appeared in the *Post* during June 1824 : " A private gentleman is at this moment actively engaged in preparing a novelty to entertain the Fashionables next season, intending to open his house with Sunday evening assemblies. We understand that it is exclusively for the *haut ton* who are to be entertained with Sacred Music, and that to gain access to these Parties will be even more difficult than it now is to become entitled to the *entrée* at Almack's." These Sunday concerts were to be conducted by Sir George Smart, and the services of Miss Stephens, Madame Vestris, Braham, and Sapio were promised. The professionals apparently were not to be trusted, the programmes having to be " submitted to a committee of Gentlemen." As a sample of the snobbishness of the " Fashionables " it would be difficult to go beyond this. No further announcement appeared, and it may be presumed that the *haut ton* did not respond.

In 1825 Madame Vestris continued her operatic work, and there was no reason why she should not, seeing that her receipts from that source in 1824 amounted to £600. Among the operas in 1825 was Mozart's *Così fan tutte*, and in this Madame was fairly successful. This was on May 13th and six days later *Sémiramide* was announced for performance with Pasta. When, however, the audience assembled, they found that *Otello* had been substituted and a scene of confusion arose, the disturbance continuing for quite an hour, half the audience expressing contentment and the other half clamouring for an explanation. At last somebody connected with the management appeared on the stage and told the malcontents that in conse-

quence of some of the performers being absent a
proper rehearsal of *Sémiramide* was not possible. This
did not suffice. There were loud cries for the names
of the absentees. The answer came after a short
pause—" Madame Vestris." The lady, he added, had
refused to attend in consequence of some misunderstanding with Ebers. The programme was then
allowed to continue, but Vestris came in for a good
deal of free comment. It was clear that, however
popular Madame was at Drury Lane and the Haymarket, the "fashionables" were not inclined to put
up with any caprice on her part.

It turned out, however, that the explanation given
from the stage was only half the truth. Madame
Vestris had really a good deal of right on her side.
The audience who packed the house four days later
did not of course know this, and when she presented
herself she was received with a volley of hisses. It
was the first time she had met with a hostile reception,
and she retired hurt and astonished. Presently,
however, she reappeared accompanied by Mr. Ayrton,
the musical director, who when he could get a hearing
explained that Madame Vestris was not at all to blame,
but as he did not go into details the clamourings were
renewed. At last Madame herself spoke—when she
had a chance of being heard. She protested that on
the rehearsal day she was at the theatre until three
o'clock, but that Mr. Ayrton would not allow *Sémiramide* to be performed that evening as it was not in
a fit state for representation. Then her self-possession
broke down, her words became incoherent, and she
burst into tears and ran from the stage. By this
time the audience were ready to forgive, and on her
return to the stage the performance was started and
the opera, to quote the *Morning Post*, " went off
with infinite *éclat*."

Reading between the lines, the real culprit appears
to have been Ebers himself, and he cannot be accused
of an excess of chivalry in leaving Vestris to fight the

battle alone. To the end of the controversy he was reluctant to face the music, and when the full story was made known through the newspapers it was Mr. Ayrton who told it. It appears that a final rehearsal of the opera was called at half-past ten, and at half-past eleven "Madame Vestris came to the theatre and sent for the Director into the housekeeper's room, and there repeated what she had declared by letter the evening before, that she would not assist at the rehearsal then going on nor perform in *La Sémiramide* at night unless Mr. Ebers fulfilled certain promises which he had made. Madame Vestris added that she would go over to the Haymarket Theatre, would there wait one hour, and that if Mr. Ebers wished to see her he might send for her. It was then too late to trust to the mere chance of Mr. Ebers's coming to the theatre. A rehearsal on an opera night was an unusual thing; it had been called early in order to afford the performers time to repose before the evening, and any further delay was out of the question. The Director therefore dismissed them all and immediately determined to give *Otello* if possible or *Così fan tutte*, either of which was ready. . . .

"It is true that by half-past twelve Madame Vestris and Mr. Ebers had settled the point in question, and that in consequence the former offered to perform at night provided she were allowed to omit an air or a duet, but it was then too late; everybody had left the theatre . . . and another rehearsal was indispensably necessary. . . . Granting Madame Vestris's claim to have been just, she was not blameable for having occasioned the change."

It may be guessed without the need of much speculation that money was at the bottom of the trouble. Ebers was embarrassed not only by the liabilities Benelli had left unfulfilled but by the necessity of making certain structural alterations in the interior of the theatre. In all probability the salaries of some of the artists were in arrears. Madame Vestris was not one to accept a position of this kind submissively. Her temper was easily aroused, and when she was put out the person who had offended her would rather run away than fight. This seems to have been the case with Ebers. Some fifteen years later Macready had a passage of arms with her in which the lady came off the victor.

Arthur Griffinhoofe asserts he was an eyewitness of a squabble at Covent Garden arising out of *The Beggar's Opera* which, according to him, showed her "overbearing conduct." Vestris was, of course, the Macheath and the individual who caused her passionate outburst was Isaacs, who was cast for Mat o' the Mint. "Madame having performed Macheath for a number of nights at the Haymarket," says Griffinhoofe, "did not think proper to attend even one rehearsal at Covent Garden. . . . It appears, however, that the prompt-book of the Haymarket had been slightly altered, at her request, in order to bring into her part what is professionally termed ' a bit of fat,' *alias* ' a clap-trap,' of which alteration Mr. Isaacs was perfectly innocent ; for such was the genuine urbanity of that gentleman, that had Madame made the circumstances known to him, he would, without a murmur, have adapted his own part to that of her Macheath.

"The performance at night proceeded steadily on till the scene when Macheath enters to the gang, to give them instructions as to their respective duties, etc. In the midst of the dialogue Madame suddenly stopped, as if waiting for a cue.

"Poor Isaacs, being rather nervous, began to fidget, while Madame, advancing towards him, exclaimed with a frown, ' Go on, sir.'

" ' Madame,' replied he, ' I have given you the cue.'

" ' 'Tis false, sir ! '

" ' I beg pardon, Madame, I have not omitted a single word.'

" She answered, in a tone so loud as to be heard by

a great portion of the audience, ' I say 'tis false, sir, and I'll not speak another line till I have my cue,' and carelessly tapping her boots with her cane, she swaggered up the stage, and, seating herself on the table, sat for some time swinging her leg to and fro.

" The audience, now perceiving very clearly that something was wrong, began to express their disapprobation by insolent hisses."

Once off the stage, Vestris pounced on the poor actor and demanded an explanation of his behaviour. He appealed to the prompter and was proved to be in the right. This so infuriated Vestris that only with difficulty could she be persuaded to go on, though the stage was waiting. In the middle of her next song she burst into tears and rushed from the stage. Fawcett, the manager, came forward and apologised, stating that she was indisposed, but would go through the dialogue of the play though she could no longer sing. Tears came to Eliza Vestris as readily as smiles, and she resembled Peg Woffington and the " combustible " Kitty Clive in many respects ; but she was more emotional and had less control over her nerves than either of these ladies, both of whom so sadly plagued Garrick with their whims and caprices.

CHAPTER X

Turmoils in the theatrical world. Stormy reception of Kean at Drury Lane. Rowdy audiences. Private and public boxes—drawbacks to the latter. Why theatre audiences had deteriorated. Maria Foote and her action for breach of promise. "Pea-green" Hayne. The notorious Colonel Berkeley. Miss Foote's love complications. The *Times* weeps. Maria Foote faces an uproarious audience at Covent Garden Theatre. Hostile reception of Madame Vestris. Theatrical squabbles and fisticuffs. Ebers and *The Barber of Seville.* Complaints that Vestris smiles and shows her teeth too much. The *claque* at the King's Theatre. Dress regulations at the opera ridiculed. A critic's facetiousness.

THE following year—1825—was one of turmoil in the theatrical world. The playgoers of George IV's time, who as a rule regarded ordinary stories of lapses from the marriage vow with complacency and found them entertaining, were indignant when the hero or heroine of one of these piquant narratives happened to be a stage favourite whom they had honoured with their applause. An actor or actress might present the gross characters of Wycherley or Farquhar with impunity, but if in their own persons they went outside the conventional confines of morality—and worse, if their peccadilloes became public property—castigation awaited them at the hands of the virtuous patrons of the theatre.

Edmund Kean, owing to proceedings instituted against him by the husband of a lady in whom Kean had taken too great an interest, met with a stormy reception on his presenting himself on the stage of Drury Lane Theatre in *Richard III* on the night of January 24th, 1825. The yelling, the execrations, the hissing, prevented a single word reaching over the footlights. The disturbance became very pronounced. One of the management attempted to remonstrate with the audience. He was saluted with an orange which struck him full in the face, and he speedily retired. Kean, however, kept on steadily, and the only notice he took of the malcontents was to flick contemptuously a piece of orange-peel into the pit with the point of Richard's sword. For nights after he was received with similar noisy demonstrations, and it was some weeks before the indignant champions of morality granted him their pardon.

When it is considered of what kind of people the average theatrical audience consisted, these protestations on behalf of public decorum, it must be confessed, savoured not a little of hypocrisy. Whatever might be the cause of affront, an audience wanted a very small excuse to descend into rowdyism. From an article published in a contemporary periodical we learn that a great change had in 1825 come over theatrical audiences.

The writer points out that owing to the fitting-up of " handsome, showy private boxes," it had become unfashionable for families to be seen in the public boxes (now called the dress circle). The people of fashion were contented to wait until they could have the use of some friend's private box or deserted the theatre altogether rather than appear in places unbecoming to their style. " Hence the front rows of the dress circle, as it is ridiculously called, at both houses are filled with extraordinary-looking people who suck oranges or munch apples between the parts and look wildly about them as if they expected to see acquaintances." A proportion of the occupants of these boxes appeared to be of the rowdy type, with the result that " women in these boxes are exposed to much that is unpleasant unless they are actually hemmed in by their male friends ; and when perchance a gentleman takes his family to the dress circle,

if he neglect the precaution of providing a rear-guard
of able-bodied men to sit behind his wife and daughters,
the chances are that some fellow comes in at half-price,
half drunk, and thrusts his dirty boots on the bench
on which they sit, to the great damage and detriment
of their petticoats, or obtrudes his nauseous ribaldry
on their ears. . . . Then the matter is taken up by
the Squire of Dames and there is a quarrel—a playhouse quarrel, the most disreputable thing in the
world ; and the women, after screaming and fainting,
form a resolution never again to put their fathers,
brothers, husbands or lovers in jeopardy in going to a
public box."

The writer deals with another cause of the deteriora-
tion of theatres. " The best and steadiest supporters
of the theatre in the olden times," he asserts, " were
the citizens and respectable tradesmen of the metropolis." But the habits of these worthy people were
changed. They now lived in retirement at Hackney,
Newington Butts, Kensington, and when business
was over they flew to their retreats and " go many
hundreds of yards into the country to sleep instead
of going to the play to laugh, and greatly is this change
in their habits, manners and customs felt and deplored
in the treasuries of the great theatres."

One of the consequences of these changes was that
a large proportion of the occupants of the pit and
" dress circle " comprised idle young men from the
Inns of Court, " apprentices always ready for horse-
play, and tradesmen who still lived in the metropolis."
As to the gallery, the less said about it the better.
Macready has described his experience when he
cleansed the Augean stable represented by this part of
Drury Lane Theatre. It will be easily seen from this
that in the theatres an unruly element was generally
present which did not need much encouragement to
show itself.

The excitement over Kean had scarcely died away
when the self-nominated theatrical censors were

again called upon to express their opinion on a " scandal " of a far more interesting nature. This time the scene of action was Covent Garden Theatre. The amatory escapades of Miss Maria Foote, a pretty, engaging, and popular comedienne, had for some time past been a favourite gossiping topic, and in the beginning of 1825 the climax of interest was reached when she was awarded £3,000 damages in an action she brought for breach of promise of marriage. The defendant was the young gentleman of fashion already alluded to of the name of Hayne, known among his associates as " Pea-green " Hayne, whether from the colour of the clothing he affected or from his facile capacity for being duped is not quite certain. " Pea-green " Hayne belonged to the set of fashionable bucks and Corinthian Toms who thirsted for notoriety, buzzed round green-rooms, gambled in the St. James's Street hells, and whose pride it was to boast of the favours of fashionable actresses. So far as can be gathered, chivalry was an unknown quantity among these " fashionables " and they had not the slightest objection to washing their dirty linen in public— indeed, they seemed to seek the opportunity. Maria Foote had had an attachment of an intimate nature previous to her engagement to Hayne, and the fact must have been well known to the green-room gossipers; but " Pea-green " Hayne appears to have been unaware of the lady's past—or said he was, an assertion which may well be doubted.

The story, however, was not public property until October 16th, 1824, when the following statement by " Pea-green " Hayne, putting his case with brutal frankness, appeared in the newspapers : " I was not aware, when I made a proposal to Miss Foote, that she had ever been under the protection of Colonel Berkeley, her father and mother having always upheld (and I believed) her to be a paragon of virtue, and had not Colonel Berkeley in the latter end of June last in the presence of James Maxe, Esq. (as the

Colonel's friend), and Thomas Best, Esq. (as my friend), owned her having had children by him, the youngest then not a month old, I should have been in ignorance of the facts until too late to retrieve my happiness."

There is no evidence that Madame Vestris was in any way connected with this curious business ; it is odd, however, to find the man Best, with whom, according to report, she had been associated, posing as Hayne's friend and witness. Whether the memory of the public was stirred by the mention of Best's name cannot now be said, but it is certain from an episode which occurred later on that some kind of ill-feeling was created against her.

Maria Foote was the daughter of Samuel Foote, an ex-officer in the Army, and Colonel Berkeley's father was the Earl of Berkeley. The two became acquainted at Cheltenham, where the young lady was acting, and the Colonel, who affected amateur theatri- cals, made furious love to her. He could have married her, so he said, but that an association with an actress would have damaged his prospects, as he was expecting a peerage, and the love-affair was kept a profound secret, save from Maria's father and mother. It was said that the Colonel never visited Maria at her mother's house in Keppel Street, but she used to pay visits to Berkeley Castle whenever he wished, her mother always accompanying her on these occasions, but hardly on account of propriety, as during the five years of this association children were born.

Differences arose between them. Whether Maria saw that the Colonel's passion was waning it is hard to say, but it is certain that in the beginning of 1824 she encouraged the advances of " Pea-green " Hayne, and, according to Colonel Berkeley, a gallant of the same " fashionable " class named Clagitt. Hayne seems to have been looked upon by Mr. and Mrs. Foote as a very desirable husband for Maria. The father borrowed money of the youthful suitor, who was about twenty-three, and the mother made herself agreeable to him; and as for Maria, she wrote Hayne many letters and, what was a somewhat remarkable thing for a love-lorn damsel to do, kept copies of her letters.

In due time Hayne proposed, all his proceedings and love-makings being, so Maria's counsel asserted, duly reported to Berkeley, who apparently had someone prying round. After his proposal Hayne repented, and the letter quoted above was published in order to justify his refusal to marry the lady. It was a mean business, and perhaps Hayne's conscience smote him, for he took back his refusal and, in spite of Maria's past, he again proposed and, what was more to the purpose, actually purchased the licence. But shortly after he once more altered his mind, and the result was an action in the Court of King's Bench for breach of promise and the defendant was cast in damages.

The affair created an immense sensation. Both sides had their adherents, but on the whole public opinion upheld Maria; the *Times* of all papers in the world bursting into tears in a gush of sympathetic sentimentality. "Poor Miss Foote!" sobbed the "Thunderer." "We are sure our hearts, and we think every heart, must bleed for her. She is a fellow-creature destroyed beyond the power of human redemption. May Eternal Mercy pardon her errors as Eternal Justice will no doubt avenge her wrongs." The *Times* must have been sorry it perpetrated such an absurdity when in after-years "human redemption" came to Maria in the person of the Earl of Harrington (once the sparkish Lord Petersham), who made her his countess. After this "Eternal Mercy" and "Eternal Justice" were hardly worth thinking about.

Miss Foote might well congratulate herself on being rid of Hayne, especially as she was £3,000 the richer by his refusal to marry her. Hayne was little more than a mere simpleton, if the author of a memoir of Miss Foote in Oxberry's *Dramatic Biographies* has not maligned him. "We are informed," he writes in 1825, " this precious youth about three years since paid his vows to Miss Bartolozzi, the sister of Madame Vestris and the object of the peculiar regard of the butterfly Petersham; that he deceived Miss B. as he did our heroine and ultimately refused to fulfil his engagements, and that the friends of that lady . . . consented to ' hush it up ' for a ' good round sum.' . . . A celebrated duellist, indeed the *best* shot in the Kingdom, is said to have been the mediator in this delicate transaction." The identity of this gentleman is sufficiently indicated by the pun on his name.

Six years later, after Miss Foote became the Countess of Harrington, Hayne wrote to her husband asking for the return of the jewels, valued at £5,000, he presented her during his courtship, but he received no satisfaction either from the Earl or the Countess. Within a year or two he became insolvent, having run through every penny of his fortune. In 1820 he came into the possession of £162,000; in 1834 he had hardly a sixpence. Miss Foote did not err on the side of generosity.

Emerging triumphantly from the law courts with all the secrets of her heart disclosed, Maria Foote appeared at Covent Garden Theatre and everybody rushed to see her. About half-past four in the afternoon of February 6th the pit doors were surrounded by an unruly mob which gradually increased, and on the doors being opened at six o'clock the rush was terrific. In a very short time it was made known that the house was full and the doorkeepers refused to take any more money. Clamorous applicants for box places were, however, told that the orchestra had been elegantly fitted up and seats could be had there for two guineas each.

The play was *The Belle's Stratagem*, possibly chosen because many of the passages put into the mouth of Letitia Hardy were appropriate to the circumstances. It was soon evident that the sympathisers were in a vast majority, and when the young lady came

upon the stage she had an uproarious reception.
What with " shouts, rapping of fans, clapping of hands,
and the rattling of the boards in the boxes, mingling
with the astounding noise that burst from the pit,"
no wonder Maria was overwhelmed and as much
frightened as pleased. After a dissentient in the
gallery had been summarily ejected, the house settled
down to enjoy the play, and every expression that
could be twisted into an allusion to the case was
boisterously approved.

The episode previously alluded to concerning
Madame Vestris was thus described by the *Morning
Post* : " After the drop-curtain fell, Madame Vestris
was discovered in the boxes and a shout was raised
against her from the pit and gallery. It did not,
however, in the least disconcert the lady. She kept
her seat as quietly as though she were the ' lion '
of the night." It is impossible to give an explanation of this expression of disapproval. One can only
conjecture either that the gossips had chosen to
assume she was in some way mixed up in the scandal
or that in the excess of their virtuous mood the censors
fastened upon Madame as a typical representation of
fashionable frivolity and frailty and condemned her
accordingly.

The readiness with which aggrieved persons took
the law into their own hands was very noticeable during
the next few weeks. As if Colonel Berkeley had not
made himself sufficiently notorious, he must needs
take umbrage at some adverse criticisms upon his
conduct in a Cheltenham paper, and accompanied
by a friend he called upon the editor and savagely
assaulted him.

Poole, the dramatist, was similarly affected by the
mania for pugnacity. Indignant at Elliston's striking
his name off the free list as a retaliation for his attack
on the Drury Lane manager contained in the introduction to his play *Married and Single*, he soothed
his feelings by the use of his walking-stick.

A squabble between Decamp, the manager of the Sheffield Theatre, and Macready happily ended without the necessity of fisticuffs; but it was the reverse at Liverpool, where a young lady, having had a difference with the management and receiving her dismissal, posted up an appeal which resulted in the audience championing her cause in very emphatic fashion. The play with which the performance commenced was allowed to proceed quietly, but when *The Forty Thieves*, from which the young lady in question had been ousted, began, the row started with a bombardment of apples, oranges, potatoes, penny pieces, and the like. In vain Vandenhoff, who was in the company, protested; the audience was out for mischief. They pulled up the seats of the gallery, they pulled down the ceiling, threw lime at the actors, and hurled the gallery benches into the pit and smashed the crystal chandelier, doing damage to the extent of about £400 in a very few minutes! A theatrical audience in the days of Madame Vestris was a veritable ogre, and little wonder when the monster was angered that managers and players did all they could to appease its wrath. The odd thing was that the violators of the law were rarely, if ever, punished.

No further disturbances of any moment occurred during the year to offend the susceptibilities of playgoers. There were annoyances, however, one of which in connection with the opera may be mentioned as typical of the theatrical management of the day. Ebers, finding he would have to close the King's Theatre, for a time, as the gallery was unsafe and threatened to give way, removed his company to what was still called by its old name of "The Little Theatre in the Haymarket." He altered the interior to suit the requirements of his aristocratic patrons, but the attractions were not quite satisfactory. For instance, the fronts of the boxes were not separated and "persons of fashion suffer the

pain of being seen by the next-door neighbours as
plainly as if they were exposing themselves in the public
boxes of vulgar theatres."

Another complaint was that the balcony, which
according to the advertisements " had been fitted
up in a commodious manner to communicate with
the boxes and pit," turned out to be the old two-
shilling gallery for seats for which ten shillings were
now charged. Pit-seat holders could transfer to
the balcony if it so pleased them, but the balconyites
were not admitted to the pit, though the price was
the same. " We observed one night," writes a
complainant, " that a servant of the house squared
himself before the pit passage and almost opposed
the entrance of individuals until they had answered
in the negative one question, whether they came from
the gallery." It is not surprising to read that " this
unusual piece of impertinence gave great disgust," and
no doubt squabblings were frequent and led to much
stormy language.

The theatre opened on March 1st with *Nozze di
Figaro*, the beautiful Ronzi de Begnis being the
Countess. Madame Vestris was Susanne, playing, so
the *London Magazine* thought, " with no great effect ;
indeed this lady seems to us altogether out of her element on the opera stage, and when she enacts Susanne
in particular we cannot help fancying that we see
' Giovanni ' in petticoats, so decidedly rakish an air
does she fling into the character. The Susanne of
Madame Vestris is in truth so exceedingly *knowing*
a waiting-woman that it appears especially wonderful
to us that she contrives to carry her virtue safe to the
end of the piece." The critic was equally dissatisfied
with Vestris's Rosina in *Il Barbiere*. He thought her
voice was not equal to the music, " but if smiles can
make amends for this deficiency it must be confessed
that ample compensation is made for it."

The opera went back to the King's Theatre in
May, and opened on the 12th with *Don Giovanni*.

Grumblings were heard at the poorness of the company. "What does Madame Vestris do here?" plaintively asked the *London Magazine*; and coming to a notice of her as Zerlina, it remarked, "In singing she was unequal to the part, but in smiling she far exceeded it. No man likes to see fine teeth more than we do, but a lady would not show her teeth to the public as she would show them to a dentist—a discovery every now and then of these beauties is very delightful, but an excessive exhibition of them destroys the effect"—an opinion which one is tempted to commend to the notice of many actresses of the present day, judging at least by their photographs. In reading the adverse criticisms of Vestris in operatic parts, one might be tempted to question the judgment of Mr. H. F. Chorley quoted in a former chapter. But if Madame persisted in singing music written for a soprano with a voice that inclined to contralto, what could she expect but unfavourable notices?

It is interesting to find that the *claque* was actively employed at the King's Theatre—that is to say, when it did not go to sleep. Apparently it had a way of doing this and then suddenly waking up and applauding in the wrong place. This fault induced one critic ironically to suggest that "to avoid accidents of this kind, which may sometimes prove extremely ridiculous, it would be well to require clappers to attend rehearsals, when they may practise applauding in the right, or to speak it more properly in the *desired* place, and may thus undergo a sort of drill which will perfect them in their manual exercise." Coffee and strong tea were also recommended, "as some of the gentlemen towards the conclusion snore very disagreeably, so much so indeed as to keep a number of people in the neighbouring boxes awake."

Continuing his facetious mood, the writer falls foul of the lax dress regulations, which, he thinks, might be omitted, "for they have only the effect of taking off the bonnets of women who go to the pit and of obliging honest men to wear shoes instead of boots. Black stocks are permitted in the pit and also shirts nearly as black as the stocks are too frequently observable, which we regard as a much more serious solecism. An order that no gentleman should be admitted in dirty linen would be much more to the purpose than the present law against boots. We would just hint too that it would be well to have a barber in attendance to trim the hair of certain foreigners who carry heads about that fill one with the most frightful apprehensions."

The same gentleman certainly did his best to add to the gaiety of nations. Remarking upon the dullness which had suddenly come upon the theatrical world, and after observing that Madame Vestris had " laid in a stock of inexpressibles for summer use," he went on to say : " Little of the usual theatrical chit-chat has been passed to and fro during the past month [April], and for want of a taste of fresh scandal people have been reduced to the necessity of combining *Foote* and *Hayne* and their pair of breaches ; Kean and his immorality and Miss Paton's answer to Malthus. . . ." (Miss Paton had the year before married Lord William Lennox.) " No new actor has made inroads upon the domestic peace of the city ; no actress has sinned herself into the sympathies of the public ; no author has rebelled against that moral beef-eater that casts jokes before the King and *damns* behind him ; no manager has horse-whipped one of the lords of the creation ; no lady behind the scenes has given being to an unstamped peer ; no gentleman has been thrown over from the gallery to the pit ; no anti-gentleman has smashed a box door in the plenitude of claret and morality to shout down Kean and uphold Miss Foote. In short, nothing in the nature of a regular novelty has transpired, and the old pleasures have therefore been mourned very tenderly."

The " moral beef-eater " was of course the censor, George Colman, against whom was raised a hearty laugh concerning a one-act farce produced during May at Covent Garden Theatre. Yates took the part of a pavior, and the author had introduced a topical joke apropos of Macadamised paving just then introduced and keeping possession of our streets until the advent of asphalt and wood blocks. " They call the roads *muck Adamed*, but I call them *damn'd muck*," Yates was to have said, but the egregious George expunged the line and wrote a letter to Fawcett on the subject. A wag protested that " Colman never spoke of any other than Macka's roads, as he could not bring himself to pollute his lips with the whole name!" George Colman was the quintessence of morality in his censorship duties. Privately he lived with Mrs. Gibbs, a popular and vivacious actress.

CHAPTER XI

VESTRIS AND "CHERRY RIPE"

The advent of Velluti. His mixed reception. Vestris in "legitimate" drama at the Haymarket. She invites criticism in Shakespeare. Paul Pry and Liston's inimitable personation. How Poole conceived the character. Madame's piquant acting as Phœbe. "Cherry Ripe" sung for the first time. Its history. Her sparkling address on the last night of the comedy. Vestris's earnings in 1825. Velluti's meanness. His squabble with the ladies of the chorus. They assert their rights and are victorious. Their small pay. The popularity of Weber in England. Der Freischutz. Weber's Oberon produced at Covent Garden by Charles Kemble. An inefficient cast. Vestris the only member who could act as well as sing. Braham no actor. Miss Paton's stupidity. Weber's disgust. Miss Goward (afterwards Mrs. Keeley) and the "Mermaid's Song." Oberon a qualified success. Weber's death.

THE operatic event of 1825 was the appearance of Velluti, the last of a class of Italian vocalists who no longer exist. For his phenomenal voice Meyerbeer wrote *Il Crociato in Egitto*. His tone was not always pleasant, but his vocalisation was superb and altogether he was an accomplished singer. The *Times* heralded his approach by a gross personal attack; the "fashionables" were uncertain whether they ought to applaud or hiss; and his fellow-artists treated him with great rudeness. The *London Magazine* remarked sarcastically : "Madame Vestris, with a consistent propriety that can only be equalled by the consistent care of the public morals lowered by Mr. Theodore Hook in the *John Bull*, offered any sum to the managers that would engage another lady to sing with him." The management was in despair and it was rumoured that the production of the opera would be abandoned;

the Duke of Wellington, however, so the report went, called Mr. Ayrton, the musical director, into his box at the opera and threatened to shut up the house if *Il Crociato* was not got out with all speed. Eventually the difficulty was overcome by the substitution of Mademoiselle Garcia (in later days the famous Madame Malibran) for the rebellious Vestris, the opera was produced, and Velluti on the whole was received with approval.

Meanwhile Madame was back at the Haymarket Theatre, which had reverted to the " legitimate " business. Apparently she was anxious to shine in pure comedy or she would scarcely have played Letitia Hardy in *The Belle's Stratagem*, a line of character for which her distinctive powers were ill fitted. But light comedy did not satisfy her, and again she essayed Shakespeare and repeated her impersonations of Mrs. Ford in *The Merry Wives of Windsor* and Rosamond in *As You Like It*, provoking the *Age* to declare that " Madame Vestris cannot play Shakespeare because she evidently cannot comprehend Shakespeare—and those who saw her Rosamond must confess this."

She was more at home in *The Lord of the Manor*, as here she had plenty of scope for her voice, among other songs singing Bishop's " Dashing White Sergeant " with immense verve and acting much to the satisfaction of the *Sovereign* " in her natural and becoming habiliments. To the shame of the age," the critic of this journal went on to remark, " we protest that we never saw this lady perform but once before in female attire ; we therefore had more than ordinary pleasure in witnessing her performance of Annette in *The Lord of the Manor*, though we thought the stamping sort of sauce-box air with which she *marched away* to the tune of the ' Dashing White Sergeant ' was too much in keeping with her notorious male-attire exhibitions." And, waxing indignant, the scribe concluded with : " *This theatrical system of putting the female sex in breeches is barbarous and abominable*." Protests on the score of propriety were, however, in vain, for during the year Madame appeared in a piece called *The Epaulette*, in which no less than seven ladies in addition to Vestris desported themselves in masculine garb !

Following *The Lord of the Manor* came *The Beggar's Opera*, in which as Macheath she was *facile princeps*. Apollo in *Midas*—a burletta noteworthy for its charming song, " Pray, Goody," in which Sinclair, a favourite Scotch tenor, made his name—was a part admirably adapted to show off Madame's figure, as one gathers from the *Mirror of the Stage*, which in a notice of Miss Foote's acting as Ariel severely observed : " Always excepting Madame Vestris's Apollo we know no dress so indelicate as that chosen by our heroine [Miss Foote] in *The Tempest*." The equanimity of the *London Magazine* was, on the other hand, by no means disturbed by the exhibition, remarking that Vestris called together all the young apprentices about town previous to their suppers at the saloons in Piccadilly. " She is," added the critic, " a very tight little personage in her dress and indeed looks a mighty dapper Daphne hunter."

In September Poole's *Paul Pry* was produced and at once took the town. It was, of course, Liston who made the play, and his queer figure, his Hessian boots, baggy breeches, black gloves, his Gampish umbrella, his whimsical humour, and the catch phrases, " I hope I don't intrude " and " I just popped in," were talked about everywhere. Never was a man better fitted by nature to be a comedian. He was irresistible. To look at him was to laugh at him. Hazlitt writes : " Mr. Liston has more comic humour, more power of face and a more genial and happy vein of folly than any other actor we remember. His face is not caricature ; his drollery oozes out of his features and trickles down his face ; his voice is a pitch-pipe for laughter. He does some characters but indifferently, other respectably, but when he *puts himself whole* into a jest it is unrivalled." Liston certainly put " himself whole " into *Paul Pry*. Paul, as the typical busybody muddling everything he touches and unintentionally making mischief everywhere, has lasted until to-day and will never be forgotten.

Poole tell us how the character suggested itself to him. "An idle old lady," he says, " being in a narrow street had passed so much of her time in watching the affairs of her neighbours that she at length acquired the power of distinguishing the sound of every knocker within hearing. It happened that she fell ill and was for some days confined to her bed. Unable to observe in person what was going on without, as a substitute for the performance of that duty she stationed her maid at the window. But Betty soon grew weary of the occupation; she became careless in her reports—impatient and touchy when reprimanded for her negligence.

" Betty, what *are* you thinking about ? Don't you hear a double knock at No. 9 ? Who is it ? "

" The first-floor lodger, ma'am."

" Betty ! " after a pause, " why don't you tell me what that knock is at No. 54 ? "

" Why, lord, ma'am, it is only the baker with pies."

" Pies, Betty ! What can they want with pies at No. 54 ? They had pies yesterday," and so on.

Poole adds that Paul Pry was never intended as the representation of any one individual, but of a class. This may be so, but in Phœbe, the pert lady's maid peculiar to " legitimate " comedy, it is pretty clear he had Madame Vestris in his mind. Her characteristics were faithfully reflected and must have been recognised and appreciated. The following scrap of dialogue between Phœbe and her mistress Laura could have lost nothing coming from Vestris's lips, emphasised by her arch looks and roguish eyes.

" *Laura.* But you know, Phœbe, Mr. Oldbutton, who is a very odd sort of man, has destined me for Sir Spangle Rainbow.

" *Phœbe*. For Sir Spangle Rainbow! Now if he were the last man in the world, I wouldn't have him !

" *Laura*. You wouldn't ?

" *Phœbe*. No. I—eh! The last man, did I say— why, perhaps that's promising too much. But lord, madame! Talking about being designed for Sir Spangle —I've no notion of such designing indeed. It's having a wife per order—it's likening us dear little women to so many parcels of grocery in thus packing us up, labelling and sending us home to the particular customer. Do you take my advice, madame—run away with Captain Haselton and get married at once.

" *Laura*. Married! I declare, Phœbe, I'm terrified at the idea.

" *Phœbe*. Why, the idea is shocking to be sure ; but I've heard say that marriage is like bathing in cold water ; we stand shivering a long time at the edge, when it's only one plunge and all is over."

Another extract, bringing in Haselton, reproduces Madame in a different aspect, but one not less pronounced :

" *Haselton*. My dear Phœbe, I can't express how much I am indebted to you ; and if I were not brought to my last five pounds——

" *Phœbe*. You'd give me the whole ; as it is, I suppose I must only hope for half.

" *Haselton*. Phœbe, you have but one error—you are too fond of money.

" *Phœbe*. My dear sir, that's the only fault I find in you. These things in us are merely the little perquisites of office : a young lady in love is as profitable to her chambermaid as a consumptive patient to the physician. All we have to do, sir, is to take the fees and let the malady work its own cure."

Laura enters and Haselton addresses her as his " charming love," on which Phœbe exclaims : " Oh, I suppose I may go now, madame ; you see the

advantage of having an intelligent waiting woman ;
I know when ' loves ' and ' doves ' begin to fly about,
the presence of a third person acts as a scarecrow ;
I wouldn't spoil the precious minutes ; I am a woman
of experience, and have my own feelings on these
occasions. I'll go watch."

Phœbe's boast that she was " a woman of experience " must have tickled the audience immensely.
It was so true. It anticipates a little conversation
of later years between Mrs. Glover, Mrs. Humby,
and Mrs. Orger (the last two ladies as pretty as Vestris
herself), reproduced by Vandenhoff in his *Recollections*.
The subject was Madame's marriage with Charles
Mathews : " They say," said Humby, with her quaint
air of assumed simplicity, " that before accepting
him Vestris made a full confession to him of all her
lovers. What touching confidence ! " she added archly.
" What needless trouble ! " said Orger drily. " What
a wonderful memory ! " wound up Glover triumphantly.

The plot of *Paul Pry* calls for no description. The
play is written round the central character and nothing
else matters. What, however, makes *Paul Pry* mem-
orable at the present day—though few people are
aware of the reason—is that in it Madame Vestris
for the first time sang that most charming of English
ballads, " Cherry Ripe." It so happened that Mr.
George Perry (a well-known musician of the day and
twenty years later the leader of the Sacred Harmonic
Society's band under Mr. Surman, and afterwards
conductor during the Society's transition period
between Surman and Costa) was going over a pile of
new songs with Vestris, and after she had sung " Cherry
Ripe," Perry exclaimed, " Really, madame, that's a
very pretty song." " I think so too," was her reply ;
" I shall sing it to-night." She did sing it, and before
many days were over everybody was humming the
delightful melody. The composer was C. E. Horn,
a melodist of no ordinary ability. The now hackneyed

duet " I know a bank " is his, and so also was " I've been roaming," almost as tuneful as " Cherry Ripe."

Paul Pry kept its place in the bills until nearly the end of the season and had not lost its popularity in 1826, when pretty Mrs. Humby played Phœbe, Madame Vestris having migrated to Covent Garden. She returned, however, to take part in the performance which wound up the 1826 season, when she delivered a sort of poetical epilogue. The moment she appeared the orchestra started " Cherry Ripe," upon which she ran forward and interrupted the music. Then with one of her most charming smiles she faced the audience and began :

" Pray don't be alarmed, but sit quietly there :
  I'm not going to sing ' Cherry Ripe,' I declare ;
  But those fiddles, though quietly placed on their shelves,
  Would from habit squeak out ' Cherry Ripe ' of themselves.
  No—my visit just now is in kindness and pity,
  To save you from almost so hackneyed a ditty.
  The tribute of thanks in the self-same dull strain
  You've endured, patient victors ! again and again.
  I saw it impending !   This ominous hat—
  A true type of the ' usual address '—' stale and flat,'
  Farren dressed all in black with a grave, solemn face
  And these four cruel pages of trite commonplace.
                           (Shows a paper.)
  Hang such dull undertakers—like work !—Whence the reason ?
  We're not going to bury the Haymarket season.
  Can't we part as we met ?   In good humour ?   If he be
  Black on this night—then—my name isn't Phœbe ! "
                             (Tears the paper.)

There was a good deal more, but it was rather laboured and may be omitted, especially as Vestris left it unspoken.

We learn from the *Mirror of the Stage* that in 1825 Madame's salary at the Haymarket was then thirty guineas a week and twenty guineas at Covent Garden, with an " understanding " at the latter theatre. By " understanding " is meant certain emoluments either at her benefit or otherwise " that shall increase the real amount of her salary, and it is thus managed because twenty guineas is said to be the *nil ultra* of Covent Garden." Nothing of importance during the winter months of 1825 was put on at Covent Garden in which Vestris had a share, save *The Rivals*, when she played Lydia Languish.

The opera season opened as usual in February 1826, but Vestris was not among the artists engaged. She had done with the King's Theatre and with Velluti too. It is more than likely that he hated her as much as she hated him. The tall, thin, pallid Italian with the singular voice which at times was distinctly repellent, disliked women, and he showed this dislike markedly on one occasion, the circumstances of which are worth relating, not merely because the episode caused no end of amusement at the time, but because it throws an interesting sidelight on the status of operatic chorus-singers and on their scale of pay.

Velluti was extremely mean, and towards the end of the season he sent to the chorus a letter which was read to them in the green-room and in which he promised a guinea each in addition to their salaries if they performed their parts well in an opera he was getting up for his own benefit. The opera was given, and the male choristers received their guinea each, but the female portion received nothing, and consequently they sued the Italian for the money. Velluti's defence was that his promise was made to the men only, he having addressed them in his letter " Signori Coristi," in other words, " Gentlemen Choristers." It was contended on behalf of the fair plaintiffs that the phrase " Signori Coristi " was addressed to the choristers in general, and that the chorus-master in reading the letter to them in English interpreted it " Ladies and Gentlemen."

Signor Velluti did not appear to defend the action, which was tried at the Middlesex County Court, but his counsel produced a letter which the ladies in chorus protested was not the one which was read to them. When called upon for the defence, Velluti's lawyer said "the fact was the Signor had a decided objection to the ladies and never allowed them to appear in any piece in which he was concerned." Upon this one of the fair claimants exclaimed, "Why, he has beat time to me," and the others chorused, "He pricks out the score for us," while the smart girl who conducted the case for herself and comrades indignantly cried, "He could not have done without us, as we had solos which could not have been omitted." At this point all the plaintiffs began talking at once, and the officers of the court had some difficulty in obtaining silence.

The judge characterised the defence as "paltry." The ladies had performed the labour, and why, if Velluti had so strong an objection to them, did he not prevent them singing? A friend of the Signor's thereupon remarked that it was not the object of the money but the mode in which it was demanded that induced Velluti to defend the present proceedings. This observation the judge brushed away contemptuously with a "Psh! psh! I do not hesitate to say I consider it a trumpery defence," and decided in favour of the plaintiffs, who were overwhelmed with compliments at their triumph.

The *Times* wound up its report of the proceedings with some information regarding the unfair treatment of the chorus ladies in force at the King's Theatre. It appeared that according to the system of screwing down the salaries of the minor performers in order to give enormous sums to the principals, the lady choristers had been paid during the first part of the season at 5s. 9½d. per night or 11s. 7d. per week (there were but two performances in the week), out of which they had to buy shoes, gloves, and flowers adapted to the costume of the various characters. They had for some months to attend the rehearsals every day from half-past nine to five; on some days dress was to be found them but was often neglected, and they

were seen performing the characters of Grecian origin
in the dresses of Spanish peasants, etc., and petticoats
of such extraordinary brevity that they might have
been mistaken for kilts were sent down to them from
the wardrobe.   In the course of the season Signor
Velluti interceded for the gentlemen and obtained
an advance in their salary to 15*s.* per night.   The
ladies struck—Madame Pasta pleaded in their behalf—
and obtained the enormous advance of 1*s.* 2½*d.*,
making altogether 7*s.* per night.

Italian opera in 1826 does not concern us.   Weber
was the rising star, and with his swan's song *Oberon*
Vestris was associated.   *Der Freischutz* had during the
past two years been a stupendous success.   It was
played at Covent Garden, at Drury Lane, at the Royal
English Opera House, otherwise the Lyceum, but,
strange to say, not at the King's Theatre.   The
Italian singers tolerated Mozart and Winter because
their operas were in the Italian style ; Meyerbeer
would have had no chance save for the specialist
Velluti ; and Weber, whose genius was essentially
dramatic and who detested ornamental music, was
taboo.   The weird, eerie music of *Der Freischutz*
appealed to the English, but they would not have
too much music, and, says Planché, " Nothing but the
Huntsmen's Chorus and the diablerie in *Der Freischutz*
saved that fine work from immediate condemnation
in England."

Charles Kemble, who was in 1826 guiding the
fortunes of Covent Garden Theatre, conceived the
idea that a new opera composed for that theatre by
Weber would be a great success.   Weber was quite
willing, negotiations were entered into, and the
result was that the libretto of *Oberon* was prepared
by J. R. Planché.

Difficulties were encountered from the very first.
Beautiful as much of the music is, the plot and action
of *Oberon* are uninteresting despite Planché's skill
in versification and in devising dramatic situations.

For the latter, Planché contended, the average British playgoer had no appreciation. " A dramatic situation in music," he says, was " caviare to the gourmet," and inevitably received with cries of " Cut it short " from the gallery and obstinate coughing or other signs of impatience from the pit. Planché thus found himself handicapped, as he was not free to indulge his own taste.

But the drawbacks of the opera itself were nothing to those presented by the company engaged to perform in it. Charles Kemble had probably had very little to do with singers or with music. No operatic entre-preneur of the least experience would have dreamed of producing a new and difficult opera with a cast only one member of which could act as well as sing. This exception was Vestris. Braham could sing gloriously—when he chose—but was a miserable actor and had a deplorable stage presence ; while the leading lady, Miss Paton, whose voice was irreproachable, had not the slightest notion of dramatic effect.

Fawcett, the stage manager, had a short way with difficulties. Everything which could not be rendered properly must be cut, and when at the first rehearsal things were not satisfactory and there was a bungle over the " Mermaid's Song," Fawcett called out roughly, " That must come out—it won't go ! " " Weber," writes Planché, " who was in the pit leaning on the back of the orchestra, so feeble that he could scarcely stand without such support, shouted, ' Wherefore shall it not go ? ' and leaping over the partition like a boy, snatched the baton from the conductor and saved from excision one of the most delicious *morceaux* in the opera." Subsequently a fitting representation of the part was found in a youthful actress who, it was discovered, had a voice. This was Miss Annie Goward, afterwards an idol of the public when she became Mrs. Keeley. The part was of no great signification, mostly dumb-show, the " Mermaid's Song " coming in the finale to the

second act. It was some time, Mrs. Keeley's biographer tells us, before Miss Goward was tried and
not until several singers had failed to satisfy the
composer. At last she was put on and went through
the song feeling horribly nervous. She was delighted
when Weber came up to her at its termination and
patting her hand said, " My child, dat song vill do."

The anxieties of the rehearsals were not lessened
by the inefficiency of Miss Paton. In the shipwreck
scene she had to wave her scarf as a signal of distress,
and her way of doing it was to catch up the short
end of a sash tied round her waist and give it a little
twist. " That woman's an inspired idiot," was Charles
Kemble's despairing cry, while Weber limped up and
down the room silently wringing his hands !

Then there was Braham craving for something
in his own particular line that would rouse the gallery
to enthusiasm. He was not contented with the fine
air Weber had written for him, as it did not give him
scope for display. Weber, after great persuasion
had been used, consented to suppress, or rather transfer
to the overture, Huon's opening song, and wrote
the warlike aria, " Oh, 'tis a glorious sight to see," for
years a stock piece of robust tenors and especially of
Sims Reeves, who used to declaim it magnificently.
Braham was successful, but his success gave no pleasure
to Weber, whose opinion of the English singer and
the English public was considerably lowered thereby.

Eleven years later Braham, who had no regard for
anything save that which kept him in the limelight,
produced at the St. James's Theatre, which he built
and which ruined him, a version of *Oberon* which was
little better than a burletta. With an eye towards
infringement of copyright he had fresh words written
for the soprano scena, " Ocean, thou mighty monster,"
and his own song, " Oh, 'tis a glorious sight to see,"
and other parts ; but his caution did not save him.
The owners of the original libretto took proceedings
against him, whereupon it was explained in defence

that the singers were so accustomed to sing the old words that they sometimes dropped into them and forgot the new ones. At other times they mixed them up! The jury at the Middlesex Sessions apparently did not think the plaintiffs had suffered much injury, and assessed the damages at 40s.

Apart from the troubles incidental to the production of the opera, Weber suffered from depression of spirits arising from a mortal disease. He was extremely sensitive, and when he arrived in London he had the mortification of seeing Rossini fêted in every direction while he himself was neglected. But Weber was in no sense fitted socially for the admiration of the "fashionables." Miss Fanny Kemble describes him as " a little thin man lame of one foot and with a slight tendency to deformed shoulder. His hollow, sallow, sickly face bore an expression of habitual suffering and ill-health, and the long hooked nose, salient cheek-bones, light prominent eyes, and spectacles were unattractive." Rossini was a *bon vivant*, gay and vivacious, and what is called " good company." The contrast was inevitable ; nevertheless Weber took it much to heart.

" One of the first visits he paid to Covent Garden," says Miss Kemble, " was in my mother's box to hear Miss Paton and Braham (his prima donna and tenor) in an oratorio followed by *Rob Roy*. He was enthusiastic in his admiration of Braham's fine performance of . . .' Deeper and deeper still,' but when in the second part of the concert Braham . . . was tumultuously encored in the pseudo-Scottish ballad ' Blue bonnets over the border,' he was extremely disgusted and exclaimed two or three times, ' Ah, that is *beast* (' *Ah, cela est bête !* ')." Later on Braham sang " Scots wha hae " with a flourish of his stick in the last verse—a piece of claptrap at which Weber expressed unbounded astonishment and contempt.

Oberon, or The Elf King's Oath, to give the opera its full title, was produced on April 12th, 1826. The

applause was tumultuous on Weber entering and
seating himself at the piano. The poetical and
picturesque overture delighted everyone who could
appreciate good music, but its full effect was spoilt
by the late arrivals and the banging of doors. The
opera as a whole was a success, though it did not appeal
to those who expected a second *Der Freischutz*. The
critics were enthusiastic in their praises, the *Morning
Post* exhausting its superlatives and speaking of the
scenery and production generally as " unequalled in
the history of the stage," but the man-in-the-street
was not impressed. There was nothing in *Oberon*
which he could take up and whistle or hum. The
music was too refined, too much above his head,
nor did the fairy-tale plot lay hold of him in any
way.

The opera ran for twenty-eight nights without
intermission, and from the sublime came a drop to
the ridiculous in the shape of *Giovanni in London*
and Joey Grimaldi in " a romantic melodrama "
entitled *Robinson Crusoe*! Charles Kemble no doubt
knew his business, but one wonders whether the
audiences which applauded those samples of vulgarity were those who had appreciated the delicate
delights of *Oberon*. The sudden thrusting of this
stuff between the performances of a work on which
Weber had lavished all his gifts of poetic genius and
his marvellous musical imagination must have embittered his closing days. He was conscious that if
Oberon was not a failure, it had not won the heart-
whole admiration of the English people.

The opera was put on again, but the composer's
vitality was at too low an ebb to care one way or the
other. His gentle soul passed away on June 3rd, at
Sir George Smart's house in Dean Street, Soho, to
the great grief of all who knew him personally and
understood his sensitiveness. *Oberon* remains to this
day one of the masterpieces of opera rarely performed
in its entirety. Its overture, matchless in its delicate

JOHN BRAHAM.
(From the collection of the late A. M. Broadley.)

fancy, is however a familiar item to-day in orchestral programmes, and never fails to delight.

Before the summer season ended, thirty-two performances were given, and during November and December twelve more, Vestris appearing as Fatima, save on two nights of indisposition when Miss Goward acted as her under-study. If the run of the opera was not that which Kemble expected, it was long enough to furnish a strong contrast to *Aladdin*, a romantic opera brought out in hot haste at Drury Lane with the amiable intention of forestalling *Oberon* and spoiling its effect. The music was by Bishop, and it had the advantage of Miss Stephens's incomparable voice, but it proved a frost and was withdrawn after five days' trial. Braham, meeting Tom Cooke, the Drury Lane musical conductor, shortly after, was asked by the latter how the Covent Garden opera was going. " Magnificently," cried Braham enthusiastically, " and not to speak profanely, it will run to the day of judgment." " Pooh, my dear fellow, that's nothing," retorted Cooke, who never could resist a joke, " ours has run five days afterwards ! "

CHAPTER XII

MADAME'S MORALS CENSURED

Vestris at the height of her popularity as a ballad singer. Poetical homage to the lively actresses of the day. Madame Vestris severely censured by the moralists. A gross attack upon her in Oxberry's *Theatrical Biographies*. Scandalous stories. Her alluring personality. The *Age* and its scurrilities. The *Morning Chronicle's* insulting allusions. A skit in the *Age* upon Madame's energies. The *Age* her champion. She performs in Dublin. A slander refuted. Hints of blackmail.

In 1826 Eliza Vestris reached the height of her popularity as a ballad singer. The music dealers vied with each other to secure the right of publishing the songs with which she was identified. " ' Buy a Broom ' with an original and finely-executed portrait of Madame Vestris (in character)," ran one advertisement. " Love's Labour Lost " and " Woman's Smiles and Tears," by Alexander Lee, " Light Guitar (4th edition), John Barnett," " Maiden, heedful be," also by John Barnett, and many more—all now forgotten—found many purchasers. Vestris, however, was not the only theatrical goddess. Other pretty, fascinating women all playing light comedy and each with individual charm sought to rival her. Probably such a galaxy of feminine beauty and liveliness has never before nor since sought to delight the British public as was on the boards at that time. But there was only one Vestris. She was imitated but not equalled. An anonymous poetaster in an attempt to describe the effect upon him of the popular stage divinities burst into the following doggerel :

For Miss Love how I languish, for Kelly feel anguish,
Then Foote too can vanquish as Hayne will declare.
I gaze on West's pretty eye, at Graddon's sweet ditty sigh,
Her dad lives in the city, I oft see him there.

My fancy still wanders on, Smithson it ponders on,
Glover, too, maunders on, ruddy and rife ;
Tree's tone enriches me, Vestris bewitches me,
Common then twitches me whispering " wife."

Tunstall has tones enough, Egerton bones enough,
Mrs. Bunn moans enough, how my heart flows ;
Waylett is bliss-able, Hollande admissable,
Mrs. Horn kiss-able, somebody knows.

Davenport's dumpy oh !   Harlowe is stumpy oh !
Miss Pearce is mumpy oh !   Yet I admire ;
Miss Chester's killing me (*maugre* dame is drilling me),
Baker's wife thrilling me through with desire.

Some of the allusions in this rigmarole are terribly puzzling and incoherent, but the greatest puzzle is that the rhymester should have omitted to mention Mrs. Humby, Mrs. Orger, and Mrs. Gibbs, compared with whom some of the ladies he glorifies are not to be named in the same breath.   And there was little Miss Goward, afterwards one of the stars of the comedy stage and better known as Mrs. Keeley.   Mrs. Humby (the subject of an audacious couplet unquotable in these pages) indeed, the *Morning Chronicle* preferred to Vestris.   But towards the latter the *Chronicle* was inclined at times to be spiteful.

Sailing smoothly as Madame was over the sea of public admiration, she was drifting perilously near the shoals of scandal.   Stories of her gallantries were being circulated, and a writer in Oxberry's *Theatrical Biographies* was moved to read her a lecture on her peccadilloes, admonishing her more, however, in sorrow than in anger.   He begins thus : " We now indeed approach the painful part of our duty.   We wish to avoid speaking harshly of the frailties of the weaker sex and we would rather draw the curtain

over their errors than expose them; but extreme cases
call for extraordinary reprehension and silence becomes
criminal where vice is notorious. . . . It must be
evident that to obtain correct information on such
subjects . . . is impossible. It is a subject on which
courts of law cannot obtain accurate evidence, and
the tales of the day are generally drawn from the
disclosures or inventions of domestics who distort
truth to give a value to their communication."

Warming to his subject, the censor proceeds in
the following caustic fashion : " Madame Vestris has
done more to degrade her profession by suffering
the impression that she could be bought than the
talents of fifty such actresses could remedy. . . . Had
the lady of whom it is our unpleasing task thus to
speak erred from the feelings of nature, had she even
emulated Catherine in the number of her lovers, as
long as passion had been her only incentive, we
should have closed our pages to her errors and cast
a sigh but no reproach over her frailties. . . . Madame
Vestris has had the misfortune to be more flattered
than perhaps any woman now in existence. Madame
Vestris had an early penchant for jewellery and finery
that has grown with her growth and strengthened
with her strength. . . ."

After a few more generalities of this sort details of
Madame's enormities are entered into, but oddly
enough with a view apparently of showing the lady
in a favourable light. We are told that " Amongst
the many charges against this fascinating woman that
of receiving a Mr. C. is the most notorious. We
happen to know the particulars of that affair well, and
if ever a gentleman was determined to be ruined and
did take a delight in it, Mr. C. was the man. What
shall be said for the folly of a being who undertook
to spend a month in Paris, and yet on the first night
of his arrival, hearing the name of his goddess mentioned at a *soirée*, exclaimed, ' Ah, I must return to
my dear little angel ! ' and actually set off instantly

back to London ? . . . The conduct of Madame Vestris to that individual was neither selfish nor mercenary; on the contrary, in one instance it was meritorious and generous."

Continuing in his extenuating vein, the writer says: " With a Captain A., who had lavished a fortune in excesses, our heroine shared a prison; she did not desert her Leander in poverty, and these traits of character should be placed against the whelming weight of her errors. We have not yet heard of any instance of Madame Vestris intruding herself into the domestic circle and deluding a husband from the arms of his wife."

In a footnote the author says : " The tales of Mr. C. Kemble and our heroine we treat as an absurd and infamous fabrication." " She has robbed no mistress of her lover, and indeed she seems rather to commit the sins that fall in her way than to seek occasion for the commission of them." Then : " We have heard instances of generosity and kindliness of heart in our heroine that would do honour to any woman. Her manners are without any tincture of affectation; to the poorer members of the theatre she is affable and kind. She is in a provincial theatre most conciliating and obliging, and in whatever theatre she appears her conduct is never such as to give the slightest offence either to the delicacy or feelings of the other ladies of the establishment."

The conclusion the self-appointed moralist arrives at is that all the lady's faults are due to her alluring personality. " We never believed in the fascinating powers of the serpent," he declares, " till we saw our heroine; and we mean this neither as a compliment nor a censure. Without beauty she allures—in spite of defects she attracts you. Madame Vestris has no one really fine feature; and when in an undress has no claim even to the negative promise of being pretty. Yet, even so, such is the witchery that hangs around her that he who converses with her for five minutes and does not feel passion rising in his frame is something more or less than man. . . ."

If Madame read this diatribe, as no doubt she did, she would be quite justified in exclaiming, " 'Twas all very well to dissemble your love, but why did you kick me downstairs ? " The question frequently asked was why did not the lady contradict, or make some protest against, the innuendoes and the scandalous stories which found their way into print ? Madame Vestris was wiser than her critics. What was the use of contradicting one false report when there were so many others which were true and which she could not contradict ? Whether this was so or not, the fact remains that while she was exceedingly sensitive to criticisms which affected her professional reputation, she was quite indifferent to those which assailed her personal character.

Another point of interest is that the *Age*, notorious for its scurrility, which made its appearance in 1825 and attacked all and sundry, was—at all events in its early years—kindly disposed towards Vestris. Its chief target of attack was Mrs. Coutts, who as Harriot Mellon married Thomas Coutts, the banker, under somewhat equivocal circumstances. Mr. Coutts died in 1822 and left his relict the richest widow in the United Kingdom. She aimed at social distinction through her wealth and her lavish and ostentatious hospitality, and Molloy Westmacott, who subsequently became editor of the *Age*, pretended that the lady's vulgar ambition justified the paper's coarse assaults. There is, however, reason to believe that his real motive was something quite different. Mrs. Coutts could have silenced him—for a time—but she never stooped to do so.

Madame Vestris stood in a different position. There was nothing to gain by attacking her—rather the reverse. Indeed, the *Age* went out of its way to shower its praises, and when the *Morning Chronicle* during August 1826, in its favouritism towards Mrs.

Humby, indulged in some remarks concerning Vestris more personal than polite, the *Age* rose in her defence. Said the *Chronicle* : " She [Vestris] is now approaching that age when, according to some, the second crop of beauty becomes ripe for the reaper, when a certain degree of plumpness makes up for the earlier graces. She never struck us as being so buxom and *en bon point* as last night, when her dress being necessarily tight showed the exact proportions of her figure. She was encored in ' Pray, Goody,' but Sinclair used invariably to be called upon to sing it three times. Madame Vestris sings to be sure sufficiently well for the part, but her claim to it *depends much more upon her legs than upon her voice.* Altogether the piece was ill got up, as the manager was aware most likely that *a pair of very nice silk stockings* for Madame Vestris *was the most important part of the property* to be employed."

In reply the *Age* lifted its bludgeon in a style that would have done credit to the " Eatanswill Gazette." " Oh, old Chronny," it lashed out, " you certainly are the greatest blockhead that ever took up the trade of critic. The flourish about Madame Vestris's age when Mrs. Humby is about two years older comes in very funnily, but it is nevertheless of a piece with the whole affair."

Vestris's work in 1826 was of a most varied character. She appeared as Fatima in *Oberon*, in Bishop's ballad opera *The Slave*, Nell in *The Devil to Pay*, Captain Macheath—" positively the last time of her ever performing that character," said the advertisement— songs at Vauxhall Gardens in the summer (the Gardens took a new lease of life in 1826 with ballet, fireworks, military and Scotch bands, suppers, and arrack punch, but that life did not last long), Lydia Languish in the *Rivals, Giovanni in London*, in *The Epaulette* with, as already mentioned, seven other ladies all in " breeches " parts, and in many other characters. Her versatility and her activity moved the *Age* to publish in its issue of October 23rd skits not, however, intended to be malicious.

"The Haymarket," it wrote, " having lost the only member which constituted its value and realised that its treasury is going on with its old tricks again, and in consequence of the appointment of Madame Vestris to the situation of stage manager, we find amongst the next week's announcements :

"'Tuesday : Letitia Hardy, Madame Vestris!
Wednesday : Donna Lorenza, Madame Vestris ! !
Thursday : Lady Elizabeth Freelove, Madame
    Vestris ! ! !
Saturday : Lady Bell, Madame Vestris ! ! ! ! '

and report says the following Monday she plays Lady Macbeth. In addition to all this a sad mutilation of the popular ballet of *Les Pages du Duc de Vendôme* (*The Epaulette*) was brought out by the Lady Manageress last night—the male characters (for the ladies at this theatre no longer support their characters) were represented, we see by the bills, by Madame Vestris, Mistress Wood, and the Madames Ebsworth, Carr, Webb, and Bailey."

On the announcement that *Pizarro* was to be played the *Chronicle* was in its element, remarking that " Among the virgins Madame Vestris will of course appear, and we have no doubt will then be more perfect in her part than she has been in most things we have lately seen her enact. After all this and well knowing what the receipts must be, we hope Madame Vestris means to pay the salaries."

Vestris's craving for versatility led her at times to misjudge her powers. She had not had the requisite training to permit her to do justice to the *bravuras* of Italian opera. Her singing of " Una voce poco fa " on one occasion was severely criticised. Apparently she was satisfied with it herself, and when " Cherry Ripe," which followed, was encored, she showed her mortification. " She absolutely returned to the front of the stage," said the *Courier*, " in a sort of pet and recommended the ballad with a ridiculous air of peevish impatience; . . . the pit only laughed at her airs, but we should not have been sorry if a more significant lesson had been taught her." Evidently she was disappointed because the encore was not given to " Una voce."

In the early part of 1826 Madame fulfilled an engagement in Dublin with Abbott, who had been a member of Covent Garden Theatre, in connection with which engagement there was a good deal of ill-natured and ill-founded gossip, Vestris being accused of having behaved shabbily over money matters. Subsequently the matter was righted, and it turned out that it was Abbott who was the shabby one in the transaction. It appeared that " she was to have £500 in advance before starting for Dublin, but this £500 was for two bills of £250 each endorsed by herself, cash for which was obtained by Mr. Abbott's agency. On settling with that gentleman in Dublin the £500 was deducted by him from the sum due to Vestris, and on her return she was applied to for the payment of the first bill of £250 which had been dishonoured by Mr. Abbott, although he had paid himself back the money from what was due to the lady."

But there seem to have been people who would not believe Vestris could be other than mercenary, and certain scribblers took advantage of this belief to make scurrilous attacks with an intimation that more might follow. Only one inference was to be drawn—Madame was to pay for their silence. The *Age*, of all papers in the world, rushed to her rescue in the following : " Madame Vestris takes her benefit to-morrow at the Haymarket and, from a report we gathered from the Box-book-keeper, a tribute fully due to her versatile and great abilities. This must be a convincing proof to the siren of May Fair that the rascally attempts of vagabonds for a pecuniary purpose to misrepresent her life so shamefully as lately has been done have no effect on public opinion. We have heard by the way that to conduct her pending actions against these fellows she has retained our friend Scarlett " (a well-known barrister of the day).

The next week the *Age* writes : " Agreeably to our predictions we find that Madame Vestris had a regular bumper on Monday last, boxes private and public, pit gallery and slips ! After this she need be under no apprehension of scurrilous publications. Among those who have been her latest persecutors are a pettifogging monkey practising the law in Water Lane, Blackfriars—whose name we will furnish her if she should desire—one McGregor Logan, who translated the English opera theme *Der Freischutz*, and John Barnett the *soi-disant* composer—nice boys all three."

In associating John Barnett with a blackmailing conspiracy the *Age* made itself ridiculous. It is incredible that the composer of *The Mountain Sylph* could be found in such a galley. The paper's assertion that Madame intended instituting proceedings against her alleged libellers was hardly better founded. She let them severely alone, both at this time and afterwards.

CHAPTER XIII

MADAME AND HER ADMIRERS

Vestris's strenuous life. Takes part in old comedies, Shakespeare, and the Italian opera. Censured for her garbled version of Susanna in *The Marriage of Figaro*. Mutilation of Mozart's *Il Seraglio*. Uproar over " I've been roaming." Vestris furious. The uproar renewed another night. Josephine Bartolozzi's first appearance on the stage. Poetical effusions concerning Vestris and her admirers. Vestris attacked by the *Times* and *Morning Chronicle*. She is defended by the *Age*. Miss Harriet Coveney as Captain Macheath. The *Chronicle* severely condemns " breeches parts " and prefers the legs of Miss Foote and Mrs. Humby to those of Vestris.

THE activity of Vestris in 1826 was continued into the following year. Never was there such an energetic woman. What with the " study " of the tremendous range of characters she attempted, the seductions of society gaiety, her endless love-affairs, and her endless want of money, no wonder her nerves frequently gave way and the announcement had often to be made that she was ill. Charles Kemble was still running opera at Covent Garden alternated with the " legitimate " drama. Vestris played Lady Teazle (at her benefit) for the first time; Lydia Languish; Zerlina (*Don Giovanni*), " first and only time," ran the announcement; she figured in the old stock comedies *Know Your Own Mind, The Way to Keep Him, The Jealous Wife*, and *She Would and she Would Not*; she was Brown in an English version of Boieldieu's *La Dame Blanche*— an odd mixture founded upon *Guy Mannering* and *The Monastery*; and she sang for the last time at the King's Theatre in her old part in *La Gazza Ladra*. In *Artaxerxes*, though she had nothing to do save look charming and sing " In Infancy," she was always triumphant, and she made a hit in Poole's comedy *The Wife's Stratagem.* Shakespeare was not forgotten, she playing Rosalind in *As You Like It.* When *The Marriage of Figaro* was produced in May she was Susanna, and in a performance of the opera later in the same year she came in for well-merited censure.

It is not a little singular that, undoubted artist as she was, Eliza Vestris could be guilty of the bad taste and impropriety of treating the great masters of music as though their compositions were not worthy of her notice. Well might one critic write indignantly of her Susanna : " She was allowed to omit ' Cruel Perche' and to substitute for one of the opera's most pleasing airs a little insignificant Spanish song." From this indifference one can understand why she could never have risen to be a great Italian opera singer. She had neither feeling nor veneration for music other than trivial, ear-catching melodies. The applause such things drew from an uneducated audience pandered to her vanity. Mozart she treated with a levity for which there was not the slightest excuse. The transpositions and interpolations in *Il Seraglio* (given in December 1827) and *Figaro* were enough to make the composer turn in his grave. In the first-named, not satisfied with the airs in her own parts, Vestris appropriated a *romanza* belonging to another character. The cast was atrocious. Wrench, an admirable comedian, should, as Pedrillo, have sung the *Romanza,* but Wrench as a singer was unendurable. Said the *Age* : " The part is unworthy of his acting talent and he takes his revenge on the music by mangling in the most horrid manner everything he touches. Why Wrench has been put into Pedrillo we cannot imagine." But is not the answer obvious ? Vestris wanted the *Romanza,* which in Wrench's voice and style would have been a hideous burlesque. Another actor might have been able to sing and so deprived

Vestris of an additional song. Hence Wrench was retained.

At last the critics rebelled against this profanation, and over a performance of *Figaro* on December 14th, when Vestris played Susanna, and Madame Sala (the mother of George Augustus, the prince of journalists) the Countess, they lost patience and smote her unsparingly. Her extraordinary vagaries were thus described :

" Madame Vestris was the Susanna, and the bills announced that she was to sing ' I've been roaming,' and some other ballad of the same class—intended, we suppose, as some sort of relief to the stupidity of Mozart. This evil is growing to such an extent that though the Managers may put a different title to their operas in the bills, they will soon all contain the same songs. Upon this occasion, immediately after the enchanting duet of ' *Sul aria* ' had been admirably sung by Madame Sala and Madame Vestris, just in the midst of the lively dialogue between these two agreeable personages and the page, the band without rhyme or reason struck up the symphony of ' I've been roaming.' An instantaneous hiss passed round the house, and Madame Vestris, taking it to herself, resented the supposed affront by retiring from the stage and leaving the performance at a stand. An uproar ensued, and Cherubino having again fetched Susanna to her post, she sang ' I've been roaming ' with much more propriety than she could have done in the first instance—not, however, without similar repeated marks of disapprobation from that foolish part of the audience who thought they had come to hear the *Marriage of Figaro*."

Vestris evidently felt this reproof keenly, and a few days later she wrote the following letter to the *Times :*

" It is with extreme reluctance that I address you on a subject which has given me great pain and uneasiness, and which in gratitude to the public whose generous applause and approbation I have so long enjoyed, I cannot pass by without expressing my regret at having incurred in any degree their displeasure. Respecting the opposition shown to my introducing the admired song ' I've been roaming ' into the opera of *Figaro*, I have only to state that Miss Stephens, Miss Paton, Miss Tree, and other ladies have introduced songs of their choice, *there being no song by Mozart* in the opera as *originally produced on the English stage*, and those composed by Mr. Bishop for Miss Stephens are quite out of the compass of my voice, that in justice to the audience whose applause I shall ever most anxiously labour to obtain, I could not presume on *attempting* to sing. Again I have been permitted to introduce ' I've been roaming,' in the same situation these last two seasons, uniformally with great success, and I must beg to call your attention to the circumstance of there being no opposition shown by admirers of Mozart to ' What can a poor maiden do ? ' a song by the same author. Most desirous that you, sir, may feel the justice of making known to the public, by the insertion of this letter, that l have only been actuated by a desire to please."

The plea that there were other sinners and that she was not worse than the rest was not a very convincing defence, but maybe it was the best she could offer.

The matter did not end here. At a repetition of the opera on January 6th, 1828, when after the fall of the curtain Wrench came on to announce the next performance, " his voice was drowned by a confused clamour from above in which now and then could be distinguished something like the word " Vestris." Wrench disappeared and the gods were silent until the scapegoat came forth to receive the benefit of a renewal of the storm. Mr. Fawcett declared that if he could form any idea of what the " ladies and gentlemen wanted he would certainly comply with their wishes if in his power." Among various shouts " I've been roaming " was at length audible. Mr. Fawcett then observed that " I've been roaming" neither belonged to the opera nor had it been promised on the bills. This was a poser and the gods were confounded ; whereupon Mr. Fawcett added, ' but if it was the wish of the public that Madame Vestris, who was now undressed—(a laugh)—should sing the song, such was his wish also—and such he was persuaded was the wish of the lady who would appear the moment she could get her clothes on.' Orator Hunt then rose and exclaimed : ' The boxes and the pit do not require it ; it is only the shilling gallery.' This happened to be so obviously true that the boxes and pit vociferously applauded the assertion, in the midst of which the lady, chancing to be at the wing, immediately approached, looking so handsome and dressed to such advantage, that no one could have the heart to object. Of course the fascinating little lady was heard with patience, though it is scarcely necessary to add that there was no attempt to encore." It is to be hoped she took the lesson to heart.

On June 17th Madame's sister, Josephine Bartolozzi, made her first appearance on the stage at Covent Garden Theatre as Rosina in the *Barber of Seville.* It was an ambitious effort, and all that can be said of it was that it gave promise of better performances in the future. Her excessive nervousness prevented her doing herself justice. Without the striking personality of her sister, she had considerable charm. We are told that " her figure is perhaps below the middle size, but is very delicately proportioned. Her hair is dark, her eyebrows are finely arched, her features are small, feminine, and pleasing, but unfitted for the varied language of the soul. Her eye is soft, but though evincing much gentleness, is never kindled with the flashing light of our divine little favourite, the female Giovanni. Her extreme timidity and agitation on her first appearance in the balcony of Bartolo's house were as painful to the audience as to herself. She looked like a beautiful little bird that is for the first time fastened in its wiry prison and, being placed in the full gaze of a crowd of people, is panting and fluttering with alarm."

During the summer Vestris was again in Dublin, where she won all hearts. It would seem that by this time the names of her chief admirers were common property. Lord Petersham, the general lover who, when he became the Earl of Harrington, made Maria Foote his countess, Tom Duncombe and " Handsome " Jack Phillipson were believed to be rivals for her favours, and journalistic poets sought the muses for appropriate verses on so taking a subject. " Handsome " Jack at this period had apparently distanced the others, according to the following effort :

> While every tongue
> Both old and young
> In Fashion's giddy pack
> Sings Petersham,
> I'll chaunt a flam
> In praise of Handsome Jack.

> Wise nature chalks
> In different walks
> Who rides on Fashion's back ;
> Let Duncombe's pride
> My beau deride,
> He's naught to Handsome Jack.

> Though Tom's the pride
> Of all the ride,
> Of Crocky's, too, the crack,
> Yet be it known
> He's quite a drone
> Compared to Handsome Jack.

In addition to Lord Petersham, other members of the aristocracy were, according to popular report, her devoted admirers. The *Age* came out with a squib which purported to give a list of articles of which Vestris had been robbed, among them an album

MISS STEPHENS.
(From the collection of the late A. M. Broadley.)

containing imaginary flowery tributes from various noble lords. Here are a few :

Lord Lyndhurst

(On seeing Vestris kill a flea)

Proud flea, thou well deserv'st thy fate
For daring to luxuriate
  On melting orbs of snow ;
No more thou'll skip from sheet to sheet,
Tasting in secret every sweet
  A god might joy to know.
Yet bliss thy fate—Eliza's nail
With one report cracked life's entail
  And sent thee down below !

Lord Lowther

(Vestris in her dressing-room)

Fine creatures, I've viewed many a one,
With lovely shapes and angel faces ;
But here I see them all outdone,
Fair Vestris's form unites the graces.

Lord Castlereagh

(To Vestris—an extempore—from the stage box)

If in that breast so soft and white
Compassion for a beau can dwell,
My pain relieve this very night ;
The cruel cause you know full well.

(To Vestris—imitated from the Kisses of Secundus)

Is there a heart Eliza's strain
Might not with love inspire,
Or breathes one of the Thespian train
So quick to cool love's fire ?

There were other effusions couched in a different strain and hinting at Madame's besetting sin, her reckless extravagance. Lord Fife, whose greatest pleasure was to spend money over ladies of the ballet, heads the list.

> Forget not, Eliza dear,
> Though false thou art and insincere ;
> Thy *costly* charms I'll ne'er forget,
> Reminded by a load of debt.

To Horatio Clagitt, one of a coterie of bucks among whom Colonel Berkeley, Captain Best, " Pea-green " Hayne, Ball Hughes, figured conspicuously, is ascribed this cynical effort :

> What is friendship ?   What is love ?
> Nought to her but empty air ;
> Such trifles Vestris is above—
> Gold, sordid gold, her only care.

Luttrell, one of the wits of the day, is supposed to give a sample of his brilliancy in the following :

> (To Vestris on her display of legs in *Don Giovanni*)
>
> When father Orpheus wanted sport, he
> By touching his piano forte
>   Drew out his brutes by millions,
> One modern Siren—the fair Eliza—
> Proves then his godship to be wiser
>   Making beaux dance to cotillions.
> Vestris beats Amphion by twelve inches,
> No " wryneck'd, squeaking fife " she pinches,
>   Discoursing 'mong the pegs.
> To animate the males at once
> And lovers make of sage and dunce
>   She need but show her legs.

The concluding quatrain is the most personal and biting, especially as it purports to come from the pen of Tom Duncombe, whose ready purse had extricated the siren from many a financial embarrassment. It is inscribed " Tom Duncombe's adieu to Vestris, then residing in Lisson Grove, enclosing an I.O.U."

> Adieu Lissonia's fatal grove,
>   Eliza dear, adieu !
> With Handsome Jack you now may rove,
>   For ought that I. O. U.

The fierce light that is said to beat on princes is dim compared with that in which pretty actresses of a hundred years ago had to bask!

It is not without interest to note that the practice —to-day carried to the point of absurdity—of advertising the tradesmen who contribute to the glories of some particular " star," from her gowns to her cosmetics, was anticipated in 1828. A piece which lent itself to gorgeous apparel and in which " our little favourite never appeared more deludingly attractive," to quote one admiring critic, stimulated the following puffing paragraph : " The dress worn by Madame Vestris in the new farce called *The Sultan and Beautiful* is made of materials of the most costly description and does credit to the taste of J. J. Valloton, of Old Cavendish Street, who also supplied Mr. Braham with the hat and feathers now worn by him in *Love's Wrinkles*, which for elegance cannot be surpassed."

Either the public in 1829 were becoming more critical or Vestris more careless about her selections. Maybe continual success was beginning to spoil her. The *Post* took her to task in connection with a musical comedy, *The £100 Note*, remarking sarcastically : " Madame Vestris gave the audience two airs and herself a great many. A few persons chose to encore a stupid song and others opposed it. Madame Vestris should have gone through the repetition without stopping every time she heard a hiss." Her temperament was ill fitted to endure rebuke, and the admiration which had been paid to her for years accentuated her sensitiveness. Naturally other actresses in her own line of " business " were envious of her success, and these had friends on the press who did not hesitate to twit the goddess whenever they had the chance.

The *Age*, however, was always ready in her defence. Her playing of Carlos in the *Duenna* furnished occasion for a gibe, and we find her advocate observing : " We are sorry to see that some of our contemporaries use this delightful favourite of the public exceedingly ill —first she has been censured for not coming on the stage before her cue, and secondly for attempting respectfully to explain to the audience that she did not deserve their censure. On Friday, the prompter having failed in his duty to call her in proper time, the stage was for a moment in waiting. When she appeared there were some few marks of disapprobation from those who did not perceive the cause. However, Vestris very significantly advanced to the prompter's entrance, and looking in a way not to be mistaken by any but the blind reporters of the *Times* and *Chronicle*, bowed to the audience and said : ' It really was not my fault.' For this short but very proper address she was yesterday censured. . . . These attacks upon a charming woman who, whatever may be her faults, is the most attentive to her public duties and always captivating performance of them, are as unjust as they are unmanly."

The *Morning Chronicle* indeed rarely lost an opportunity of snarling at Vestris and appeared to see little merit in her beyond the possession of her symmetrical legs. Apparently the critic who represented the *Chronicle* prided himself on being a judge. Take this notice of a musical piece called *The Nymph of the Grotto, or The Daughter's Vow* (Covent Garden), in which the principal female characters were played by Miss Jarman and Madame Vestris. " We really wish she [Miss Jarman] would take a few lessons in pronouncing what the children call round O. . . . In other respects there was little to complain of, but that her legs are by no means well-shaped. Madame Vestris seemed to like her part and was in good humour, excepting when (as deputy stage manager, we conclude) she audibly abused the stage-keepers for removing two chairs that ought to have remained." In a parting fling, the critic wound up with " she was encored in only one song."

A performance of *The Beggar's Opera* at Covent Garden in June 1829, in which Miss Harriet Coveney, who as a woman blossomed as a genuine comedy actress and remained a great favourite with the public to the last day of her long career, gave the *Chronicle* a chance of descanting on its favourite topic : " We are always enemies," it wrote, " to the assumption of male attire by woman on the stage, and we have always resisted it on the score of decency and modesty, but still it is constantly endured, and Madame Vestris and Miss Love have been allowed night after night to exhibit almost *in puris naturalibus* as Apollo and Giovanni. It savours therefore a little of mock modesty and pretended puritanism now to raise a cry because Miss Coveney is required to put on a pair of trousers and to act Macheath. We should like to know how many times Madame Vestris has performed the same part in the very tightest buckskins she could obtain to fit her shape. To us the exposure was always offensive. . . .We should be glad to see this practice abolished, but while it is continued, let us be consistent, . . . do not let us applaud Madame Vestris . . . and be ' struck on a heap with horror ' because Miss Coveney, a child under fourteen years old, puts on a pair of trousers."

The legitimate objection was surely not the question of legs, but the absurdity of a girl in her early 'teens playing Captain Macheath. When such things were suffered, one wonders of what a British audience in the old days was made and how theatrical managers could perpetrate such enormities.

The *Chronicle* gave a further sign of its obsession a fortnight later when, noticing Planché's *The Green-eyed Monster*, produced at the Haymarket, it said : " We were glad to see Mrs. Humby again as Louisa. We cannot help thinking the manager will ere long have good reason to congratulate himself that he had not to lay out £60 a week upon Madame Vestris. She is really not wanted, and she will thus have an opportunity of exhibiting herself (not her legs merely) for the gratification of gaping gawkers in the provinces." If Madame was at all ruffled by these pinpricks she had ample compensation in the deluge of enthusiasm which poured upon her at every provincial town she played in during the summer of 1829. On this tour she was accompanied by her sister Josephine.

On her return to London she found the *Chronicle* carping at her in its old style on the question of legs. When *Giovanni in London* was revived with Vestris, it ironically expressed a hope that Vestris would secure a permanent engagement and not be banished and legs be forbidden, " because they are certainly still very pretty ones, though somewhat shrunken in the calf, a perfection which Miss Foote still retains and which Mrs. G. Calcraft never possessed," and maliciously quoting the words of the churlish philosopher Apemantus :

> I doubt whether their legs be worth the sum
> That are given for 'em,

observed that this was the point the manager would have to decide after he should have engaged Madame Vestris.

Provoked by these aspersions on its favourite, the *Age* protested that it " knew as much of the fair proportions of the fair Vestris's legs as any man breathing—we have a cast of one of Madame's legs in our possession, and on comparison with the Medicean Venus we pronounce that of the living Venus to be faultless." Really in matters theatrical at this moment the only thing worth discussing appeared to be actresses' legs !

CHAPTER XIV

MORE THEATRICAL SCANDALS

London theatres at a low ebb. Covent Garden Theatre closed. Failure of Charles Kemble's management. A subscription fund started. The King's Theatre in difficulties. Laporte converts pit rows into stalls. Mutiny in the orchestra. Vestris complains she has no new parts to play. Kemble impersonates William Shakespeare in *Shakespeare's Early Days*. Various remedies proposed to restore theatrical prosperity. A quarrel on the stage between Vestris and her future brother-in-law. A ludicrous scene. Vestris threatens legal proceedings. Alexander Lee, the musical composer, manager of Drury Lane. His curious history. Elopement of Lady William Lennox (Miss Paton) with Wood, the tenor singer. Molloy Westmacott thrashed by Charles Kemble. Vestris engaged at the Tottenham Street Theatre. The managers of the patent theatres, frightened by Vestris's success, take action. Vestris leases the Olympic Theatre. Its varied history.

THE English stage in 1829 was in rather a bad way. Of the Shakespearean actors Miss O'Neill rarely appeared. Edmund Kean was approaching his decadent days and Macready had not at that time made his reputation. The theatres were thinly attended and managers had a difficulty in making both ends meet. Drury Lane had not recovered from the effects of Elliston's bankruptcy; and Stephen Price, who followed him, though fairly successful during his first season, was subsequently little more fortunate. The season of 1829–30 ended the venture. The rent, says Planché, was certain to ruin any lessee in the long run. Mr. Price had deserved well of the public, and his experience stood him in good stead, despite his lack of education and his occasional want of taste. Planché tells how an eminent tragedian once suggested to him the omission of Locke's music in *Macbeth*, as the words were not Shakespeare's. Price listened attentively, apparently considering the argument, and then remarked, "Well, look here, sir, I don't think it would do to omit the music, but if you think it would be an improvement I've no objection to leave out the *Macbeth*."

Covent Garden was in worse case than Drury Lane. Charles Kemble's management of Covent Garden had been so disastrous that insolvency faced the lessees. Rates and taxes were unpaid, two years' ground-rent was owing, and in default of payment the Duke of Bedford threatened to take possession of the building. In June the theatre was closed. This state of things was all the more puzzling because during the thirteen years of Harris's control little short of a million sterling, so it was said, had been taken at the doors. A fund was started to restore its fortunes, and the profession were not backward in their help. Among other contributors Vestris figures. She sent a subscription of £40. A notable performance was that of *Nozze di Figaro* in the autumn, when all the artistes gave their services, and Malibran, hearing that Miss Paton (now Lady William Lennox) was to be the Countess, came expressly from Paris to show her sympathy by playing Susanna.

The vicissitudes of the King's Theatre continued. Laporte had no greater success than his predecessors Velluti and Ebers, and the treasury at the end of the season showed a deficit of £13,000. Under Laporte's régime the pit rows nearest the orchestra were converted into stalls and the price raised from half a guinea to a guinea, greatly to the dissatisfaction of the patrons. He was unfortunate in his choice of Bochsa, the harpist, as musical director. Bochsa, a vain and self-opinionated man, issued arbitrary orders to the band which caused rebellion, and the principal members, headed by Lindley, the celebrated 'cellist, sent in their resignations. Bochsa was held in no particular respect outside the theatre if we may believe the *Age*, which wrote : " We wish Laporte well because we believe he deserves our best wishes, but let him keep that fellow Bochsa in the background. We neither want to see nor hear anything of his interference."

It is not surprising that at this time much discontent prevailed in the profession. Vestris complained of the paucity of new parts. Those given to her, she said, were feeble and unattractive, and she was compelled to rely upon impersonations with which the public were thoroughly familiar and of which she was heartily tired.

Towards the end of the year Covent Garden had, with the aid of subscriptions, tided over its difficulties to some extent, and the advent of Fanny Kemble and her success helped considerably, but the lessees were still anxious about the future. In default of Shakespeare, which appeared to be beyond the powers of the company, Charles Kemble produced a play founded upon a well-known episode in the poet's career—his stealing a buck and his appearance in consequence before Sir Thomas Lucy. This effort to give a Shakespearean air to the season was entitled *Shakespeare's Early Days*. Kemble played William Shakespeare and the piece ran for several nights. It is probable that this is the first time Shakespeare in person was introduced on the stage.

The next year failed to bring any improvement. The question was anxiously discussed by the profession and the public. Various theories as to the cause of the depression were put forward. One error, it was suggested, was making the theatres when rebuilt of too great a size. Another idea was that shareholders and proprietors should content themselves with less interest. Such a diminution, it was pointed out, would be scarcely felt, though of sterling benefit to managers. One person thought theatre rents should be reduced, private boxes done away with as much as possible, and in the dress circle " the places should become the private property of those who pay for these places and tickets "—in other words, seats should be booked. " This," the proposer went on to say, " would bring the fashion of twenty years since back again, when merchants' families who are engaged in business until six or seven o'clock would then arrive about eight o'clock and have their places secured for the end of the first act." A drastic proposition was that actors' salaries must come down, " particularly those of the nightly stars," and, to sum up, " retrenchment must be the *order* of the day and no further *orders* pass current." Apart from these reforms, dramatists, it was contended, ought to be more generously remunerated. As things stood, it paid an author much better to write novels than to write plays, and the result was the production of very inferior dramas.

As might be expected, nothing was done. Matters drifted on and were allowed to right themselves as best they could, and as the public mind was suddenly diverted to a much more important circumstance— the death of George IV on June 26th—theatres and their troubles retired into the background for the time being.

Nothing of special interest concerning Madame Vestris occurred during the first six months of 1830. It may, however, be mentioned that in April she played Captain Macheath at Drury Lane, in spite of the announcement some time before that she would never again appear in that character. This revival, of no particular moment by itself, gave rise a few evenings later to an unrehearsed scene on the stage which for some days was the talk of the town. Madame Vestris and a Mr. Joshua Rose Anderson were performing together in *Guy Mannering* when the audience were startled by an exchange of violent words between Lucy and Henry Bertram which certainly did not belong to the play. Some squabble apparently had occurred before the performance, and this squabbling was resumed on the stage, ending in an appeal to the audience. Both made speeches and both were hissed and applauded by their respective friends. The dispute ended seemingly by the lady being the victor. Then they went back to the play and made love to each other, though their feelings were evidently the reverse of their words and actions. At last Madame could restrain herself no longer and told Mr. Anderson that she would not stay there to be insulted by him, and after allowing the hand which he essayed to take to hang by her side she rushed from the stage.

The sequel took place when Madame Vestris attended before the grand jury and preferred a bill of indictment against Mr. Anderson and William Hopkinson, in which she charged them with having gone to the theatre for the express purpose of hissing her, thereby endeavouring to intimidate her from exercising her profession. The grand jury returned a true bill against both.

A day or two after Madame wrote to the papers a letter of which the following is an extract : " I hope that it is unnecessary for me to assert that I have not been influenced by any private feelings in the measures I have been advised to adopt against that gentleman [Mr. Anderson], for if such were the case no grand jury would have granted the indictment that has in the present instance been preferred. The performance of Captain Macheath, out of which has arisen all this irritation, was undertaken by me (with extreme reluctance from the prejudice I have to the character) to prevent any disappointment to the public in witnessing Miss Stephens's established representation of Polly ; and in that or in any other instance the idea of deterring Mr. Anderson's ' advancement in his profession ' was never in the remotest degree contemplated."

There was, however, much in the background which Madame did not think it necessary to divulge. It was really a family affair. Anderson was one of Josephine Bartolozzi's admirers, and indeed married her in 1831. It was said that he owed his introduction to the stage to the influence of Vestris, but what the exact cause of quarrel was no one knew. The bill of indictment, to the public disappointment, went no further. The difference was made up through the services of a mutual friend, both sides admitted that there had been "misrepresentations," and so the matter ended and the Lady Sneerwells and Sir Benjamin Backbites were deprived of a piquant dish of gossip.

After her benefit at Drury Lane on June 4th, when Meyer's opera *Romeo e Giulietta*—about which one may venture to assert no one knows anything to-day—was produced for Malibran, who sang a duet with the *bénéficiaire*, Vestris departed for a long provincial tour. Hitherto she had played at the "summer" theatre in the Haymarket, but managers were tightening their purse-strings and Madame's terms were high. For the same reason Covent Garden was not assailable—indeed, it was stated in one paper that "Madame Vestris, the fascinating little Venus, threatens, we hear, to cross the Atlantic if Kemble or Lee does not behave more liberally."

Alexander Lee had succeeded Price as lessee (jointly with a Captain Polhill) of Drury Lane Theatre at a rental of £9,000 a year, and was the composer of "The Soldier's Tear," "Meet me in the Willow Glen," and other sentimentalities then much in favour. His history is rather a curious one. After many vicissitudes he became very low in the world, and his last engagement was the direction of an entertainment of *tableaux vivants* given at the "Garrick's Head," Bow Street, with which Renton Nicholson (Baron Nicholson of *Judge and Jury* fame) had something to do. His passion for Mrs. Waylett, who became his wife, amounted to madness. She was a drunkard, had a very bad temper, and led him a terrible life.

Yet when she died he was inconsolable, and was found a corpse doubled up on a chair beside the bed on which his wife had a short time before expired.

Alexander Lee is entitled to a niche in the temple of fame enshrining the fashionable follies of Vestris's time. He was the first " tiger," then the outward and visible sign of the man about town, as Dickens did not fail to note. The picture of " Montague Tigg, Esq.," in the days of his flash prosperity behind his highstepper and attended by his " tiger," Bailey junior, is one of the most vivid in that wonderful collection of character-sketches contained in *Martin Chuzzlewit*. The " tiger " was the invention of Lord Barrymore, one of the family trio, two brothers and one sister, respectively dubbed " Hellgate," " Cripplegate," and " Billingsgate." " Cripplegate" claims the introduction of the " tiger " in the person of Alexander Lee.

The Rev. John Richardson (*Recollections*), to whom we are indebted for this information, tells us that the " tiger " at first sat by the side of his master, but afterwards he sat behind him. The " tiger's " most important duty was to keep his eyes on the watch for any pretty woman who might pass, and at a signal from his master jump down, accost the lady respectfully and ascertain if possible her name and address, follow her if need be, and perform generally the functions of a youthful Pandarus. There is nothing in the subsequent career of Lee to show that he did not perform the part satisfactorily. He was a weak-minded creature, the tool of everyone who chose to make use of him.

There appears to be some ground for the rumour that Vestris, in default of obtaining an engagement in London, contemplated crossing the Atlantic. A semi-theatrical paper which had adopted the name of Poole's popular comedy *Paul Pry* had this paragraph bearing on the subject : " We hear that Miss Paton and Mr. Wood contemplate an expedition to America.

The undertaking would be somewhat perilous—for the Yankees are ' pretty particular scrupulous.' Indeed it is pretty well understood that the reason why Madame Vestris does not accept the larger offers which have been made to her to go there is that she could not go with any reasonable degree of comfort, as she would be obliged to leave her friend P. [Jack Phillipson ?] behind her." Madame eventually did undertake an American tour, but not until after she married Mr. Charles J. Mathews.

The dullness which generally followed Vestris's departure from the metropolis was this year greatly relieved by two episodes—the elopement of Lady William Lennox, better known as Miss Paton, with Wood, a popular tenor singer, and the thrashing Molloy Westmacott, as he was pleased to call himself, received at the hands of Charles Kemble. Westmacott, who had the knack of thrusting his nose into theatrical scandals, no doubt for his own journalistic purposes, also figured as the friend and whitewasher of Lord William Lennox.

Molloy Westmacott was now the proprietor and editor of the *Age*, which was started by one Richard Richards, who was mostly in financial difficulties and not infrequently edited his paper in the seclusion of the Fleet prison. The tone of the *Age* was always extremely personal, and as such, at times, offensive, but under the management of Richards it was mild in comparison to what it became when Westmacott had a free hand. The man was a combination of venom and greed. He had not the slightest conscience and never sought to curb his coarseness if coarseness would serve his purpose—generally blackmail.

There is no necessity to go into the merits or demerits of the popular soprano's matrimonial differences beyond noting the lofty attitude of the press generally, which under the cloak of a homily indulged in gross abuse of the lady. Lord William Lennox was, according to the censors of morals, a model of a good husband;

Lady Lennox was all she should not be. Subsequently this verdict was reversed, but for the time being the papers vied with each other in raking up the garbage-heap, and their wrath was only appeased when the erring couple were decently married, Mrs. Wood at her first public appearance being overwhelmed with praise.

Westmacott's castigation concerned himself only, and the contemporaries of the *Age* left him severely alone. He deserved punishment for his repeated attacks on Fanny Kemble, but it may be doubted whether her father took the right method of dealing with her detractor. Westmacott, at the end of the first act of the piece, was passing in front of the stage towards the entrance, when Kemble quitted his box, rushed at him, and felled him with a stick, continuing to belabour him while he was on the ground. There was certainly nothing heroic in the assault, for Kemble was an athletic man of over six feet while Westmacott was but five-feet-five. The behaviour of the police superintendent who witnessed the scene was somewhat singular, and Westmacott had good reason to complain. The man not only did not interfere, but refused his assistance when Westmacott begged for his arm, his reason being that he saw the sympathy of the audience was in favour of Kemble.

Westmacott made the most of the affair in the *Age* and wanted to challenge his assailant, but, so he said, was dissuaded from this course by his friends, and he contented himself with legal proceedings, which, however, came to nothing, Kemble apologising and accepting Westmacott's assurance that he never insinuated anything against the young lady's honour and that his criticisms were strictly confined to her histrionic abilities. It can hardly be said that the lesson, severe as it was, made any difference to the scurrilities of the *Age*. They continued to appear, and as time went on they became coarser and more malevolent.

In the late autumn Vestris returned to London and failed to obtain an engagement at any of the larger theatres. But she was not the only actress of light comedy who was compelled to " rest." A newspaper paragraph runs : " Stars out of place, Foote, Vestris, Paton, Stephens, Mrs. Bunn, Miss F. H. Kelly, Mrs. Humby, Miss Kelly." But Vestris was not left unemployed for long. The enterprising manager of the Tottenham Street Theatre—doomed in after-years to suffer many changes of fortune, at one period sinking so low as to be called the " Dust Hole," from which it emerged in butterfly fashion as " The Prince of Wales," and under the brilliant management of the Bancrofts drew all fashionable London to its doors, and has now settled down as the " Scala "— offered her an engagement and she accepted it.

In the estimation of the play-going world the little Tottenham Street Theatre was much beneath the great patent theatres, Drury Lane and Covent Garden, but this made no difference to Madame Vestris. She probably was of the same opinion as Mrs. Siddons, who, when reproached by Fanny Burney for playing at so inferior a place as Sadler's Wells, retorted, " I will play anywhere so long as I am paid." Directly it was noised abroad that the public's idol was at Tottenham Street, the house was packed nightly, although at first nothing more novel than the almost worn-out *Lord of the Manor* was produced, and subsequently a version of Auber's *Fra Diavolo*—Madame of course in the title-rôle; that the music of the first was written for a tenor made no difference to her, nor to the audience either, and she continued her successes until December, when other ambitions began to occupy her mind.

The effect of her popularity was to raise the Tottenham Street Theatre into a position which frightened the magnates of the patent theatres. They discovered that their exclusive privilege was being encroached upon, and they pretended that their scanty audiences

MADAME VESTRIS,
As Apollo in *Midas*.

were due to the rivalry of this presumptuous " minor " theatre. Proceedings were instituted against Chapman, the lessee, restraining him from " acting any Interlude, Tragedy, Comedy, Opera, Farce, Play or other entertainment of the stage," and notwithstanding that the theatre had been properly licensed by the magistrates, a fine of £50 was imposed.

There may have been something more than a dog-in-the-manger spirit at the back of the prosecution. The patent lessees could not have been unconscious that a strong feeling against their ridiculous monopoly was rising and that before long active hostilities might leak out. There is little doubt that they hoped, by pouncing upon the Tottenham Street Theatre, to stifle the growing ferment. In this they totally failed. The time was rapidly approaching for the establishment of free trade in theatres, and on December 24th a meeting of the theatrical profession was held and a memorial was drawn up for presentation to the King, in addition to a petition to Parliament calling for an abolition of the restrictive laws.

Meanwhile a powerful competition for public favour was being prepared which neither Charles Kemble nor Alexander Lee anticipated. It was rumoured that Madame Vestris intended taking the Olympic Theatre and running it under her own management. The rumour proved true, and on December 5th a paragraph to the effect appeared in all the papers. We quote the announcement in the *Age*, because it shows unmistakably that at this time Westmacott was disposed to be extremely friendly towards the budding manageress. The announcement was the following : " La Belle, late the Olympic. Madame Vestris, assisted by Miss Foote and we hope all the other eminent actors and actresses who are at present prohibited from appearing before their patrons the public by the patent monopolists of the two major theatres, will shortly open the above house in a style of elegance combined with attractive pieces and

performances that will be worthy of the British metropolis. It will be admitted that these fascinating
and favourite performers have been driven to this
measure of self-defence by a most unfair combination
equally opposed to the interests of the public and
themselves." It was not long before Westmacott
entirely changed his tone and became one of Madame's
bitterest enemies.

The Olympic had not had a very prosperous past,
but its history was not without interest. It was built
on the site of Craven House, Wych Street, and was
a speculation of Philip Astley, of circus fame. Astley
had an eye to economy, and coming across a captured
French man-of-war, the *Ville de Paris*, about to be
broken up, he purchased the timbers and with them
built the little theatre, superintending the operations
personally and keeping a sharp eye on his workmen.
Hardly any brickwork was used ; the yards and bow-
sprit of the vessel formed the uprights and supports,
the deck was converted into the stage and flooring,
the sides for the outward walls, while the roof was
of tin. It had no orchestra in front of the stage,
the musicians occupying a sort of stage box, one on
each side of the house. It was thus admirably adapted
for a conflagration.

Astley's building bill amounted to £800, and he
opened the house in September 1808. He styled it
" The Olympic Pavilion," and described it as " a
house of public exhibition of horsemanship and droll."
Astley's venture was a failure. He lost £10,000 and
sold the building to Elliston for £2,800 and an
annuity of £20. Astley lived only a year, so that
Elliston got a bargain.

The new owner altered the original title to the
" Little Drury Lane Theatre," forgetful of, or more
likely indifferent to, the patent monopolists of Drury
Lane and Covent Garden. The Lord Chamberlain
was at once approached, and it was pointed out that
Astley's licence, which Elliston had taken over, was

for equestrian entertainments only, and even this was only operative when the amphitheatre in the Westminster Bridge Road was closed. Elliston consequently had to revert to the old title and depend upon *burlettas*, upon the exact meaning of which the authorities could never agree. He opened the theatre in 1813, and five years later rebuilt it at a cost of £2,500. He migrated to Drury Lane in 1819, and the Olympic became a sort of white elephant, as the articles of the Drury Lane lease precluded him from active interest in any other theatre. After his bankruptcy in 1824 the mortgagees sold the property and its accessories for £4,860.

Then following a period of lurid melodrama under the management of John Scott, the builder of the Sans Pareil, afterwards the Adelphi, and it was from Scott that Madame obtained a lease of the building, the scene, by an odd coincidence, of the first performance of *Giovanni in London* with the notorious Miss Goold, in which piece, when it was transferred to Drury Lane, Vestris laid the foundation of her fame.

CHAPTER XV

Madame opens the Olympic with great *éclat*. The theatre entirely remodelled and redecorated. Maria Foote and Colonel Berkeley. Liston and Count D'Orsay. Vestris surrounded by men of fashion. Theodore Hook and an "impromptu." Tremendous excitement on the first night. *The Olympic Revels*—the first of Planché's "extravaganza burlettas." The Duke of Devonshire's compliment to Vestris. An innovation—the entertainment shortened. The *Age* abusively attacks Vestris and Planché. The attacks increase in vulgarity. Westmacott suddenly becomes complimentary. Captain Phillipson ("Handsome Jack") charged with threatening to "whop" Westmacott. A lively verbal duel at Bow Street. The *Age* renews its offensiveness. The paper's lying statements. Blackmail the probable motive.

How Madame obtained the funds for the necessary outlay in decoration and other things connected with the Olympic can only be surmised. Probably she was dependent upon no one man for pecuniary assistance. The generosity of Tom Duncombe we may be sure was not lacking, and there were others. It is not a little singular—and it is a tribute to Madame's cleverness—that she contrived to keep peace among her large circle of admirers. She was never the subject of ill-feeling, no duels were ever fought about her, and all were ready to be her champion. She was not of the sentimental temperament which demands the solace of an absorbing passion. When she had the money she was as ready to give as to receive. She took life lightly, and men thronged round her for the amusement she gave them. Yet, as will be seen, she stepped aside in one instance from this butterfly existence, and with disastrous results. But at first all went well, and the Olympic green-room was the nightly resort of, among others, the Duke of Brunswick, who rented a box, Lord Chesterfield, Count D'Orsay, Lord Harrington, and their friends. The too-notorious Colonel Berkeley (afterwards Lord Fitzhardinge) was one of her supporters, but owing to Miss Foote being a member of the company he absented himself. Liston was engaged, but did not appear for some time, having given offence to D'Orsay (according to Mr. T. H. Duncombe) by wearing a coat similar to that favoured by the Count.

Mr. Duncombe's statement is difficult to reconcile with a paragraph in the *Satirist* of November 9th, 1834, wherein we are told : " Liston in the *Retort Courteous* in his costume hits off the ' Royal ' Count to a hair ; his looks do not bear the same resemblance, as the initiated well know. Lest the public, however, should imagine the contrary, we advise D'Orsay to plant himself in the stage box for a few evenings in order to its being seen that he is the handsomer of the two." The Count appears to have taken the hint, for in the following week the *Satirist* noted that he was present and was highly amused. However this may be, it is certain that Liston was not included in the company until October 23rd, 1834, when he made his first appearance in the above-mentioned play. The theatre had then been run by Vestris some three years and nine months.

When Madame took upon herself the responsibility of running a theatre, she was sure of a big following among ordinary playgoers. But she had another string to her bow. At this time she was pre-eminently the " toast " of men of wealth and fashion, who divided their homage between her and Crockford, who started as a fishmonger and became the owner of the most sumptuous gambling-house to be found in London or the Continent. There were many other gaming resorts, and one of them, at 14, Park Place, St. James's, found its patrons among high-class

" punters." Four men ran the establishment, one of them being the brother of Mazzinghi, the composer of the music to Dibdin's opera *The Cabinet*, made famous by Braham, and of a pretty pastoral trio, " The Wreath," very popular once but long since forgotten. Theodore Hook was a constant visitor here. Tom Duncombe, Horace Clagitt, Jack Phillipson ("Handsome Jack"), and other admirers of Madame Vestris were also often to be seen. Hook was sometimes persuaded to give one of his extemporaneous poetic effusions for which he was so celebrated. One of these efforts, bringing in most of the men present, ended with a reference to the " bucks " and Vestris, running thus :

> And the first in my fist
> I will place on the list
> Is ' D'Orsay," that beau of renown.
> Oh, him I've oft met—
> Lady Blessington's pet—
> At her ladyship's soirées and meetings,
> When all eyes would scan
> The elegant man
> Who receives with much grace all their greetings.
> There are " Duncombe " and " Clagitt,"
> When bitten by maggot
> Would venture to Vestris select,
> Though parochial duty
> Is performed in its beauty
> By Phillipson, tall and erect.

The fair manageress and her lieutenant, William Vining, were in attendance at the theatre every day planning and devising attractions, improvements, and decorations. Planché was at hand whenever there were difficulties or when new effects were desired, and public curiosity was kept on the qui vive. Among the profession not less interest was excited. The *Memoirs of an Old Stager* (whose identity we have been unable to fix), quoted in John Coleman's *Plays and Playwrights*, contains a vivid picture of the commotion created. He writes : " The morning following the appearance of the announce bills the stage door was surrounded by a motley group, composed of almost every grade in the profession, from the decayed Hamlet downwards, all applying for situations.   There were heavy fathers, and ditto villains, utility men, chamber-maids, chorus singers, ballet-girls, etc., not forgetting the materials for organising an army of ' sandwich-men,' or board bearers.   The names of the most likely of the lot were taken down by Ireland, the copyist of the theatre, and a selection made from the list by Madame herself.   Meanwhile, artists and tradesmen were busy at work, both inside and outside the build-ing, getting it into order for opening.   Planché and Charles Dance prepared a burlesque-extravaganza, called *Olympic Revels*, which was to have been pre-ceded on the opening night by *A Roland for an Oliver* had not the Covent Garden management interdicted its performance. . . . On the Saturday prior to the opening, the liberal lessee presented to every member of the company a week's salary."

Nothing was heard but praise for the transformation which had been brought about.   The ceiling repre-sented an ornamental silk canopy, drawn tight by garlands of flowers held by flying cupids.   The pros-cenium was divided by gilt beading into panels each containing flowers.   The door at the side opening on to the stage, as was the fashion in those days, had been removed and proscenium boxes substituted. Emblematical figures set in panels surrounded by an arabesque scroll ornament decorated the fronts of the upper tiers of boxes, and those of the lower tier had their subjects selected from the works of Bartolozzi, Vestris's grandfather.   There were many other decorative details, but these may be passed over.   The general effect was so novel and so different from the heavy crimson and gold in vogue that the audience who crowded into the building on the night of January 3rd, 1831, was taken by surprise.

As early as from four o'clock the house was besieged.

Bell's Life in London informs us : " The boxes had all been engaged by fashionable company for some time past, and the train of carriages before seven o'clock, unable to set down their company, owing to the thronging and confusion at the doors, completely blocked Wych Street, and extended up Drury Lane beyond Drury Lane Theatre. Very soon after the opening of the doors, the boxes, pit, and gallery were completely filled, and boards were exhibited outside to that effect, but numbers still continued to pass in and pay their money, though only to crowd the lobbies and stairs. The box office was the scene of the greatest confusion. . . . Immediately after the overture Madame Vestris entered amid universal acclamations and spoke with her usual grace and *naïveté* an introductory address, written of course for the occasion. She was interrupted at every pause with plaudits, bestowed as much upon her pleasing assurance as the witty point of her prologue." The opening lines of this prologue or address ran thus :

> Noble and gentle—matrons—patrons—friends !
> Before you here a venturous woman bends !
> A warrior woman—that in strife embarks,
> The first of all dramatic Joan of Arcs.
> Cheer on the enterprise thus dared by me !
> The first that ever led a company.

And this was true. Never before had a woman essayed the management of a theatre.

The piece chosen to inaugurate the new venture was a pot-pourri entitled *The Olympic Revels*. Planché, who wrote it, tells how he ran across Vestris in Long Acre and how Madame told him she had taken the Olympic with Miss Foote and would be glad if he had anything ready for immediate production. It so happened that he had a classical burlesque which he could never get accepted. This was altered and brought up to date, and was put on as the opening piece, Vestris sustaining the part of Pandora. Planché says : " The extraordinary success of this experiment —for it may justly so be termed—was due not only to the admirable singing and piquant performance of that gifted lady, but also to the charm of novelty imparted to it by the elegance and accuracy of the costume, it having been previously the practice to dress a burlesque in the most *outré* and ridiculous fashion." *The Olympic Revels* caught on, and was the first of a series which the public appreciated for upwards of thirty years.

The *Age* was foremost in its congratulations and prognostications of future success. " Madame Vestris," it proclaimed previous to the opening, " is fairly enthroned in managerial state, directing the most active preparations for opening her theatre on a style of supreme elegance. The female Giovanni deserves the greatest praise for the spirited manner in which she contrived to overcome the combined tactics of the two great monopolists who had petitioned the Duke of Devonshire, as Lord Chamberlain, to refuse her licence. Nor must we withhold the praise due to his Grace for his independent and gallant conduct upon the occasion. ' There is your licence,' said the generous nobleman; ' I cannot refuse to Madame Vestris what would have been granted to any person of less powerful attractions. I shall come and see you often and bring all my friends, and I have no doubt your speculation will prove eminently successful.' "

Westmacott, however, had his own schemes in regard to Vestris and her venture, and when these schemes proved abortive he came out a few weeks later in his true colours, as will be seen.

The theatre was crowded every night, the papers were enthusiastic in their praise, and all went well. Quite by accident an innovation was introduced which was at once accepted by the public. The fashion of the theatrical managers in those days was to give plenty for the money. The performances commenced as a rule at half-past six and did not end much before midnight. A "three," sometimes a "four-piece bill," was a common thing. The Olympic had a four-piece bill, one of the items being a drama in two acts entitled *Mary Queen of Scots*, Miss Foote taking the part of the heroine. One night, for some reason, the drama had to be removed and the performance terminated at eleven instead of twelve. The difficulty of reaching the suburbs late at night was at that time considerable, and the extra hour for the journey was so much appreciated that the abridgment was adopted permanently and continued during the whole period of Vestris's lesseeship.

Towards the end of January the tone of the *Age's* criticisms suddenly changed and Molloy Westmacott exhibited the spite and vulgarity which he always had at hand when he was so inclined. The first missile was hurled at Planché on January 23rd, in the following, apropos of a translation from the French under the English title of *The Chaste Salute* : "*Chaste Salute* is the worst of the bad, without point and without plot," declared the critic. "We have not heard who is the perpetrator of this ' villainous compound,' but we shrewdly suspect it has emanated from the person whom the carpenters call *Plank*, and if so we can only say that his name and his nature cannot be more wooden than this miserable translation."

A fortnight later Westmacott returned to the charge, and this time Vestris was the object of attack : "Widow Vestris," wrote the virulent scribbler, " is going it, at least so the large placards in the street tell us. Four *new pieces* in addition to the attraction of the beautiful Miss Sydney, the widow herself, and grandmama Edwin. By the bye, we heard that the widow and Miss Sydney have been rehearsing a one-act *serious* burletta called the *Jealous Rivals*. *Prenez garde*, Miss Sydney, ' two stars shine not in the same hemisphere.' The widow's company have obtained the *nom de guerre* of the *Olympic Devils* ! and truly they are for the most part eminently entitled to this distinction; but surely the lady herself might have managed with the assistance of her treasurer and Mr. Stage-manager Vining without an acting manager, Mr. Raymond, and a master-manager, Mr. Plank, who gives it out that he is lord paramount and intends to regulate *all* the lady's affairs next season. This is just the error that the best friends of the widow cautioned her to avoid. Once let one of these *Wooden* translators or dramatic cobblers of French pieces into power and there is an end to your success, Madame." The sting contained in this effusion is evident— Westmacott hoped to wound Vestris's vanity by praising Miss Sydney, and he worked in this vein whenever he had the chance, on one occasion going so far as to say that Miss Sydney had " all the talent of Widow Vestris with a more beautiful person than the widow ever possessed."

Vestris went on her provincial tour as usual when the Olympic season ended, but Westmacott continued to pour out his venom, which became more and more offensive. On her return to town in June she was assailed with this piece of abuse : " Widow Vestris, her foreign friend Monsieur Jouez-là (the monkey), her two men-servants and suite have arrived at the cottage at Mitcham Common. We regret to learn that the widow's tour has been a decided failure— we cannot attribute this to the sedate habits which have necessarily grown on her with advancing years and which are so much opposed to her former gay manners and sprightly flirtations, her ' nods and becks and wreathèd smiles,' that she has lost the admiration of millions of her fluttering and flattering beaux— and has ceased to be the idol of the *Age*." On the identity of " Jouez-là " (the monkey) we are unable to throw any light. Possibly Planché, who was of French origin and whom Westmacott hated because of his position at the Olympic, was intended.

In July Madame obtained a lease of the Olympic

for five years, and it was stated she intended enlarging and improving the theatre. Meanwhile Anderson, the adventurer with whom she had the squabble on the Drury Lane stage, had married Josephine Bartolozzi and set sail with her to America. At the end of July something had happened either to pacify or frighten the pest of the *Age*, and it went back to some extent to its former adulation, as this paragraph indicates : " Madame Vestris, our elegant little widow, has returned to town after her provincial trip and is setting every wheel in motion for the success of her ensuing campaign. With such eminent talent as her own, let her have but a good cabinet and success is fully before her."

This tolerant mood was probably due to a letter from Bunn, who afterwards came to the front as a writer of operatic librettos, and subsequently as manager of Drury Lane Theatre, and exploiter of Jenny Lind. Bunn was running a theatre in Dublin and was acquainted with " Handsome Jack Phillipson." It was perfectly obvious that Vestris could make no answer to Westmacott's cowardly onslaughts, but it was otherwise with her friends, and Phillipson in a conversation with Bunn made no secret of his intention to inflict punishment on the maligner. If the soft paragraph was intended to turn away the wrath of Madame's defender, it utterly failed. On October 9th the theatrical world was startled by reading in the *Times* that Captain Phillipson had the day previous appeared before Sir R. Birnie at Bow Street to answer a complaint of Mr. C. M. Westmacott, by whom he was charged with having " threatened to ' whop ' him," or in other words to beat him with a stick. Westmacott explained about the letter from Bunn reporting Phillipson's threats, but that of these threats he took no notice. Some weeks after Phillipson came to his house flourishing a stick and using threats of violence. Westmacott was not at home and nothing happened, but as he went in fear of his life he made the present complaint as he might be assaulted, which led Phillipson to remark that it would be rather hard if he were to be held responsible for whatever chastisement Westmacott might receive, seeing that he was a gentleman who had been horse-whipped so often. Thereupon following this lively interchange :

Mr. Westmacott. I never was horsewhipped by mortal man without having taken prompt and effectual means of resenting it.

Captain Phillipson. Everyone knows that you have been horsewhipped more than twenty times and that you are too much of a coward to act as another man would.

Mr. Westmacott. You know that you were horse-whipped by Mr. Anderson.

Captain Phillipson. Produce one person besides your lying self who can say so.

Mr. Westmacott. The fact is sufficiently notorious, for it was witnessed by several persons at Drury Lane Theatre.

Captain Phillipson. You never open your mouth without uttering some gross and barefaced lie, and that which you have just uttered is in character with the rest.

The upshot of the affair was that Phillipson was bound over in his own recognizances of £40 and two sureties of £20 each to keep the peace until the sessions, and, according to the *Satirist* (a rival to the *Age* in its own particular line), Sir R. Birnie is made to observe of Westmacott, " Well, he is a strange fellow—I have seen him horsewhipped twice myself." This tale, however, sounds remarkably like the *Satirist's* own invention. It is not to be supposed a magistrate would commit himself in this fashion.

Westmacott, having put himself under the protection of the law, had no scruple about flinging more mud, and in his braggadocio, street-gutter style explained " why we were compelled to make our exhibition of

Widow Vestris's groom of the chamber, Mister John Burton Phillipson, therein described as Captain, but who never held a commission in His Majesty's service and was therefore most improperly so described, unless indeed he be Captain of Madame's Corps de ballet at the Olympic and examiner of legs in ordinary to the Widow's establishment. . . . Of this same bullying fancy gentleman 'Handsome Jack' (as the man is called in derision) we could say a great deal, but as what we allude to would wound the feelings of more than one lady and one of those whose professional talents, seriously speaking, we are very great admirers of, we shall on those points make sacrifice of our indignation upon the altar of gallantry and so far let the booby escape. Before, however, he enters upon another *fracas* we recommend him to settle his differences—first with Mr. T. Duncombe and secondly with Mr. Anderson. . . . How he induced the *Times* reporter, a man of the name of Archbold, to dub him Captain we neither know nor care, but we are not equally indifferent to that part which concerns ourselves. In that report he, Phillipson, is made to say that Mr. Westmacott had been horse-whipped several times. Now, we have been assailed several times and always by very powerful men like the Widow's Jack, armed too like him with bludgeons but in no instance with a horsewhip."

The satisfaction of Mr. Westmacott at having been thrashed by a stick and not by a horsewhip has something unconsciously humorous about it; but Westmacott was as dull as he was degraded and his self-complacency was not to be penetrated. His inordinate vanity and the motive which actuated him in attacking Madame Vestris peeped out in the next issue thus:

" The Widow has fallen into the error of all her predecessors in management—she commenced under *our* auspices and was successful for a season. Success produced the common disease of her class in gratitude.

She took unto herself *other* counsellors, and they have beguiled her into profligate expenses which her establishment can never repay. The last week has been fifty per cent. worse than the preceding, and the ensuing may perhaps produce half of the last. It is not too late, however, for her to alter and improve her plan. If Vestris will produce pieces in which Mrs. Glover, Miss Sydney, and herself have good parts, we venture to promise good houses; but she must not depend upon Liston, who is quite out of his element at the Olympic. . . ." The end was a typical Westmacott stab: "We do not wish to say anything ungallant of the little Widow, but her mirror must inform her that ' the days are gone when beauty bright our heart's chain wove.' "

The statement that the Olympic was doing badly was a bare-faced untruth. Its business, on the contrary, was exceedingly good, so much so that owing to the demand for the higher-priced seats it was proposed to take in a portion of the gallery, much to the indignation of the gods, and to abolish the shilling seats altogether. But truth had no place in the columns of the *Age*.

Meanwhile the *Satirist* was doing its best to rake up the inner history of Westmacott's enmity towards Madame and everybody connected with her. On October 16 it alleged that the reason why Westmacott was so bitter against Vestris was that when she took over the Olympic " the sweep proffered his valuable services. . . . But what will our readers think that he demanded in return? . . . a private box to his own sole and particular use. . . . We need hardly say that Madame Vestris distinctly and directly refused to accede to his demand, and the consequence has been that he has ever since turned the paltry influence of his paper against her. It is disgusting to think that such a man, utterly void as he is of all liberal feelings, but ever actuated by selfishness and malevolence, should have the power to frighten others into concession to

his impudent and base demands. . . . However, the
dog has had his day."

Westmacott's reply was a piece of coarse abuse
directed against his only vulnerable target. " Mrs.
Vestris," he remarked, " has favoured the town this
week, under the idea of starting an opposition to the
other theatres, with a stated version of the *Philtre*,
even stealing the very title adopted at Drury Lane
Theatre. It is, of course, nonsense to talk of such
a little Fantoccini hole as the Olympic interfering
with, or rather forestalling, the performance of the
larger houses ; but it is diverting to fancy the Widow
herself *fancies* it does (and we know what *things she*
fancies at times). We had the curiosity to go and
see her *Love Spell* on Thursday, and we can only say,
as we have before recorded, that she may throw them
around her with perfect impunity. . . . The only
thing well done throughout the whole was a song by
the Widow, which was not Auber's, called ' Man's
Conundrum.' It is a very funny name to call it,
but Mrs. V. knows more about these matters than
we do, so we have no doubt she was quite right. The
opera was delayed for two days owing to the inability
(with all Horn's teaching) of the lessee to get the
music into her head. . . . The sole prerogative of
her little theatre is burletta—let her stick to them
and her monkey ; and in God's name do not let us
hear for the future of a person producing musical
pieces who (though she manage fifty theatres) cannot
play a note on the pianoforte. A more ignorant
compilation or one more impudent in its adaptation
than this we never sat out ; it is from the regular
Vamp, Vamp, Gag & Co. School, and Mrs. V. has
made a great mistake if she thinks to *Filter* the public
with it, for though she long has been the *Flirt of the
Village*, her day has gone by for possessing any ' *Love
Spell*.' "

The *Age's* persecution never ceased during the
year. Madame, alluded to as " our *passée* friend,"

was requested to take a leaf out of Miss Paton's " book of acting " at Drury Lane (another version of Auber's *Le Philtre* was being played here under the name of *The Love Charm*), and better still to study her costume. The absurdity of this was patent, as Miss Paton had no notion of acting and was not celebrated for her taste in dress. But absurdity was nothing to this detestable fellow. He would write anything so long as it wounded. Madame chanced to be in a box at Drury Lane with Sir Andrew Barnard, a well-known banker of the day, upon which the *Age* declared : " There is nothing like having a friend at court, and although Barnard only comes in at the fag end of the list of courtiers, he must be a much better speculation than the Olympic this year is likely to turn out."

After reading this and other spiteful snarls it is amazing to come across the following on December 18th : " The pretty widow's *Dumb Belle* has been received with the favour we predicted, and although we cannot say a great deal for the piece, we cannot say too much for the fair lady. . . . There is a *tone*, after all, about Vestris that none others possess, and it is no wonder therefore that the people go where fame and fashion both preside."

Bludgeons could not silence the pest, but bank-notes could. Westmacott was as mercenary as he was malevolent. A passage in one of her letters, to be quoted later on, seems to indicate that Vestris had convinced herself of this.

CHAPTER XVI

A DISASTROUS LOVE INTRIGUE

Madame Vestris's régime at the Olympic. Her novelties and innovations. J. R. Planché installed as her adviser. *The Olympic Revels* and *The Olympic Devils*. Puzzling *volte face* of Molloy Westmacott. The 1832 season ends successfully. Vestris's address. Season 1832–3. Great attraction of Planché's *Court of Queen's Bench* and *The Paphian Bower*. Madame's anxieties and luxuries. Her inner life. Impending misfortunes. A disastrous intrigue. Sudden disappearance of Vestris. Fracas between Mr. T. S. Duncombe and Molloy Westmacott. Westmacott's cunning to obtain credit for preventing a duel. Westmacott's insinuations against Vestris. Big sums of money paid to Vestris. Vestris, saddled with debts, takes flight with an aristocratic admirer to Devonshire. Vestris's despairing letters. Westmacott paid to hold his tongue. Vestris appeals to Harris to send her money. Vestris's bitterness at having been duped.

MADAME VESTRIS'S management of the Olympic marked the beginning of a new era not only in stagecraft but in drama itself. She began by abolishing the worn stock pieces, whether of the so-called " legitimate " variety or of the musical play of which the public had had more than enough. Madame herself had long been heartily sick of both. *The Lord of the Manor, The Siege of Belgrade, Artaxerxes,* and other productions of a similar class she resolutely banished from her programme. Even *Giovanni in London* she cast behind her, and it was years before she again looked at *The Beggar's Opera,* and when she did it was a *Beggar's Opera* different from that the public had been accustomed to which she put on the stage. Nearly all the pieces she produced— mostly with the aid of Planché—were novelties, not perhaps so novel in themselves as in their mounting. Managers, owing to ignorance, indifference, and cheese-paring economy, had lowered stage accessories to a deplorable level. Anything was considered good enough. When a new play was produced, old, battered scenery had to do duty. In dramas of a bygone period dresses were a ridiculous medley of anachronism and shabbiness. Vestris would have none of this. Her innovations might be costly, but she never permitted money to stand in the way of anything she wanted.

No one was better qualified to act as adviser to Madame than Planché. He was an authority on costume, he had a fertile and poetical fancy and a peculiar faculty in adapting classical stories and old fairy-tales to modern taste   At first his or her ambition had to be modified : " The scenery of the *Revels*," says Planché, " had been limited to a few clouds, the interior of a cottage, and a well-used London street which was made a joke of in the bill to anticipate criticism. Haste and lack of funds had something to do with it." But the *Revels* was a tremendous success notwithstanding, and when the season of 1831–2 commenced and *The Olympic Revels* was followed by *The Olympic Devils*, there was time to devote to the mounting and money forthcoming to pay for it. " It was suggested," writes Planché, " that the scenery should be picturesque and in keeping with the dresses. We had a most infernal Tartarus, a very gloomy sty, and a really beautiful Greek landscape with the portico of the Temple of Bacchus, the colours of which joined in the general dance when

Orpheus with his lute made trees, etc.

to the great delight of the audience. . . . The success of *Olympic Devils* exceeded, if possible, that of its predecessor, and the popularity of this new class of entertainment was thoroughly established."

Meanwhile the position of Madame Vestris at this time was beset by anxiety. She had embarked upon a hazardous enterprise the result of which she could not foresee. The incessant excitement of her adventurous life ever since she was a child, its ups and downs, its jealousies, its monetary difficulties, must have made great demands upon her wondrous vitality, and as time went on a penalty would have to be paid. Maybe her sybaritic tendencies came to her rescue. She lived for the moment and did not meet troubles half-way. It was written of her in after-years that " her reckless personal expenditure often brought her into untoward circumstances. But even when the wolf was at the door the butter on her breakfast table had to be trimmed with roses as early as the month of March, on the plea that she had been so long deprived of them, and throughout the winter her home was scented from attic to base-ment with violets." She adored flowers, and at one period of her Olympic management she owed a florist in Covent Garden £300 for bouquets. So says Edward Sterling in his *Recollections of Drury Lane Theatre.* Whether these bouquets were for presenta-tions to herself on the stage he does not tell us. Probably they were. Her disregard for money was a growth of many years. Clement Scott, in his *Drama of Yesterday and To-day*, says that Vestris " was known to have cut up a three-hundred-guinea Indian shawl merely to use a portion of it for a tartan and sash in *Oberon*."

Vestris was in truth a creature of refinement, and herein we suspect was her attractiveness to men of intellect and education, and so enabled her to retain their fidelity despite her frailties. With all her faults and caprices she was free from the weakness of intemperance. In not one of the many stories told of her by those whose only object was to bring her into disrepute has this reproach ever been hurled against her.

In one direction, however, she was spared an inflic-
tion. At the beginning of 1832 Westmacott suddenly
ceased his persecution and throughout the year his
comments were entirely complimentary. Madame,
in his opinion, was now the best of manageresses and
everything she did met with his approval. What had
brought about this change can only be conjectured.
The fact remains that hostilities had ceased. No more
was heard of the Phillipson episode and apparently
Westmacott and Vestris were friends.

The record of the pieces in which Madame Vestris
appeared during her first Olympic season is represented
by *The Olympic Revels, Fra Diavolo, The Grenadier*,
and *A Duke for a Day*. There were many other novelties, but these concerned other members of the company. The season ended on March 30th, 1832, when
Vestris delivered an address couched in the form of
a parody of the terms of a prorogation of Parliament.
The only part that need be quoted ran : " Gentlemen
of the Pit and Galleries,—I thank you for the cheerful-
ness with which you have furnished the supplies, and
I have the highest satisfaction in informing you that
they have not only been adequate to our current
expenses but that a surplus remains. This surplus
I have directed to be funded and it will remain
applicable to the future exigencies of my management."

There is no reason to doubt this statement. Madame
filled up the summer months with provincial engagements, and the winter season of 1832–3 commenced
on September 30th, and so far as outside appearances
were concerned, prosperity was attending her. The
usual tour in the country was successfully accomplished,
and the third season commenced with one of Planché's
fanciful burlettas, *The Court of Queen's Bench*,
in which the jury of women were, said the *Age*,
" composed of all the flowers in the garden, the
Widow as a full-blown rose and Miss Murray as a
tulip."

In the early part of November the *Age* was extremely suave and complimentary, declaring that " the dramas produced at this theatre must be admired ; they are not too long and generally of a light and pleasing character." A classical extravaganza of Planché with the taking title of *The Paphian Bower* took the town mightily. It had quite a long run and the treasury must have benefited accordingly.

Despite this satisfactory result, a storm was gathering for Madame and burst upon her in full force during the summer of 1833. It is impossible to gather the facts which brought about this catastrophe, even if it were desirable so to do. The story relates to one of the inner passages of Vestris's life and probably only a few of her most intimate friends knew what was happening. This at least can be said—her misfortunes were the result of her own folly and of her weakness in acts of misplaced generosity. The truth seems to be that she departed from the gaiety and frivolity which had marked her former love-affairs and engaged in one in which she showed a blindness and a sentimentality altogether surprising in a woman of her level-headedness. The young nobleman upon whom she bestowed her affection was not worthy of her. He appears to have been one of the reckless spendthrifts characteristic of the times. He was living apart from his wife, and from the very first he was the source of embarrassment and worry to Madame, who sacrificed herself and her fortune in his behalf. Her association with him seems to have lasted from 1833 until the catastrophe came in 1837. But in the interval the public knew nothing of this. The two were rarely seen together, and it is by no means certain that the gay Lothario's wife was aware that her husband had formed a liaison with the idol of the theatrical world until the matter became known through the newspapers. From the very first the unfaithful husband was overwhelmed with debt and there is cause to believe that a portion of Vestris's earnings went into his pocket. Her generosity was a saving grace in her character and she could be easily imposed upon.

At what period the unlucky intrigue began, or how, it is impossible to say; but the unusual absence of any provincial tour during the 1833 summer vacation was noted. Neither was she engaged at the Haymarket as in former years. As a matter of fact, she had vanished, and no one could say why or wherefore. It may be suspected, however, that Vestris's dark shadow, Westmacott, pursued her. An incident, the scene of which was Drury Lane Theatre, suggests as much.

It was on the night of February 15th, 1833. Westmacott was, to quote his own words, " standing in the front wing P.S. during the last act of the ballet when T. S. Duncombe approached him, and after a few words of general abuse he collared Mr. W., who returned the compliment by seizing him (Mr. D.) in the same way. In the scuffle Mr. W.'s hat was knocked off and Mr. Duncombe aimed a blow at him which was parried and returned." The result was bloodless, says Westmacott. The *Satirist* gave a different version. According to this print, which was of the same disreputable class as the *Age*, Duncombe's blow landed on Westmacott's face, a black eye being the result. The words that passed previous to the " scuffle " are not recorded. Apparently Duncombe's grievance was a personal one, but in reality he was acting as champion for Vestris, for whom there is every reason to believe he had a sincere affection.

The encounter was purely accidental. Mr. Duncombe, with Lord William Lennox, Captain Gronow, and other friends, had come from the Garrick Club, where probably champagne had been flowing, and when Captain Polhill, the Drury Lane lessee, sought to quell the disturbance, it is highly probable some intemperate language was used on both sides. The

Satirist says that Duncombe and his party retired, the *Age* had it that he was " expelled." The result was that Lord William Lennox waited upon Polhill, the inference being that he bore a challenge from Mr. Duncombe. Anyhow, Westmacott chose to assume as much, and at once rushed off to Bow Street, not to apply for a summons against Duncombe for assaulting him—oh dear, no !—but to lay information that a duel between Mr. Duncombe and Captain Polhill was contemplated ! The alleged belligerents were accordingly summoned before the Bow Street magistrate, Sir R. Birnie, who investigated the matter in a private room, but on receiving their assurance that nothing hostile was intended, did not think it necessary to hold them to bail.

Westmacott exhibited all his low cunning. He was invited to attend the police court to prefer any charge he might have to make against Mr. Duncombe, but he declined to do so on the ground that he " did not wish to be misrepresented by the reporters and that he intended to proceed against Mr. Duncombe in another court." Westmacott, however, always had more discretion than valour, and nothing further was heard of the matter. He did not even adopt his usual method of retaliation. He was very cautious and mildly commendatory in his brief notices of the Olympic performances, and maybe that, having suffered so little from the threats of Phillipson and Duncombe, he feared he might not be so fortunate on a third occasion.

In view of Vestris's doings in the autumn it is pretty clear that he was not letting her alone. In the *Age* of April 7th came the following cryptic intimation : " Madame Vestris, having passed the Passion week with young Rapid in Chesham Place, appeared in the *Invincibles* at Covent Garden." Chesham Place was where she was living at this time.

Mr. T. H. Duncombe, in his biography of his father,

Thomas Slingsby Duncombe, throws a lurid light on the mystery. To begin with, Vestris was embarrassed pecuniarily, notwithstanding the large sums of money which had poured into the Olympic coffers. Mr. C. Harris, who for years had acted as her confidential agent, financial and otherwise, was still the one to whom she turned when in difficulties. Mr. Duncombe gives the following memorandum of sums received by her from Mr. Harris during the two years 1833 and 1834. In 1833 she had from him : July 17th £3,000 ; November 29th £989 18s. 6d. ; in 1834, March 13th £4,140 ; March 15th, £900 ; April 23rd, £200 ; September 15th, £1,050—in all, £10,279 18s. 6d.

Where Harris obtained this money—whether from loans or that it was due to Vestris from engagements outside the Olympic—Mr. Duncombe does not explain. It is one of the mysteries surrounding the whole business. It may be assumed, however, that in the early summer Vestris and her new alliance were spending money merrily, and that the £3,000 she received in July did not go very far in discharge of their debts and in defraying current expenses. Most probably, after the fashion of the day, their debts were left unpaid. We do not know whether Mr. T. S. Duncombe acted the part of a generous friend. It was like him to do so. At any rate, it is certain the young gentleman owed him a considerable sum. Tom Duncombe was an easy man, but the other creditors were just the reverse. Vestris was as hard up as his lordship, and to avoid arrest they left London secretly and hid themselves in an obscure Devonshire village.

At this time Madame must have been in dire distress. She was saddled with the inevitable expenses which would fall upon her when the Olympic opened in October for the winter season, and *not* to open would be her ruin. She had deprived herself of the substantial sum which would have been hers had she gone into the provinces or played at the Haymarket, and maybe she had tired out her many friends who in former days readily opened their purses to gratify her slightest whim. It is quite within the bounds of possibility that some of these had found the attractions of Crockford's gambling saloon, then in the height of its palatial folly, too costly an amusement. Moreover, it is obvious that to pay a lady's own debts is one thing, but it is quite a different matter when to these debts are tacked on those of somebody else— and that somebody else a man.

Vestris, it was clear, was helpless, and her companion set his wits to work to raise money. He accordingly wrote to the Duke of Buccleuch asking for a loan of £3,500, and apparently he unbosomed himself sufficiently to let his Grace know that the money was not for himself but for a friend. The Duke sent the £3,500 and advised his correspondent to have " the proper receipt given for the money before you part with it to your friend's creditor." The " friend " presumably was Madame Vestris, and had her companion in misfortune acted honourably she would have been saved much worry, but that is what he refrained from doing. He converted the money to his own use! Practically the Duke was deceived, as a letter from Mr. T. S. Duncombe clearly shows .

We are indebted to Mr. T. H. Duncombe's book for some letters of Madame Vestris to Harris, from which we take the liberty of quoting. Here is an appealing one dated September 9th and written from London, the couple having apparently returned from their hiding-place in Devonshire :

" LONDON, *September 9th.*

" DEAR MASTER DEVIL,

"—— is writing to you at this moment. He is staying here a close prisoner. I believe he returns to Lady —— at Hastings on Sunday next. He is quite unchanged and perfectly happy where he is, but he still talks about cutting Richmond Terrace. I say all I can to induce him to have patience, but he will hardly listen to me on that subject.

" You ask me why I at first said I should want £600 or £700 and then mentioned £1,000. The fact is, I mentioned the first sum without looking at my book, which I did before I wrote again. The following is a list of all I owe . . . [the debts are given in detail]. The amount of all, you will see, is £1,313, therefore nothing under £1,000 would be of service to me. . . . I give you my honour that I have at this moment only between £30 and £40 in the world. Therefore my friend must go before Saturday next. . . . What do you think of the *Age* ? I intend to see Westmacott to-morrow or next day, but money is no use to him unless a very large sum, which I have not got to give. I do not grumble at not playing at the Haymarket, but I think it a pity under existing circumstances to lose so much money. . . . All is going on well at the Olympic. W—— accepts the terms of £6 per week, but altogether I am not pleased with him. I wish you were here, but it is of no use wishing. If I could leave town I would go down to you ; I would give anything to have a good long chat with you ; it would do me good. . . .Write ! write ! write !

" Yours sincerely,

" E. V."

Despite her embarrassments Vestris, it appears to us, writes with vigour and determination. She certainly was a good fighter. The reference to Westmacott and the large sum of money which alone would satisfy him is very significant. It seems to suggest that a repetition of his fulsome, hypocritical compliments throughout 1832 would have to be purchased, or something very different might appear. Here was a private scandal to which his victim had no defence. He was able to dictate his own terms, and dictate them doubtless he did. Surely a more despicable fellow than Molloy Westmacott never handled a pen.

The following letter is undated, but the context shows that it was written at the end of September :

" DEAR HARRIS,

" In the name of all that is *mysterious* what is become of you ? It is now nearly three weeks since you wrote to me to say that you intended paying me a visit in the course of a *week* or a *fortnight.* I think you might have written a few lines to say when we were to see you. Although you say that you do not receive any letters now, I will run the risk of this reaching you somehow or other. If I do not hear from you shortly, God only knows what I am to do or what will become of me. My cash is getting very low ; I have only between £20 and £30 in the world. My mother's quarter (£50) was due the first of this month, my rent in Chesham Place was due the 25th of last month, £500 for the Olympic must be paid on the first of next month. You clearly and distinctly told me before I left town that I was to have the money to pay all these. If you had not done so, *nothing under heaven* would have induced me to come into the country. I could have made money enough to meet all these demands (and more too) in the country theatres during the summer. I cannot even stir from this place, which you know I *must* do before the end of next month, until I receive some money. Have you sent *him* any since he met you at Collumpton, or do you know if he has any ? If he has, for God's sake send him a cover and tell him to let me have some. . . . I fear I shall require very nearly £1,000 before I can open the Olympic, that is if I mean to keep out of debt, and I hope to God I shall never get into difficulties again. . . . Under *any circumstances* I must have some conversation with you and that soon.

" Sincerely yours,

" E. V."

Keep out of debt! As if such a happy state of things could possibly happen to one so extravagant and so generous. She seems to have had a real affection for the worthless gentleman, and with a woman of her nature in love with a man younger than herself this would mean a sacrifice which possibly was accepted with indifference. Upon a woman of Vestris's temperament a sense of ingratitude would be certain to inflict much bitterness.

CHAPTER XVII

MADAME'S CHARACTERISTIC LETTERS

Madame Vestris as a letter-writer. The inner history of the Montagu Gore affair. Madame's dependence on Charles Harris. Her amusing notes to him. A sidelight on her last amatory escapade. Card debts and plain speaking. A curious epistolary list.

MADAME when in the mood was a sprightly correspondent. She did not waste words, and expressed her thoughts without restraint. She seemed always in a hurry, and dashed off her notes heedless of her writing and indifferent to the quality and size of the paper. Any quill pen that chanced to be handy sufficed, and at times the result was a shocking scrawl. Those belonging to the Montagu Gore affair were stilted and artificial and evidently written for a purpose. Many were corrected and a fair copy made (apparently by Charles Harris or someone employed by him) and the language was invariably guarded. The true Vestris is carefully concealed.

In dealing previously with this matter (see Chapters VII and VIII) the statement in the auction catalogue that the letters were written for her by Harris was accepted, but subsequently a mass of correspondence came into the possession of the present writer which indicates that the former statements must be modified. A few undoubtedly were written by Harris at the lady's request, but the majority were her own composition. There is no sign in any one letter of the slightest tinge of real emotion. Montagu Gore, on the other hand, plunged into passion, or what he took to be passion. His language is excessively flowery

190

and reads as if taken from a sentimental novel of the period before Sir Walter Scott revolutionised taste in fiction. Here is one written in the very early stages of his amatory advances :

" Tribute of respect to Madame Vestris. In the person of Madame Vestris are united all those attractions which have often flitted as phantoms in the brains of poets and artists, but were never before embodied in the full reality of Nature. Lives there the man with breast so cold as to view unmoved her countenance, which is tinged with the fairest and most delicate hues of Beauty's pencil, her glossy locks parted in graceful ringlets over her unruffled forehead, her ebon eyes that shed around the loveliness of their brilliancy, or the pure marble of her breast ? Breathes there the wretch of so degraded a taste as not to gaze with respectful rapture on the symmetry of her person—and the graces of her mien ? "—and so on, and so on.

Montagu probably followed the " tribute " with material proof of his adoration. Madame's letters are undated and it is impossible to establish their sequence. They are all in the same strain. " How to thank you I know not," she writes. " Your kindness distresses me, not because I believe myself incapable of feeling your goodness, but I know no terms to express my gratitude, and write what I will I feel dissatisfied. Were I to thank you again and again my pen would never do justice to my heart, but pray accept them and give me credit for the rest."

In another letter is more gratitude. " You overwhelm me with kindness, which I feel I can never repay ; still, while I am tortured with feelings of gratitude I can neither shew nor express, I have one pleasing reflection left, that you have a heart that will give me credit for more than I deserve. My cold is better." All very prim and proper, but one is inclined to echo Goldsmith's Mr. Burchell and ejaculate " Fudge ! "

The following is an acceptable bit of spontaneity addressed to the faithful Harris : " With the enclosure I received a Beautiful Diamond comb. Pray write an answer as quick as possible and I will send it. I go to the rehearsal at twelve. Adieu. Ever yours, E. V." Apparently Harris asked to see the comb or, what is more likely, Madame wanted his opinion as to its value. Anyhow we have her writing : " I have sent you the comb and would have sent it before but I have been so engaged with the oratorio. I am unexpectedly going to play this evening at the opera." Another letter (both this and the foregoing are written in a hurried scrawl indicative of excitement) says to Harris : " I have just received the enclosed with a beautiful pair of bracelets. Pray write an answer and send it to me. Do you think we ought to see Chippendale to-day ? I shall go to Theatre to-night. Ever yours truly, E. V."

The reference to the " oratorio " in the first letter seems to fix the date some time in March. Rossini's so-called oratorio *Cyrus in Babylon* was publicly rehearsed on March 28th, 1823, and Vestris took part in it. But in December 1822 a serious rupture occurred between her and Gore and for a while their relations were somewhat strained. The inference is that the quarrel was made up and that the comb and bracelets were peace-offerings. It is the fact, however, that while Madame was " carrying on " with Gore there was another Richmond in the field (for whom she did not care, or said she did not) who had settled money upon her, but it is hardly likely the presents were his. Madame, it was clear, was very anxious that no one should know anything of her liaison with Gore. She never signed her name nor did he his. Moreover, she repeatedly asks for the return of her letters.

As to the estrangement alluded to above, it would seem, from one or two passages in Gore's letters, that he was to blame. So far as can be gathered

ISAAC NATHAN,
Composer of *Sweethearts and Wives*.

from the fugitive dates, matters had gone on amiably until the beginning of December 1822, by which time Gore had engaged to settle upon her £300 per annum. Then something happened which caused him to write thus : " Mr. Montagu Gore presents his compliments to Madame Vestris and regrets that (since the date of his last note) circumstances have occurred which preclude the possibility of any further connexion between Madame Vestris and himself."

This stiff epistle is dated December 2nd, 1822, and is addressed from 5 St. James's Place. It was written in the morning, and by the evening the gentleman had changed his mind and he then wrote : " Mr. Montagu Gore presents his compliments to Madame Vestris and is sorry his servant should have taken a letter before he was up this Morning which is founded on circumstances that Mr. Gore now believes may be obviated ; and which he will explain if she still deigns to meet him this day, in Half Moon St. where he will be at 3 o'clock."

Madame was not one to receive a letter of this kind tamely. Her first impulse was to scribble the following : " I cannot explain to you more than that from some unfortunate circumstances our meeting is suspended so things must remain as they are until you hear again from me to-morrow. This is the last I must beg of you to return." Like the gentleman, however, the lady altered her mind. She did not send this letter, but, her anger rising, she wrote a second, dated Tuesday, December 3rd, 1822. It ran : " Your first note this morning has excited a feeling in me which nothing but a full explanation of those circumstances can remove. I cannot fulfil my engagement to-day. This is the last I must beg of you to return."

What Gore's reply to this was does not appear. Presumably it was of an apologetic character, but Madame was not to be pacified easily. She wrote in a fury : " Madame Vestris presents her compliments to Mr. Montagu Gore and feels sorry (that subsequent to her note which was written yesterday Evening and which she now finds was not delivered until this Evening) that Mr. Montagu Gore has by his two last notes since received assumed a totally different character and which compels Madame Vestris to decline a correspondence which proves uncongenial to her feelings, which Mr. M. G. must be perfectly aware is utterly impossible Madame Vestris can continue. Sunday Evening Curzon Street." The sprawling calligraphy and the equally sprawling syntax show Madame's towering passion. No doubt, however, the invaluable Harris put something like order into the wording.

This emphatic dismissal probably drew further apologies and maybe an entreaty for forgiveness, and the lady changed her tone and wrote—not without a suspicion of irony: " Madame Vestris presents her Compliments to Mr. Montagu Gore and though M. V. is of opinion that Mr. Montagu Gore's note of yesterday renders a reply unnecessary still M. Vestris would regret to lose this last opportunity of showing her gratitude for the manner and the sincerity with which Mr. Montagu Gore has conveyed to Madame Vestris his esteem for her humble talents and so Madame Vestris impelled by that gratitude begs leave once more to present to Mr. M. Gore her sincere thanks for his esteem and that honourable feeling which Mr. Montagu has expressed in his note of yesterday." Nothing could be more polite. The letter might have been written by Sir Charles Grandison.

Bereavement occurring in his family, Gore took advantage of it to appeal to Madame's sympathies. Vestris was always generous-hearted and never bore malice. She wrote: " Although you have forbid me to write unless something immediately connected with myself should render it necessary still I cannot refrain from offering my condolence on the present occasion. Let me shew that I am not unmindful of those moments when you have studied with so much care the feelings of her who now seeks to appease your own and if it can afford the slightest consolation to know that I am alive to your misfortunes be assured that I am. Yes, I am bound by every tie and though last, not least the gratitude I owe." This letter, submitted as usual to Harris, was evidently an ungrateful task and caused Vestris some trouble to compose. It abounds in erasures and rewritings.

Before the year was out the breach seems to have been healed, though matters were not quite on the same footing as before, and Gore returns to his proposition of a settlement. Madame, meanwhile, had one of her frequent illnesses—probably due to nerves—and Gore wrote to " enquire of your health " and regretting that " I cannot in person offer you that consolation which it would be my heart's warmest wish to give but I beg of you, to remove my anxiety by writing to me to-morrow to inform me how you are." Gore had ever a stock of sentimentality at his command and he declares : " There is not a pang you can command which does not affect me and I have no doubt whatever that everything will be settled in a day or two and depend upon me that you shall never know what sorrow is." After this rhapsody he descends to bathos by telling her, " I have hurried the Jeweller about the Ear Rings and hope to have them on Monday."

In her reply to Gore's effusion Madame is at great pains to make it clear that she had no feelings for him other than what she called " gratitude." At the end of the letter she drops without scruple into the business woman.

" Perhaps," she writes, " I shall not deceive myself by thinking you will be better pleased if first I commence my note by speaking of myself and tell you that though I am not well I am much better. I can easily imagine that it must frequently have occurred to you that there has been a coldness in my notes when compared to those you have written but it would ill have become me to have expressed more than esteem and gratitude which your extreme kindness has not made difficult to feel but if it had been possible to have excited a passion of a more exalted kind "—the words first written and crossed out were " the exalted passion of love "—" in one to whom the other was almost a stranger your goodness would have made it perfect and secure "—first version, " would have secured to you all that you have desired "—" but to have written in other terms would have been the height of hypocrrisy, to have felt less would have been the blackest ingratitude. I hope you clearly understand that I have left everything to my solicitor with reference to the settlement and pardon me if I say I cannot consent to any pecuniary assistance whatever from you until all is complete when I may renounce the settlement I hold and him that gave it. Monday morning." In a postscript she adds : " In the meanwhile rest assured though I can do no more than express my sincere thanks for every sacrifice you have made for me I am not the less grateful nor unmindful of their worth."

The reference to the " settlement I hold " is explained in a letter which, like all the rest, is undated. It runs : " Your conduct is so truly honourable that I feel I can communicate with safety and will be brief. The fact is I have already a settlement of £500 but to be compelled to live in the same house with a person whose ideas and pursuits are so totally different to my own leads me (though not to decide) to listen to the offer of another. I will see you this week. I must return the enclosed. Pray send my letter back."

What Gore thought of his rival is not made clear, but it probably influenced him in drawing up his own deed of settlement. Some condition he laid down was not acceptable to Madame and she wrote to him on the matter. The letter is not in existence, but from Gore's reply its purport can be imagined. Gore writes : " I return your Note and am unable to understand it. If you wish the words of the settlement altered in the words ' as long as she is faithful ' I will annex an explanation that I renounce all power of keeping you under restraint of any kind but that I shall consider any positive proof of your giving the preference to another as rendering the bond nugatory. Or if you will send me a written pledge that you will be faithful I will send you a paper that shall give you command of the money for ever instead of its being dependant on contingencies. I have now done everything that it is possible for a man of honour and a gentleman to do and I must confess myself curious to see your Note to-morrow."

Protestations of love and constancy and reminders of what he has done for her follow and the letter winds up with : " Forgive me these expressions I entreat you ; Dissipate by your Note to-morrow my wayward ideas and they shall never be revived. Name your own terms, I assent to anything except that you give another the preference in your affections."

Two letters from Madame Vestris are extant, either of which might be construed into a reply, but they are not conclusive and probably the actual answer is missing. One says : " There are so many things required of me were I to accept your offer and your previous note is still fresh in my recollection. Were I to make one move and you recede I am ruined. In your hands and at your mercy I must therefore place myself and so for a few minutes on Thursday evening I will see you in a private box at Covent Garden. If you will send your servant at six o'clock on Thursday you shall know the rest. Sunday morning. I beg to have my note returned."

The other runs : " I shall ever feel grateful for your kind attention to me and to-day I have directed my solicitor to wait on yours. I have great difficulty in fixing on two friends as my trustees as I find it would be impossible to avoid at least communicating in part to them what my own feelings would rather decline. Still I will begin. I have conveyed to him to whom I alluded yesterday in my letter my intentions and my determination. Upon this I will make no comment. Your goodness lightens every difficulty. Tuesday Evening. Please return this." Whether the condition as to "faithfulness" was retained or expunged cannot be said, nor is there any clue to the identity of "him" whom Madame threw over in favour of Gore.

These points are, however, of little importance, as before the document was signed a serious hitch occurred. It is pretty certain Vestris did not care a rap for Gore. If the man who had been allowing her £500 a year was uncongenial to her, Montagu Gore could not have been less so. He was an ass, as Disraeli called him, and a bore into the bargain, if his conversation was anything like his long-winded letters. Vestris was under no illusions. Writing to Harris, she says: "I have seen Chippendale"— presumably her solicitor—" and I can assure you that from what he says I think Mr. G. has it not in his power to make the settlement, however he intends calling on him to-morrow evening and will let me know the result."

Judging by her subsequent letters this result was not satisfactory. Virtually she gave Gore the cold shoulder. "If you should see Mr. G. to-night at the opera," she writes Harris, "pray be so kind as to beg of him not to come on the stage to-night. Tell him *anything you like*. I am half mad with anxiety concerning this new part, indeed my good friend I am very unhappy."

Gore apparently would not be shaken off. "I found the enclosed," she tells Harris, " on my return home this moment. He has already sent for an answer, pray write one immediately and tell him that I cannot see C—— [Chippendale] to-night."

A few days later she writes : " I have not heard from Mr. G., but I have received a very curious letter from a Mr. Vernon of Lincoln's Inn which I intend to show Mr. Chippendale."

Harris writes in return : " I wish you would let me have a sight of that very curious letter you speak of in your note—before you take it to *Chippendale* that is if the new year has not destroyed that confidence you were once wont to repose in me, for come what may you shall ever find me your most faithful and sincere friend, C. H." This would appear to be interesting, but there is nothing to throw any light upon Mr. Vernon and his " very curious letter."

It was some time before Vestris was free from the Gore entanglement. " More letters when will they cease, indeed I am quite tired of the *Maypole* pray write the *dear* creature an answer." In the same note she alludes to another friend, possibly an admirer : " I saw Horace yesterday. Poor fellow he is very unhappy. What am I to do ? but I will not be a fool and for *the first time in my life* think of the future. Oh dear." A very characteristic touch this. Finally, in desperation, she scribbles : " I have just received the enclosed. Will you answer it for me, request him to Return my letter and I will do the same. I will not be bothered any more by him." With this disappears Montagu Gore and no one was more likely to be pleased at his exit than the much-badgered Charles Harris.

Harris's relations with Vestris were apparently those of close friendship and nothing more. It may be pretty safe to assume that he was an easy-going, good-natured man with a sincere affection for the wayward, fascinating Vestris. Her hasty notes to Harris are very different from her stilted epistles to Montagu Gore. " Pray how did you get on last night ? " commences one, the writing of which bears no resemblance to her agitated scrawls. " Oh dear. I will call on you after the Rehearsal if I can. Will you come and dine with me at six but I shall turn you out very early for *I must study*."

Another runs : " I was out all the day and remained out untill late in the evening when I found your letter. A fish dinner with cup well iced and excellent fruit is the sort of repast for this season of the year. Broadwood gives a dinner to Plaguemedamnable at Greenwich on Sunday." Plaguemedamnable is of course Vestris herself, and a very good name for her too, her friends must have thought.

Two letters throw an instructive light on a strange fashion of the day—snuff-taking. Queen Charlotte, we know, was a prodigious snuff-taker, and George IV's snuff-cellar at his death realised £400. Every male " fashionable " had his collection of snuff-boxes and favourite mixtures, and elderly dowagers did not disdain the refreshment. It is startling to find the dainty, elegant Vestris indulging in the objectionable practice. But it was so. Of one kind of snuff she writes to Harris : " It has no freshness ; I do not like it but I like what I now send to you ; so much so indeed as to have ordered twenty four pounds of it, tho it requires *age* : Pray give me your opinion of it. I like it as a *foundation* for other snuffs having a sound agreeable flavour." Madame was evidently a connoisseur, but twenty-four pounds ! It almost makes one sneeze to think of it.

The other letter shows that she had a vast acquaintance with the different varieties of snuffs in vogue. The first part of the letter is missing. In what remains she says : " It is excellent in these proportions. I should perhaps like it as well with rather less of the Montagu. They are the *same* snuffs I have frequently sent you samples of and which I mentioned having purchased largely of : it is the warm weather that has improved them. Yes ! I have promised to dine at Greenwich to-morrow." The reference to " Montagu " suggests that the gentleman had also his fancy in snuffs. One can quite sympathise with Vestris. It must have been an extreme annoyance every time she took a pinch to be reminded of a vexatious love-affair.

One half of the following may be taken as a bit of harmless banter, the other half shows pretty clearly that Harris was expected to do what he was told to further Madame's intrigues : " I hope," she writes, " your Harem was all harmony, that your Sultana's [*sic*] agreed—and that you passed the night between them. Pray direct three or four covers as before for me (you remember 18 Harley Street in your common hand not your feigned one)—and send them to me."

Here is a note in which she pours out her troubles. It was written at Oxford and the post-mark is July 10, 1833, just when she was at the height of her embarrassments, what with the Olympic expenses and those relating to the enamoured young nobleman. In July she was in fear of arrest, as her letter indicates. Harris was then living or lodging at Chesham Place, Belgrave Square. The letter indicates infinite distress of mind. She writes :

" I am now on my road to Hertford to meet Duthie and the *libelled*. You are a most extraordinary and *unsatisfactory* commissioner, *no* letter again this Mng, but a sort of message per Duthie to desire me to come to the *Square*. Why that is of no use, it is too late to-day as I must be so early at Hertford to-morrow Mng—I am in a dreadful fright in going there unless you have sent by him the needful—I suppose the best thing I can do, if you have not, will be to return to the *Square* on Thursday night or Friday Mng— This suspense is destroying me, I wish to God I had known there was to be this delay, I should have known the worst and should have extricated myself but here I am a prisoner (unable to assist myself) relying upon you and Gibb's resources (of which I have no opinion) I may be utterly ruined and things accumulating—You led me to understand that Gibbs could command *any sum* therefore a few thousands ought not to have delayed it so long—and even a letter to inform me of the *worst* would be better than this suspense but if it is not done this week I shall give it up—either I or Duthie or both shall be up on Thursday night—I will send to you immediately. . . . [word indecipherable] I hope to God you have sent me the needful by him. In haste my Dear H. Yours always E. Vestris."

Harris, as mentioned in the preceding chapter, managed to send her £3,000 on July 17th, but probably the most pressing of her debts absorbed the greater part of this and her position was still precarious. Then came the desperate flight to Devonshire with her companion, and her return to London in the autumn to plunge into the vicissitudes of theatrical management.

Madame was now thirty-six, and this unhappy amatory entanglement reveals an infatuation which one would hardly expect from the Vestris who ten years before had shown herself to be so calculating and level-headed. A curious sidelight on the state of affairs is thrown by a letter to Harris dated May 18th, 1833, from 65 Gilbert Street, two months previous to the crisis at Oxford. Both the handwriting and the general incoherence of the epistle indicate a woman friend greatly troubled. She writes :

" Never was anything so unfortunate as your going away at the moment you did—last night at eleven o'clock I was desired to go into the Parlour to speak to a Gentleman when who should I find but our friend Tommy [T. Duncombe ?] of course I was sure all was not right and he told me there was a Blow up in Chesham Place, there had been a terrible quarrel all night about Ld. E. T. who came into our Box at the Haymarket and a promise exacted on the reconciliation yesterday never to go to Tommy's again as he is supposed to encourage the Meagre (?) Lord—in spite of which promise she goes there to dinner and as she arrives at the door arrives the Chateau also who civilly pulls of [*sic*] his hat and bids her good bye telling her he has found her out and all is at an end. She goes to his House tries all in her power to lure him back without the least effect and when at supper I am sent for again by her and T. D. to tell me all is over and no chance of reconciliation from there being no mediator and you are the only one that could undertake the task but you are not here and I fear cannot come.   I told them the fact that your circumstances I was sure made it impossible.   Whether they mean to put that or not I do not know but I expect a Letter for you from D. every moment which I promised to forward and shall if it comes—I presume it will explain all to you though as usual I should not understood [*sic*] half I do but from my previous conversations with you—It is a dreadfull blow at this moment and I fear will be the cause of serious consequences in various ways—they think I know nothing of what is carrying on in Arlington Street and I do not try to undeceive them but I fear if all comes to light it may hurt D. with Miss M. L. and not show him in a very high light to the world.   It is now past three and she was to let me know if anything had happened and I have heard nothing so shall go there at four o'clock and you shall hear from me on monday.   If she goes to Bath I think I shall go with her will you come there.   I sincerely hope you will arrive here as without your advice I know not what she will do.   I see nothing but ruin before her this is no little quarrel to be made up he treated her with perfect *good temper* and *contempt* this she says herself.   If D——'s letter does not come in time I shall send this but of course you will take no notice of it to the party send me a line by return of post and Believe me ever most sincerely yours A. H."

This is as much as the letters reveal.   The main fact is that the whole business was one of complications, enbarrassments, tempests, and rages, and it may be left at that.

Madame's laconic epistles are more interesting than her lengthy ones. This is what she wrote to a friend of many years' standing—Lord William Lennox : " Madame Vestris's compliments to Lord Will Lennox — and it having been a maxim with Madame Vestris from her earliest days always to give to the poor whatever fortune should bestow when courted with a pack of cards Madame Vestris having innumerable objects of charity waiting her pittance during this inclement season of the year and Lord William Lennox having had to lose to Madame Vestris four pounds about six weeks ago Madame Vestris begs Lord William will enable her to proceed in her charitable purpose." This was only " Pretty Fanny's way " : she meant nothing, for she winds up by asking his lordship to visit her and " lose some more money."

The last letter that need be quoted is somewhat puzzling, as it is not certain whether it was written by Madame Vestris or *to* her. The writing resembles hers, but it is signed " A. H.," the signature of the correspondent at 65 Gilbert Street. From certain erasures it would appear that the note also refers to a card debt. Whoever wrote it was in deadly earnest. It runs : " Madam when I received your last note I concluded I should never hear or see anything more of you. I therefore determined not to notice it. But now that I am compelled to acknowledge the receipt of the six pounds eleven I will take this opportunity of telling you that a more rude impertinent letter I never recollect to have received. Excuse me but you really appear to be ill bred—wanting in principle and unfit for society."

The following list (apparently referring to letters) drawn up by Madame stimulates a curiosity which cannot be gratified :

" No. 1 Mellish's death, etc.
    2 To my wife, etc.

3 Preparing to come.
4 Arrest, etc., etc.
5 A little swindling.
6 Mellish's death—begging me to come
    again.
7 Most material.
8 Duthie's rect. for Eddington's bond not
    sent.
9 Almost too bad to shew—marked 8.
10 Not material.
11 More entreaties to come. Blow up with
    his Governor (? illegible).
12 The money sent for the Horses to A.
    Smith.
13 Rect. for Money.
14 Not material abt. the *Satirist*.
15 My answer to E. T. when the war was
    about to commence.

" Wednesday January 29th 1835. Copy of Eddington's rect. sent to Duncombe.

" Memorandum. Mr. Harris has this day paid me five thousand six hundred pounds July 3rd 1833. E. Vestris, 2 Chesham Place Belgrave Square."

How this amount and date are to be reconciled with the £3,000 stated by Mr. T. D. Duncombe (see Chapter XVI) to have been sent by Harris on July 17th and with Vestris's despairing appeals for money on July 10th we cannot pretend to explain.

CHAPTER XVIII

THE CLIMAX OF EMBARRASSMENTS

The third Olympic season opens. Madame's management thorough and efficient. Alfred Bunn's muddling manœuvres. Scenery and dresses at the Olympic never allowed to be shabby. Spiteful personal attacks on Vestris in the *Age* and in *Figaro in London*. Vestris powdered, but did not paint. Offensive aspersions. Her brother-in-law Joseph Anderson behaves treacherously. Madame sues Anderson. A complicated negotiation. Westmacott flings mud. The climax of Madame's difficulties—Vestris announces bankruptcy. She asks the public to suspend its judgment. Her examination in the Bankruptcy Court. Grasping money-lenders. A sordid story.

THOUGH Vestris's affairs were rapidly hastening towards catastrophe, there was certainly no trace of worry or anxiety in her demeanour when she faced the audience on September 30th, 1833, the opening night of her third season. The piece was an extravaganza entitled *High, Low, Jack, and the Game*, on which Planché had lavished all his fancy and knowledge of effect. The dresses in imitation of the cards were, in the opinion of the *Morning Chronicle*, splendid and the scenery excellent. " The drop-scene of the Great Mogul's Head which usually figures on the wrapper of a pack of cards," the *Chronicle* remarked, " is really ingenious. . . . The season has commenced auspiciously, for the house was crowded to excess and numbers were obliged to content themselves with only an occasional glimpse of the performance."

Madame set an example of thoroughness which other managers would have done well to follow. Bunn at this time was endeavouring to manage both Drury Lane and Covent Garden, and spoilt his chances by making use of one company to play at both houses.

Raymond, in his *Life of Elliston*, describes how he effected this arrangement : " Broad Court and Market Buildings (Drury Lane) from about half-past nine at night to a quarter from ten exhibited a most extra-ordinary scene. Actors half attired with enamelled faces and loaded with the paraphernalia of their art were passing and re-passing, . . . while the hurried interchange of quaint words—' stage waits '—' music on '—' ring up,' etc., would have perplexed the stranger with a thousand surmises. . . . At the season of Christmas when this state of alternation was at its height the female figure-dancers pattered from one house to another six times during the evening and underwent the operation of dressing and undressing no less than eight."

The result of this "management" was the dissatis-faction of the public and poor houses. Bunn's idea of management was only equalled by his want of judgment. Planché, who was writing for Bunn, bitterly complains of his fatuous policy, which was especially vexing to him who " had worked in a theatre managed by Madame Vestris. That lady," he goes on to say, " when on the stage was constantly in her private box watching the performance, noticing the slightest imperfection and seeking to increase effects instead of allowing them to be gradually de-stroyed by time and carelessness. Many of our Christmas pieces were thoroughly re-dressed twice during their run, and consequently as brilliant on the last as on the first night of their performance. Bunn, on the contrary, whose hobby was spectacle and who occasionally expended considerable sums on ' mount-ing ' it, took not the slightest care of the poor thing afterwards, but rode it to death, starved, ragged and shoeless. . . . That such false economy or dis-creditable negligence recoils upon a manager there can be no doubt, and Mr. Bunn suffered more than once from it accordingly—while Madame Vestris was a gainer both in purse and reputation by the contrary policy and but for other circumstances might have realised a splendid fortune."

Vestris's responsibilities may have kept her mind from dwelling on her worries—for that she had worries is certain, and these were not lessened by the stings of journalistic gad-flies. Westmacott, who had been quiet for some weeks after the reopening of the Olympic, suddenly woke up and recommenced offensive personal paragraphs of a kind deadly to any woman and especially a woman like Eliza Vestris. What could be more irritating than this of November 10th ?—" We regret to observe that our fair friend the once pretty widow, was out of voice and out of spirits. The house was not so well attended as usual, . . . that wretched affair, the card piece, is withdrawn." By a disagreeable coincidence a play called *Hush Money* was produced. Westmacott made no comment. Perhaps the title touched him home. In January 1834 he wrote : " The Widow wags on but slowly and is obliged to have recourse to new pieces to keep up the attraction. She has produced more this season up to the present period than she did during the whole of the last or former one. Her *Deep Sea* grows stale and cannot continue to attract for any length of time." At other times he was fairly complaisant ; then a fit of bile or spite overcame him, and he alluded to her as " The widow of forty "—she was then thirty-seven, but the fellow was not likely to be punctilious on such a point.

The *Age* was not the only paper to sneer and carp. *Figaro in London*, an obscure sheet with a solitary claim to attention in that its woodcut caricatures were drawn by Seymour, whose coloured sporting sketches were very popular and really were the origin of *Pickwick*, which was originally intended to chronicle the doings of a Cockney sporting club to be illustrated by Seymour.—*Figaro in London* thought it funny to remark of *The Paphian Bower* : " Madame is still charming though old . . . rouge and carmine are

MISS MARIA FOOTE.
(From a painting by G. Clint, A.R.A.)

very good substitutes for nature, while enamel may serve for the neck as well as unpurchased whiteness." This was written in 1832, when Madame was but thirty-five; but, unfair as the statement was, it was not less so than the reference to paint and enamel. If she used rouge on the stage, she was quite entitled to do so. Of pearl powder she made prodigal use, but enamel was one of the many fictions of which Madame was the subject. It was currently believed that her arms, neck, and face were covered with a coat of enamel " which required her to sit for an hour before the fire to dry." A writer in the *Cornhill Magazine* (March 1863) says : " Those who knew that agreeable and accomplished actress off the stage are aware that she allowed the brown of her brunette complexion to appear undisguised, however liberally she might have applied rouge and pearl powder when on the stage." But anything served the purpose of the " smart " journals of those days so long as it was rudely personal.

Figaro in London was an insignificant effusion, but it added to the annoyances of 1833. The paper's main object, theatrically speaking, was to laud the superiority of the theatre in Tottenham Street (then known as the Fitzroy) to the detriment of the Olympic. " The new pieces," it wrote of the latter in the spring of 1833, " are particularly poor and seem often written to puff off the at last fading attractions of Madame Vestris. . . . It is absurd to hear an old woman in the immediate precincts of forty constantly referred to as a goddess " ; and of the final night it remarked that " the Olympic has closed after a season not quite so prosperous as the two that have preceded, but Madame Vestris still contrives to reap a tolerably abundant harvest from her very amiable reputation. Her personal attractions are, however, rapidly declining and as she has been content to trust to them more than to any other resource the Olympic may soon be in want of another manager."

How silly and futile were these assertions and prognostications was proved by the twenty years of triumph in store for the indefatigable woman. This after-career is all the more remarkable because, as already intimated, for three years she was continually being harassed by monetary difficulties arising out of her unhappy connection with the spendthrift aristocrat.

If Madame Vestris was fortunate in some of her friendships with men, she was unfortunate in others. In her early years it was Captain Best who influenced her, hardly for her good ; in the period we are now dealing with, Anderson, who married her sister Josephine, was her evil genius. With all her shrewdness she could not prevent herself trusting the wrong people. About Anderson little definite information is forthcoming. When he was paying court to Josephine he was believed to possess means, but this is very doubtful. Most likely he was an adventurer and lived on his wits—a method of livelihood extremely common in the thirties. It is certain Vestris at one time was not on good terms with him, as the squabble between the two on the stage of Drury Lane amply proves. He went with his wife to America, and on his return was employed in some business capacity by Vestris, probably because she wanted to help her sister. From what appeared in the newspapers in 1837 it is perfectly clear that either the young nobleman already alluded to made use of him or, what was more probable, Anderson made use of the nobleman.

However this may be, the public, who were always ready to swallow scandal, were highly interested when the *Times* of February 25th, 1837, contained a report of an application made by Madame Vestris in the Vice-Chancellor's Court to restrain the negotiation of certain bills of exchange. " Anderson, who was the plaintiff's brother-in-law," so the report ran, " had been employed by her as an agent in the general management of her affairs and in such character had been entrusted with certain bills of exchange and several blank acceptances which were to be used in a particular way specified. The affidavit stated that on the 13th inst. a letter was received by Madame Vestris from a money-lender setting forth the particulars of a certain bill of exchange which bore her acceptance. Madame Vestris, however, swore she was quite ignorant of the matter and that the acceptance had been made use of in a way not authorised by her. As she had reason to believe there were many other bills drawn under similar circumstances she now applied for the injunction of the Court to restrain the defendant from drawing any more bills in her name as her agent, and also to restrain the negotiation of those already in circulation." The injunction was granted.

Westmacott pounced upon this piece of information and made use of it to deliver one of his characteristic stabs : " The injunction," he pointed out, " is only *ex parte*, consequently Mr. Anderson will show cause against it, when we are authorised to state, he will prove that he never was her agent, but as her friend and brother-in-law he has at various times up to October lent upwards of £3,000 and £550 more to enable her to pay the rent of her theatre, besides various other sums to " (the spendthrift nobleman) " at her particular request to liquidate her inamorato's board and lodging bills while at *hide and seek* from unpleasant visitors who troubled him at her residence in Chesham Place." The assertion that Anderson lent Madame money was subsequently proved to be wholly untrue ; but of course truth was a matter of no moment to Westmacott; and the following week he returned to the charge in this paragraph : " We are informed Mr. Anderson is preparing his answer to this bill and that it will shortly be on the files of the Court, disclosing all the transactions between himself and the *fair enchantress* and that outlawed magician. . . ."

This " answer " was probably bounce. At all

events, before Anderson made any move the daily papers of April 23rd came out with the following frank declaration :

"MADAME VESTRIS TO THE PUBLIC

" Gratitude for the unceasing favour bestowed upon my efforts as actress and manager will not suffer me to remain silent while an event on the result of which my character depends is made known to you through other channels.

" Painful but mature consideration has convinced me that this address is called for by respect for you— by respect for myself.

" An unfortunate entanglement in a series of bill transactions, the first step in which no one can regret more than myself, has lately drawn itself so closely round me as to preclude all hope of extrication by private means, though none which honour, honesty, and self-sacrifice could dictate have been left untried and my name is about to appear in the *Gazette* as a bankrupt.

" I shall carefully and respectfully abstain from all attempt to forestall or to influence the result of the coming enquiry, but calumny will doubtless be busy with my name and I ask you, the kind dispensers of the popularity I enjoy, to suspend your judgment and to protect me against the penalties to which your envied favour is sure to expose me.

" The two reports most obvious for malevolence to fix on are—personal extravagance and failure of the Olympic Theatre, and these I shall briefly answer by anticipation.

" My *bona fide* creditors have shown every con- fidence in me and have cheerfully and unanimously agreed to every proposition made with a view to my avoiding the step now forced upon me, and with a full knowledge of the receipts and expenditure of the theatre they have been willing to allow me an ample annual income out of the profits and to receive the remainder and gradual liquidation of their claims.

" These are facts and enquiry cannot shake them. Their intentions for my good and for their own have been frustrated by persons who have purchased my acceptances which I was incautious enough to sign in blank. Indeed to such an extent has misplaced confidence blinded me that I await the coming investigation to ascertain their number and amount.

" My first impulse was to withdraw myself from the stage until the ordeal should have been passed through, but the claims of all those who are dependent on the theatre remaining open—claims which, be it remembered, have never during seven seasons been one houi in arrear, came forcibly to my mind and I did not hesitate to sacrifice my private feelings to my public duty.

" You will, I am assured, put the most generous construction on my motives. You will remember when I present myself before you that I am labouring for others in a field where I must not reap for myself and you will receive me not only with your usual kindness, but with all needful indulgence.

" Eliza L. Vestris.

" Story's Gate, *April 19th,* 1837."

Westmacott was not pleased. He had apparently constituted himself a sort of father-confessor to the lady, and anything she did without telling him beforehand was wrong. He was inordinately jealous of Planché, and saw in the announcement an opportunity of a gibe at the dramatist's expense. He " strongly condemned the advice which caused its publication and the person who composed it, the adviser and composer being of course J. R. Planché." He questioned Madame Vestris's facts and wanted to know what had become of the profits of £16,000 or £17,000 the theatre yielded in 1834. He hinted at a " recent remittance " from Bath. Where had *that* gone to ?

He wound up by a belief that there " must be something wrong somewhere "—a tolerably safe assertion as matters stood.

Her examination in bankruptcy came on in due course, when the court was packed not only with members of the theatrical world, but with the outside public, anxious to see what the famous actress looked like *off* the stage. Her debts, considering her mode of life, were not large—some £1,300—but these were the " proved" debts. There were probably others which did not figure in the schedule, while certain creditors who would possibly have proved their debts were unable to gain admission to the court by reason of its crowded condition.

The story of Madame's financial embarrassments does not differ very much from hundreds of others of a similar character. The principal creditors were money-lenders, and their methods of business were those which Thackeray so graphically describes in *The Newcomes*. These gentry rarely called themselves money-lenders. They were bill discounters, wine merchants, cigar merchants, picture-dealers, anything which suited their purpose and enabled them to make a little extra profit. One of the fraternity who appeared to prove his debt against Vestris dabbled in wine. He discounted one bill for £250 and £100 worth of wine—of very doubtful vintage, one may be sure. Madame denied all knowledge of this transaction, but the merchant (?) protested that the wine was sent to her residence in Chesham Place. Another discounter gave £180 for a bill for £200, and this was paid to Anderson, though the discounter imagined the money was for Madame Vestris. About this transaction also Madame said she knew nothing.

The key to the mystery seems to be that Anderson prepared a number of bills with the amounts not filled up which Vestris accepted, the idea being that Anderson or the titled spendthrift should insert the figures according to circumstances. The whole thing was

concocted between these two, and Vestris's name
appearing as the acceptor there was no difficulty in
getting the bills discounted. How much went into
her pocket and how much was lost on the way thither
for the benefit of the two men cannot be said—not
that it is of the least consequence at this distance of
time. The affair was unsavoury from beginning to
end whichever way it is looked at ; and apart from the
initial mistake of compromising herself with a reckless
and unscrupulous spendthrift, it is but fair to regard
Madame Vestris as more sinned against than sinning.

It is pretty clear that Madame Vestris was as ignorant
as a child in purely business matters. There was
no difficulty in deceiving her and imposing upon her
good-nature. One of her box-keepers absconded
with all the money he could lay his hands upon, and
at the time of her bankruptcy she had taken legal
action against a treasurer over a matter of £500 alleged
to be owing her. Disagreeable as was the ordeal of
disclosing her affairs—amatory as well as monetary—
to the public, she must have been thankful that she
had the courage to cut the Gordian knot of her
troubles. Bankruptcy cleared away her load of debts
incurred, as she probably would be the first to admit,
through her own folly, and when a few weeks after
her examination the bankruptcy was annulled—the
proceedings were in private—and she returned to
the theatre a free woman, we may well believe that she
repeated her words in her letter to Harris : " I hope
to God I shall never get into difficulties again."

Anderson and his aristocratic partner also went
through the purifying process of bankruptcy. In
the affairs of the first no one took the slightest interest.
The second was a very different personage in the
eyes of the public, and his association with Madame
Vestris gave him an importance which he did not
merit personally. He had behaved badly to his friend
T. S. Duncombe ; so much so that Westmacott in
September 1835 wrote : " We have read a letter

bearing Lord ——'s signature . . . attempting a
vindication of himself and an aspersion of his guardian
friend. We could *if we chose* give a better history
of the whole transaction than has yet appeared, but
n'importe at present. . . . Mr. Duncombe is uni-
versally liked by all parties, and we will never submit
to see even a party enemy borne down by the intrigues
of an ungrateful and heartless courtezan and the
trickery of her titled paramour." Pleasant reading
for poor Vestris !

The noble bankrupt, however, had the grace to
write (in September 1837) offering his " sincere expressions of regret for any trouble or annoyance "
that he might have occasioned Mr. Duncombe. This
letter was published in the *Times* and was dated from
the King's Bench Prison, where his lordship was
awaiting the benefit of the Insolvent Debtors Act.
Mr. Duncombe's reply was that of a generous gentleman. He accepted the apology, expressing his opinion
that his debtor " would never have pursued a hostile
course towards him had he not been influenced by
misrepresentations and unfounded statements." The
proceedings in bankruptcy showed that the nobleman's
debts amounted to £221,000. He owed £8,200 to
Mr. Duncombe, of which the latter saw no return.
The *Times* inferentially called the bankrupt a " noble
dupe," a description which was probably very near
the mark.

CHAPTER XIX

MADAME'S MARRIAGE. THE AMERICAN TOUR

The retirement of Liston. The end of the seventh Olympic season.
Madame turns over a new leaf and contemplates a serious step.
Charles James Mathews. He sends a drama to Vestris, which she
accepts. Mathews's first appearance at the Olympic. Enthusiastic
reception. Mathews's genius as a comedian. His wonderful per-
sonality. Antiquated stage methods swept away at the Olympic.
Madame Vestris married to Mathews. Engaged for a tour in America.
Unfavourable reception owing to scandalous gossip. Prejudice in
New York against Vestris. The Mathewses take farewell of America
at Philadelphia. Criticism of the American Press. Mathews and
Vestris return to the Olympic. A hearty welcome.

ON June 1st, 1836, while Madame Vestris was at
the height of her troubles, came a notable event in
the history of English comedy—the retirement of
Liston, whose personality as well as his art had drawn
forth more laughter from his audiences than perhaps
any other humorous actor in the annals of the stage.
His farewell performance was in the character of
Monsieur Champignon in the burletta *A Peculiar
Position*, and in the farce of *A Gentleman in Difficulties*, in which his ludicrous woes when dressed
in the red plush inexpressibles and other paraphernalia of a full-blown lacquey were irresistible. "He
seemed on this occasion to put forth all his powers—
to play if possible with more than his usual excellence
in order that the public might feel the more sensibly
the great loss they were about to sustain by his retirement" (*Morning Chronicle*). The fall of the curtain
was the signal for tumultuous applause and cries for
"Mr. Liston." He was led forward by Mr. Vining,

but was too overcome to say a word. All he could do was to bow again and again. When the audience was sufficiently quiet, Mr. Vining delivered a farewell address terminating the seventh Olympic season— an address which was listened to with sympathetic attention.

"Aware," said Mr. Vining, "how much less graceful is my bow than Madame Vestris's courtesy, I would willingly have escaped from being her deputy upon the present occasion. To the causes which have led to my being so it is not her wish that I should make more allusion than to express to you her deep sense of your generous sympathy and support at a most trying period. She will ever be delighted to share with you the hours of merriment, but she is unwilling to intrude upon you her moments of depression. Most truly cheering has it been to her, and to us all, that a two-months' extra season has brought with it a two-months' extra success. The gracious condescension of His Majesty by permitting the extension of the present season has hastened the approach of the next, and for four months, therefore, ladies and gentlemen, instead of six, in the name of Madame Vestris, and of a company which feels justly proud of its female captain, I respectfully and most gratefully bid you farewell." The season, it may be remarked, should have ended as heretofore in April, but representations were made to the Lord Chamberlain, and in view of Madame Vestris's difficulties and of the fact that during the investigation of her affairs she would be absent from the stage, the date of the closing of the theatre was deferred as stated.

The crisis Vestris had passed through must have told upon her emotional temperament. She resumed her work at the Olympic, and on the opening night of her eighth season (1837–8) played in *The Country Squire*. After this her appearances were few. She had had a severe lesson, but her resolution once decided upon was not easily shaken. Frivolity and determination were strangely mixed in her nature, and having arrived at the conclusion that her time of philandering was past and that she could no longer face her responsibilities in haphazard fashion, what was to be her next step ?

She was not one to live alone. Companionship was vital to her existence. Her irregular associations had lost their charm and her last experience must have sickened her. Marriage was the best solution of the problem, not because it was respectable but because it would give her a stability of position which was essential to her business undertakings. It is pretty certain that she had no illusions about love, and one can imagine that her ideal of the man she would mate must possess qualities to interest her. Her unbounded energy and restlessness demanded appreciation and encouragement, and unless he was of the same mind as her own in dramatic art she would have none of him. Wealth, even a title, possessed for her no attraction. Her world was not that of the aristocracy. No one knew better than she that no matter to what rank a husband might raise her in the social scale, she would be ostracised by those who moved in it by right of birth. She was not of the class to which Miss Farren, Miss Bolton, and Miss Stephens belonged. It is true that Maria Foote had, like herself, a questionable " past," but it may be doubted whether Maria was welcomed with open arms by aristocratic dowagers, matrons, and their daughters.

There chanced to be a member of her company who, like herself, was mercurial and took monetary troubles lightly. He was withal a gentleman, well-educated, and clever. This was Charles James Mathews, the son of the wonderful mimic and entertainer, Charles Mathews. Charles James was intended for an architect, but considering the strain in his blood it was not extraordinary that he should have a leaning towards the stage. He began by writing a play, under

an assumed name, on Planché lines, with an eye to
getting it produced at the Olympic. He sent it to
Liston, who handed it to Madame Vestris, with the
result detailed in this letter :

"33 BROMPTON SQUARE, December 9th, 1831.

"DEAR CHARLES,

"I gave <i>Pyramus and Thisbe</i> to Madame
Vestris, as I promised you, but heard nothing further
about it, till last night, very unexpectedly, they informed me it is their intention to put it in hand immediately ; but previously they wished to communicate
with the author, and asked his name and address.
This was a poser—as I could give neither without
compromising your incognito. I told them, however,
I would direct a letter to the Post Office, Brighton,
upon the chance of its reaching you. You had better
write without delay to Madame, 13 Craven Buildings,
as doubtless they wish to arrange the terms before
they put the piece into rehearsal.

"Give our love to your mother. Mrs. Liston
wrote to her some time back, not knowing she was
gone to Brighton. How do you get on ?

"Yours truly,
"J. LISTON."

Mathews accordingly wrote to Vestris, who replied
very promptly as follows :

"OLYMPIC THEATRE,
"<i>Monday, December 12th,</i> 1831.</div>

"SIR,

"I received your letter this morning, and
have read your piece, <i>Pyramus and Thisbe</i>, which I
approve of much, as well as Mr. Liston, who has also
read it.

"My usual terms for a one-act piece are twenty-five
pounds, and if this meets your views I shall be glad
to hear from you immediately, as I shall put it into
hand without loss of time.

" Your request as to the *nom de guerre* shall be most faithfully attended to.

" I am, Sir,

" Your very obedient Servant,

" E. Vestris."

The play does not seem to have been produced. Mathews in his *Life* does not explain why. Perhaps he and Madame could not come to terms, or it may have been due to his ill-health, which sent him to Italy to recuperate. On his return to England he went with his father and mother to the Olympic. " At the end of the performance," he writes, " I was carried down from the box in the arms of my Italian servant, and we were invited to wait in the little treasure of the theatre, in order to escape the crowd at the doors. After our departure a lady remarked to the stage manager (looking after me, as I was lifted into the carriage), ' Ah ! poor young man ! it's all over with him—he's not long for this world.' How astonished would that lady have been had she been told that she would be my wife for eighteen years, which, however, turned out to be the case."

Charles Mathews made his first appearance on the stage (he was engaged at £6 a week) at the Olympic on December 7th, 1835, in *The Hunchback Lover*, written for the occasion. In the latter his old friend Liston also played, and John Coleman in *Players and Playwrights* tells how that when in the course of the piece the two were at work in the stable yard, " the old coachman brushing up his hammer-cloth, and the young tiger cleaning his cabriolet—the house rose at them, and the excitement intensified when Liston took Mathews by the hand and led him down to the footlights. The enthusiasm thus commenced culminated at the close of the piece, and when the old stager told the young one that he had reached home at last, and that he hoped his friends would be kind to him ' for the sake of his father,' the curtain fell amidst such a tempest of applause that Liston was overcome by emotion, and sank down almost fainting in an arm-chair. After the play there was a regular levee on the stage, assisted at by some of the most distinguished men of the day in art, letters, and fashion."

The critics were as pleased as the audience. " He is an actor by nature as well as by art," wrote the *Morning Chronicle*. " . . . He now and then reminded us of his father, but more in manner than in face or person."   With this favourable start Mathews soon made good his footing, and in the various pieces in which he acted and displayed his budding personality he strengthened his hold on the public—a hold which was not relaxed even when as a septuagenarian he made his final bow to an audience.   Mathews established his reputation as a light comedian of no common order.   He was without a rival in his own particular line.

" Charles Mathews has more graceful ease, more untiring vivacity, more general comprehension, than the very finest of the Parisians," says a writer in *Blackwood's Magazine*.   " For ninety-five nights he has held a hushed theatre in the most complete subjection to his magic art and was as fresh and forcible on the last night of the course as at its beginning.   Yet never once does he raise his voice above drawing-room pitch ; no reliance has he on silver shoe-buckles or slashed doublets ; he wears the same coat and other habiliments in which he breakfasts at home or dines with a friend.   Never once does he point an epigram with a grimace or even emphasise a sentiment with a shrug of his shoulders.   The marvel is how the effect is created, for there is no outward sign of effort or intention.   That the effect is there is manifest from pit to gallery."

This was written in 1852, when Mathews had polished and concentrated his style until he was complete master of the difficult art of concealing art.

Yet in his early days his acting was marked by a finish which so excellent a judge as Madame Vestris must at once have appreciated. It is more than probable that in his desire to be natural he saw the necessity of having natural surroundings, and it is worthy of note than when the *Old and Young Stager* was revived on September 29th, 1836, the floor of the various apartments in which the scenes were enacted was covered with suitable carpets—an accessory never before seen on the stage.

Apropos of this innovation Mathews says that at the Olympic was " introduced for the first time in England that reform in all theatrical matters which has since been adopted in every theatre in the kingdom. Drawing-rooms were fitted up like drawing-rooms, and furnished with care and taste. Two chairs no longer indicated that two persons were to be seated, the two chairs being removed indicating that the two persons were not to be seated. A claret-coloured coat, salmon-coloured trousers with a broad black stripe, a sky-blue neckcloth with large paste brooch, and a cut-steel eye-glass with a pink ribbon no longer marked the ' light comedy gentleman,' and the public at once recognised and appreciated the change."

What brought about Madame's marriage with Charles Mathews is not of much consequence. Their tastes were congenial, both were enthusiastically devoted to their art, and nothing seems to have happened in their after-lives to make them regret the step. When troubles fell upon them they faced them together without mutual reproaches, and probably this is as good a test of married felicity as any. They were married at Kensington Church on July 18th, 1838, and soon after started to fulfil an engagement in America. This engagement was negotiated by Stephen Price, who had run Drury Lane for a couple of seasons and who previously had had considerable experience as manager of one of the principal theatres in New York. The various engagements of the

Mathewses in America promised to bring in £20,000, with power to prolong their stay if so inclined.

George Vandenhoff, an American actor, who joined the Olympic company in 1839, remarks of the newly married couple with not the best of taste : " Price the old Park Theatre (New York) manager had them . . . married as a necessary preliminary sort of *purification* before their being admitted to the rarefied atmosphere of New York." The Puritanic prudishness of America was, as Charles Dickens did not fail to record in *Martin Chuzzlewit,* easily outraged, and no doubt certain sections of society were somewhat ruffled by the prospect of so notorious a lady presuming to appear before the decorous citizens of New York. Marriage would hardly have altered their sentiments —it certainly did not in later times when one of the most gifted comediennes of the twentieth century (now passed away, alas !) was received with rabid hostility. This attitude had probably much to do with the failure of the Mathewses' tour in 1838.

Some of the preliminary paragraphs in the American newspapers were anything but encouraging. " After twenty years of ' mad, lurid joys,' " ran one, " Madame Vestris has actually wheedled into wedlock the very convenient semi-daft son of the mimic who had once enjoyed American hospitality of the kindest sort and then caricatured his friendly entertainers by making them the jest or laughing-stock of stupid John Bull." "Horribly personal," as young Martin Chuzzlewit told the editor after reading a sample of American journalism. Mr. and Mrs. Mathews's experience of American manners was not less unpleasant. To prepare for their professional ordeal the couple went for rest and quiet to the little village of Poughkeepsie. They found neither. Tired to death with a fatiguing journey and covered from head to foot with dust, they found the " summer retreat " ablaze with light and noisy with revelry.

" A host of elegantly dressed men and women,"

MADAME VESTRIS,
As the Buy-a-broom girl.

says Mathews, " abandoned the illuminated ball-room and lined the piazzas and corridors, to inspect the new arrivals. Through this bevy of strangers we sneaked as quickly as we could in search of a room. A room! What an idea! The whole place was brimful and over-full, and every bed doubly occupied. Sitting-rooms were unknown ; the public saloons were the only resorts for meals and conversation, and repose and quiet were things never even inquired for. After writing our names in the book, for public inspection, the whole party was in a state of tumult, and ' The Mathooses ! ' travelled from mouth to mouth with electric speed. A small bedroom was given up by one of the officials of the house. It was divided by a scanty Venetian blind from the public corridor, or piazza as they called it ; and we were allowed, on the plea of ill-health, to have a cup of tea in it alone. This, it appeared, gave great offence ; and there is no doubt we were greatly to blame in not at once putting on our ball dresses and joining the dancers.

" It was clear this was no place for us, and a carriage was ordered to be ready immediately after breakfast, to bump us down again. This was not to be done privately. The guests were all up in arms and indig-nation. At the moment of departure, as we sallied forth into the corridor, we found it lined on each side with eager faces turned towards us, to get at least one good stare at parting. We retreated for a moment, to hold a council of war, when a sympathising coloured waiter grinned with delight as he beckoned us down a back staircase to a lower corridor, through which we passed, leaving the mob of starers over our heads, popped into the carriage, and off we drove.

" I need scarcely say this flagrant act was never forgiven,and what was worse,actually cost us £20,000."

Vestris and Mathews started their repertoire at the Park Theatre, New York, on September 17th, 1838. The notice in the *New York Mirror* was on the whole complimentary, but remarked that, while the audience was " in raptures, the critics were in a quandary about her." The *Mirror* itself did not consider Madame Vestris superior even in her most favourite parts to Miss Tree and Mrs. Keeley. " The principal charm of her performance is in her singing. Nothing can exceed the effect of the execution of the beautiful little song ' I've No Money ' in the *Loan of a Lover*. It excites the enthusiasm of the audience to the highest pitch. In *Don Giovanni*, which is rich in beautiful and popular airs, Madame Vestris is deservedly celebrated."

But for some reason there seems to have been a prejudice against Vestris. She herself probably did not feel at home, and it was not easy for her to conceal her feelings. She would be quick to see that her dash and sparkle were lost upon an audience which was not in sympathy with her. A significant feature was that after a few nights the seats were mainly occupied by men. Mathews says : " We played our first engagement to good houses, the ladies gradually making their appearance, and all seemed right again. But a damp was thrown over the whole affair, and as a commercial speculation it turned out a failure to the management.

" We then went to Philadelphia, where we had the same ordeal to go through, and to complete the matter, a great monetary crisis arrived, which struck a still more fatal blow to theatrical amusements generally ; and, in short, after two or three months, I determined to abandon all further attempt, and a farewell engagement was announced in New York. A better feeling now began to manifest itself, and I really believe the public became ashamed of the absurdity of the whole transaction. However, I was firm in my determination to return, and a crammed house, with a brilliant assemblage of ladies, graced our last appearance. At the conclusion of the performance, in a long speech, I related all the facts I have mentioned, and bade them (as I then supposed) farewell for ever.

" The effect was everything that could be desired, and I was cheered and applauded as if I had been the greatest favourite in the world, and I verily believe that if I had been allowed to address them in the same straightforward manner on the first night that I insisted on doing on the last, the scale would have turned at once in my favour."

Commenting on Mathews's farewell address, the *Mirror* expressed its opinion that the cause of the failure was " to be found in the inadequacy of their attractions. . . . Had Mr. Mathews made his appearance here alone in fashionable comedy he would have stood a much better chance of success. Mrs. Mathews wholly failed in equalling the extravagant expectations which had been raised in regard to her ; while her youthful husband much surpassed the anticipations of the public."

The *New York Star* sounded the same note. " It has been said," it asserted, " that conspiracies were set on foot against them, that they had committed themselves disrespectfully in one of the hotels in a travelling excursion—that pamphlets impugning the lady's character had been set afloat, and a riot was expected. All this, however, amounted to nothing— their reception was warm and enthusiastic—their performances entirely free from disturbances of any kind—every possible chance was afforded them, but they did not make that impression on the public which had been anticipated. Madame Vestris is a very pleasing actress—quiet, natural, easy, and un- affected, with a sweet ballad voice—but Time, that enslaving monster, has passed his icy finger over her brow ; and although she looks uncommonly well in face and figure, and her constitution appears to have masked all the shocks of a long theatrical life, still it is evident that Madame Vestris could not possibly be in 1838 what she had been in 1818."

The *Star's* greatest complaint, however, was that there had been too much Vestris. " They might have succeeded admirably as auxiliaries, as sauces to other rich viands, but alone and nothing else and they too with a stock company whittled almost down to nothing, made the whole affair cold, clammy, and unpalatable." The truth of the matter seems to be that individual characteristics which have fastened themselves upon English taste by the process of growth do not succeed when transplanted. During recent years the experience of many popular favourites of the English theatres and halls who have appeared before American audiences has been mainly that of Madame Vestris and Charles Mathews. Every nationality has its own ideas of humour, and humour, it may be said, is a question of habit. Old jokes are generally better appreciated than new ones.

While the Mathewses were away, Planché took the management of the Olympic. A strong company, including Farren, in place of Liston, and Mrs. Nesbitt, an accomplished actress but without the attractive personality of Vestris, Mrs. Humby, Mrs. Orger, and Mrs. Waylett in purely comedy parts, had been engaged; but without the all-pervading influence of Vestris the fortunes of the theatre languished. "On our return to London," says Mathews, "we found the Olympic in a fainting state. During the five months we had been absent it had incurred a large amount of debt, besides having swallowed up the large sums I had remitted from America to bolster it up."

Vestris did not make her appearance on the stage for some nights after resuming management. One of the pieces identified with Mathews, *Patter* v. *Clatter*, maintaining its hold for many years, was put on for his reintroduction. The house does not appear to have been crowded save the pit. Rank and fashion at that time had no particular interest in Mathews, and the boxes were but scantily filled—a fact which was more apparent as the shilling gallery had been abolished some two or three seasons before and four-shilling boxes substituted.

But he had a hearty reception from the pittites, was called for at the close of the piece, and he uttered a few broken words of thanks. Vestris, who was in a box consumed by anxiety, must have been thankful that all went off well.

The theatre presented a very different aspect when Vestris herself appeared to receive the welcome of her London admirers. They had remained faithful to their allegiance. Long before the opening of the doors Wych Street was impassable and the rush for entrance was so great that one of the doors was broken.

Blue Beard, an extravaganza burlesque of the type identified with the Olympic, was the play in which she elected to show herself, and when she entered to the playing of " Home, Sweet Home," the audience rose, burst into a continuous roar of applause, waved their hats, beaver and gossamer, their handkerchiefs, " tails of coats, mackintoshes," says *Figaro in London*, " and in one instance a lady's cap on an umbrella." The stage was strewn with flowers, and when a large bouquet fell at her feet she caught it up and kissed the blooms, completely overcome by emotion. With a violent effort she regained her self-possession and dashed into her part. She no longer had any doubt that her popularity had in the slightest degree diminished, and the warmth of her reception did much to compensate for her depressing American experience.

It was remarked that Madame looked thinner but otherwise no alteration was perceptible. Her voice had retained all its lusciousness, her movements their accustomed grace, and her acting all its fascinating archness.

Blue Beard was not the Bluebeard of the nursery tale. The spectacle was not intended, as it would be in the present day, for juveniles. Planché treated his subject reverently and in his zeal for accuracy laid the scene according to the original legend of Brittany and dressed the characters in the costume of the fifteenth century. Whether for this reason or any other, *Blue Beard* was a great success and ran to the end of the season. In addition to *Blue Beard*, Madame Vestris put on other new pieces, among them *Our Cousin German* (evidently intended to be apropos to the marriage of Queen Victoria with her cousin), *or I did it for the Best*, *Faint Heart Never Won Fair Lady*, *Petticoat Government*, *Izaac Walton* (Farren and Vestris), *Meet Me by Moonlight* (Keeley), alternated with revivals of old successes, *High, Low, Jack, and the Game*, and *The Two Figaros*, and for a time she acted at the little theatre in Tottenham Street (formerly the Fitzroy and then called the Prince's) in dramas which the Lord Chamberlain's licence would not permit at the Olympic.

The ninth season at the Olympic ended on May 31st, 1839, and with it Madame Vestris's tenancy. The receipts had been satisfactory so far as the capacity of the house would allow, but, as Mathews points out, it was apparent that in so small a theatre there was no chance of recouping the heavy loss that had been incurred during his and Madame's absence in America, and Covent Garden Theatre being available, the entire company with scenery, dresses, and properties removed to that house.

Just before the theatre closed, James Smith, one of the two brothers who wrote the famous *Rejected Addresses*, sent a poetical tribute to Vestris, which, coming from a man of recognised literary taste, must have pleased her highly. It was contained in a letter he wrote to Planché, and ran :

> Though not with lace bedizened o'er
>   From James and from Howell's,
> Ah, don't despise us twenty-four
>   Poor conson*ants* and vowels.
> Though critics may your powers discuss,
>   Your charms applauding men see,
> Remember you from four of us
>   Derive your X. L. N. C.

Planché passed the lines on to the lady for whom they were intended, and she asked him to reply for her, which he did in this happy way :

Madame Vestris's Answer to the Alphabet

Dear friends, although no more a dunce
    Than many of my betters,
I'm puzzled to reply at once
    To four-and-twenty letters !

Perhaps you'll think that may not be
    So hard a thing to do,
For what is difficult to me
    Is A.B.C. to you.

However, pray dismiss your fears,
    Nor fancy you have lost me,
Though many, many bitter tears
    Your first acquaintance cost me.

Believe me, till existence ends
    Whatever ills beset you,
My oldest literary friends,
    I never can forget you.

CHAPTER XX

The Olympic management reviewed. A wonderful record. West-land Marston's analysis of Vestris's dramatic art. Her amazing versatility. How *The Court Beauties* was produced. A model of realism. Novelties in *The Olympic Picture*. *Riquet with the Tuft*, the pioneer of the modern gorgeous pantomime. The pantomime of the thirties little more than a harlequinade. Vestris's clear articulation highly praised. End of the ninth season of the Olympic and Vestris's farewell address. She and Charles Mathews become lessees of Covent Garden Theatre.

A REVIEW of the arduous work undertaken by Vestris during her nine seasons at the Olympic from January 3rd, 1831, to May 31st, 1839, discloses a truly astonishing number of new pieces put on by her, in many of which she enacted the chief part. Nothing old was attempted; the programme of novelty and completeness of detail in every department, histrionic and mechanical, was rigidly adhered to. It is doubtful whether Vestris's record at the Olympic, of enterprise, energy, and untiring efforts to put on the best entertainment possible, can be paralleled. Her insistence on accuracy in costume and scenic effects, irrespective of cost, paved the way for Charles Kean, Henry Irving, and Beerbohm Tree. Vestris was unquestionably the pioneer of the modern stage.

The list of new pieces, burlettas, extravaganzas, musical farces, etc., is far too long to find a place here, and it is to be regretted that Genest's *History of the Stage* ended before Vestris's régime. Otherwise the meticulous care with which the work is compiled would have been of great value to the student of the theatre, could it have had within its scope the chronicles of the Vestris period. A few of the principal productions are entitled to more than a passing reference, partly because of the personality which Vestris infused into them and partly because of their own merits as examples of care and completeness. *The Olympic Revels*, with which she inaugurated her management, gave occasion for a discriminating study of the actress and her methods, by Westland Marston, which is worth quotation, as it brings her very vividly before us.

" She never failed," Marston points out, " to give her personal attention to the advantage of rich and tasteful costume, and she was such a votary of elegance in dress, that she could display it even in rustic or humble characters. That a silk shirt, a lace-edged petticoat, a silk stocking, a stock of satin or patent leather would never have been worn by some of the characters she personated, was of no more concern to her on the ground of consistency than were their rich attires to Marie Antoinette and the ladies of her Court, when they masqueraded as shepherdesses and milkmaids in the grounds of the Petit Trianon. . . .

" It was, I fancy, her practice of taking the house into her confidence, combined with her coquetry and personal attractions, that rendered Vestris so bewitching to the public. When she sang, she looked with a questioning archness at her audience, as if to ask, ' Do you enjoy that as I do ? Did I give it with tolerable effect ? ' And though in the delivery of dialogue she could hardly be called keen or brilliant, she knew what mischief and retort meant. When she had given a sting to the latter, she could glance round, as to ask for approval, with a smile that seemed to say, ' I was a little severe there. He felt that, I suppose ? ' She had on the stage, either real or assumed, the abstraction of a spoiled favourite. Then, on the night of my first seeing her—as Psyche, I think, in *Olympic Revels*—she could at times seem absorbed

in contemplating her dress, in adjusting a sleeve or
a fold of the skirt, or she would drop her eye in reverie
upon the point of her pink satin *bottines*.   Of a sudden
she would affect to wake to consciousness, and cast
a trustful and appealing glance on the house, then
become demure and staid as one who felt she had taxed
indulgence.   She had skill enough not to carry these
little pantomimic contrasts too far and to enhance
them by fits of reserve."

The completeness with which *Mary Queen of Scots*
was put upon the stage and its strict attention to
accuracy in the appointments and costumes was a
revelation to the managers of the old school.   The
picture presented by Queen Mary's room in Lochleven
Castle may be taken as an example.   Every single
thing in it was in perfect keeping with the period.
The tables, chairs, couches, etc., were all of genuine
carved oak, and everything bore the arms or emblazon-
ment of the Stuarts.   The window curtains, table
and chair covers, drinking goblets, candlesticks, knives
and forks, nay, even to the very carpet on the floor,
were thus marked.   The result was a picture which
would have borne the scrutiny of an archæologist or
an antiquary, though intended merely as a background
to the work of the dramatist and the acting of Miss
Foote.   The " Old Stager," from whose records
(quoted by John Coleman) this description is
taken, sums up thus : " With a full recollection of
all that has been done since by Macready, Madame
herself, and Mr. Charles Kean, I believe that no
more elaborately perfect ' set ' was ever seen on the
stage."

In the days of *Giovanni in London* and *The Beggar's
Opera*, Vestris never excited more enthusiasm than
during her reign at the Olympic.   She seemed en-
dowed with personal youth, beauty, and vivacity.
Here are a few of the compliments showered upon
her by the Press :

" Madame in all the radiance of her own beauty

and with the additional ornament of one of the most splendid costumes we ever saw (*The Deep, Deep Sea*) ; Vestris as a hurdy-gurdy scraper dancing a *pas de deux* with Pincott (*The Retort Courteous*), one of the most effective exhibitions of its kind that we have seen for years." Madame's performance in *How to Get Off* was pronounced " a great treat—an admirable personi- fication of that strange race of beings called ladies' maids." In *Telemachus* Madame Vestris's voice was declared to be as fine as ever and she herself as charming. " No wonder this theatre succeeds. She played to perfection the wicked-eyed, black-haired, short-petticoated, handsome-legged coquette Lisette Giserestein, in *Why Don't She Marry ?* "

The Court Beauties of the fifth season was an enor- mous success. It was just one of the pieces in which Vestris revelled. Planché was indebted for the idea to Douglas Jerrold, and the scene in which " King Charles II's Beauties " were represented in their frames from Sir Peter Lely's luscious pictures at Hampton Court by ladies of the company really anticipated the " living pictures " in favour a few years ago.

The " Old Stager " has much to say about the pro- duction of *The Court Beauties*, over which no end of trouble was taken and money spent with an audacity and a desire for accuracy which were part of Madame's character. " The scene painter, machinest, costumier, and property-man of the theatre were despatched to Hampton Court to take notes of everything necessary from the original paintings deposited in the picture- gallery there. We had hardly commenced work when one of the attendants stopped us, saying that no one could be allowed to copy anything there without special permission of the Lord Chamberlain, so we had to return to London with our purpose unful- filled.

" This hitch in the business, however, was soon re- moved. The same evening, Lord Adolphus Fitzclarence was behind the scenes, to whom Madame related the circumstances and expressed her disappointment at the result. . . . ' Dolly ' drove straight down to St. James's Palace, saw the King, his father, and then came back with an order bearing the signature of the Sovereign, ordering the attendants at Hampton Court to allow us to copy what we pleased. . . ."

" The first scene was the Mall in St. James's Park, beautifully reproduced from a print of the period of the play. The effect of this scene was much heightened by our making use of a passage, fully one hundred feet in length, which led from the back of the stage to Craven Buildings, and by which the Mall was represented going away into perspective, with wonderful appearance of reality.

" On wires hung between the trees were suspended numerous cages with various kinds of singing birds, whose St. Giles's owners managed to make them sing to perfection. On the rising of the curtain this scene used to call forth the most enthusiastic applause, and the demonstration certainly did not diminish when Mr. Hooper, looking the Merry Monarch to the life, came on, followed by his attendants, all in gorgeous and scrupulously correct costumes of the reign of Charles II.

" True to the life, the King was accompanied moreover by a number of King Charles's spaniels. There were twelve in all of these little brutes, and one couple of them alone—named respectively ' Nell Gwynne ' and ' Old Noll '—cost no less a sum than seventy pounds sterling !

" The second scene showed the fruits of our labours at Hampton Court. It was a correct model of the room in the Palace there called the ' King Charles's Beauty Room,' the back of it representing the wall with the eight life-size pictures by Lely, each in its massive frame. The sides were hung with beautiful tapestry, which, though now used for the purposes of stage illusion merely, was the bona-fide article, the real handiwork of ladies at King Charles II's Court. For many years it had adorned the walls of Carlton House, and had now been purchased by Madame for a pretty roundish sum, to contribute to the vraisemblance of this piece.   Nay, more, the curtain which I have mentioned as concealing this picture while the King and Sir Godfrey were at supper, was the identical stuff, green with gold embroidery, which has for years covered the original portraits at Hampton Court. Having been replaced at the Palace by a new one, the discarded article came into the possession of a valet of the Lord Chamberlain, who sold it to us.

" The ceiling of the scene was a painted representation of the twelve signs of the Zodiac, and from the centre there hung a massive old crystal chandelier with no less than fifty wax tapers burning in it.   For the miscellaneous furniture and properties we had searched the chief curiosity-shops in London until the smallest item required was procured in keeping with the rest.   Such, as briefly as I could well give it, is a sample of the means which Madame Vestris took to *deserve* that success which, as a rule, she managed to command."

The Olympic Picnic (December 26th, 1835) contained certain novel features which in modern times have been carried to excess.   Well-advertised nostrums were engrafted on to a pseudo-classical story. Psyche (Madame Vestris), having incurred the anger of Jupiter and Venus, is consigned to search for the box of beauty, which she finds in what the Olympic deities called " Lower Pall Mall," in reality Crockford's gambling-house.

This box provided by Pluto, on being opened by Psyche, is found to contain an eighteen-penny bottle of Warren's blacking, then all the vogue, as the admirers of Sam Weller will remember.   In some magical way the blacking transfers itself to the face of the lovely Psyche and gives it the lustrous appearance of patent leather.   Wandering in this plight,

Psyche comes upon a party of gods and goddesses picknicking, and among the company is Zephyr, represented as a lady of fashion. Zephyr proclaims the virtues of Rowland's Kalydor, which she asserts has the power of converting the ugliest object into the most beautiful. The sable-faced Psyche is selected as a test, the Kalydor is applied, she is transformed, recognised, received with joy and forgiveness. All very absurd and even childish, but this was of no moment. The burlesque served as a vehicle for splendid scenery, gorgeous dresses, pretty faces and figures, and tuneful music. " Vestris," one reads without surprise, " was the life and soul of the piece."

Riquet with the Tuft, put on as a Christmas piece in 1836, was the first of a series of fairy extravaganzas, followed by many others and afterwards identified with Madame Vestris's management of the Lyceum. It was an adaptation from the French, and when Planché proposed it to Vestris, both she and Charles Mathews, by this time a member of the company, were doubtful of the success of what they called a new experiment, for hitherto the subject of the Christmas pieces for six years had been invariably classical. It so happened that the author of *The Olympic Picnic* was Samuel Lover, who wrote a once-popular comic novel, *Handy Andy*, and many humorous songs, the music as well as the words. Both Charles Dance and Planché, fearing that Lover was trenching on their ground, determined to strike out a new line. Vestris and Mathews allowed themselves to be persuaded, but at the eleventh hour they hesitated and were inclined to revive one of the classical favourites rather than risk the ruin of the whole season by the failure of this untried species of entertainment. Planché and Dance, however, held out; the piece was produced and the success was tremendous.

As a sort of apology for and explanation of the departure from the usual Christmas programme, Vestris as the Princess Esmeralda sang this parody of the song which Henry Phillips made famous, " The Fine Old English Gentleman " :

Old friends, I've the old prayer to make before it is too late,
With your bold kindness please to view this change in our old state,
Our old mythology, we thought, was getting out of date,
And so we've left Olympic old and all its gods so great
For a fine old English fairy-tale, one of the olden time.

It is interesting to note that the criticisms of Vestris after she became manageress and acted in plays which appealed to her sense of art changed in tone.   She was no longer praised because of her beauty of face and figure, her fascinations, her charm of voice.   She was now regarded as an actress who aimed at a high standard, albeit that standard did not go beyond imagination and fancy.   The notice of *Riquet with the Tuft* in the *Morning Chronicle* may be taken as an example : " Madame Vestris was the beautiful but half-witted Esmeralda.   She acted the part admirably ; we hardly thought she could have made the character so strikingly interesting as she did.   In the first part of the piece she came on the stage bounding after a butterfly and exhibiting endless absurdities of manner and expression; then came her restoration to reason by the hump-backed invisible Riquet, and then she displayed a warmth of tone and soundness of expression and delicacy of feeling which proved a complete and striking contrast to the absurdities which had passed. Nothing could exceed the beautiful pathos and richness of tone which she threw into the melody ' The Light of Other Days has Faded.' "

For the extravaganza as a whole the *Chronicle* had quite a song of praise.   " What," it wrote, " could be more enlivening than the scene of Fairyland with scores of little fairies dancing a true fairy round ? What more inviting than the fairy kitchen scene with all the little pigmy cooks frying, stewing, peppering; basting and tasting the delicacies preparing for her highness's wedding breakfast ?   What could be more imposing than the grand review of all the com-

bined heroes of fairy romance, from Jack the Giant
Killer to the Seven Champions—from Cinderella to
Beauty and the Beast, which concluded the enter-
tainment ? "

The production and success of *Riquet with the Tuft*
have a significant bearing upon the pantomimes of
later years. Mr. Dutton Cook (*Book of the Play*)
says that up to the year 1850 the harlequinade was
announced by a series of dioramic views, mostly
the work of Clarkson Stanfield. This bald and uninteresting expedient then gave place to the " gorgeous transformation scenes traceable to the grand
displays which were wont to conclude Mr. Planché's
extravaganzas." The employment of fairy-tales as
themes for pantomimes was thus instrumentally due
to Madame Vestris, thanks to her acceptance of
Planché's ideas. The pantomime of Joey Grimaldi
and his immediate successors was a totally different
affair from that of the present day. The old clowns
played to audiences of adults ; children are now only
considered, or should be. But it may be that pantomimes, like a good many other things theatrical, have
now had their day.

Among Vestris's other successes *A Duke for a Day*
(January 24th, 1831), founded on Boieldieu's *Le Seigneur
du village*, is notable for a criticism which in a way
was the foundation of her hold upon the public. They
could always hear every word she uttered, whether
spoken or sung—an accomplishment which too many
actresses and singers nowadays quite ignore. " The
rich tones of her voice," wrote the critic, " are poured
forth without exertion ; moreover, her pronunciation
of the words renders them as familiar to the audience
as if they were exhibited in melodramatic letters of
fire upon a flat scene. If she goes on in this way, she
will ruin the fruit-women, for nobody will buy a
book of the songs." Of how many singers now before
the public can this be said ? Yet it is in clear articulation that all great vocalists have excelled.

MADAME VESTRIS'S HANDWRITING.
(From a letter to Charles Harris.)

In the farewell address on May 31st, 1839, Vestris would have been fully entitled to recapitulate some of her triumphs, but she was one to look forward to fresh successes rather than to go back to old ones, and it will be seen from the following that she started upon her new venture full of hope and confidence :

" LADIES AND GENTLEMEN,—For the ninth time I have the honour to drop my curtsey and my curtain at the close of a prosperous season, for which, in Mr. Mathews's name and my own, I beg to offer you our best acknowledgements.

" There have been peculiar circumstances connected with the season about to conclude which I conceive I had better say but little about. I may, however, safely and truly say that I left you with unfeigned regret and returned to you with unbounded joy, and though it must be confessed that the mode in which you manifested your regret at my absence was more calculated to feed my vanity than my treasury, your kindness since my return has left the latter nothing to complain of.

" Encouraged by the approbation my managerial efforts have received, we have become lessees of the Theatre Royal, Covent Garden. I am aware that we shall have many difficulties to contend with. We propose to face them manfully and womanfully— to preserve the good points of former managements and reject the bad—to take with us the best results of my experience here, and to trust to the public to do the rest.

" Some kind friends have already prophesied that I shall not succeed there. My only answer is, that nine years ago they said I should never succeed *here*.

" The most absurd reports are in circulation about the characters which we mean to appropriate to ourselves ; two of them, and only two, I shall notice, for if allowed to remain uncontradicted they may do us serious injury—Mr. Mathews will *not* play Macbeth, and I have positively refused Queen Catherine.

" In conclusion, ladies and gentlemen, I beg to state that the great increase of our business having justified us in taking more extensive premises, I most respectfully, for the performers and myself, bid you farewell until we meet in September next at the Theatre Royal, Covent Garden, where I entreat a continuance of your custom and recommendation for the house of Mathews, Vestris, and Company."

CHAPTER XXI

DIFFICULTIES OF THEATRICAL MANAGEMENT

Vestris at Covent Garden Theatre. Her prospects. Qualifications as a theatrical manageress. Westmacott's attacks cease. Difficulties in the way of the new enterprise. Vestris's superiority to Macready as a manager. *Love's Labour's Lost*, the opening piece. First night uproar. Shakespeare a failure. Sheridan Knowles's play, *Love*. Financial Embarrassments. *The Beggar's Opera* put on as a last resource, dressed in the proper eighteenth-century fashion. The house packed nightly, but embarrassments continue.

MADAME VESTRIS'S decision to embark her and her husband's fortunes at Covent Garden was a venture which demanded boldness, energy, and belief in success. But she was nothing if not sanguine, and her policy of no half-measures was the only safe one where so big an undertaking was concerned. She was fortunate in her partner. Charles Mathews had established his popularity in a certain line of character-acting in which he had no rival, and that popularity was increasing. His buoyancy of spirits was equal to hers, and this was a great asset.

The greatest point in her favour, however, was that her management of the Olympic had shown that she was not the frivolous, capricious light o' love that scandal had represented her. Her delight in pleasure was the outcome of a vivacious, restless nature which could not tolerate dullness and monotony, while her innate love of art and all that was beautiful in art was her protection against vulgarity of any kind. The exception which the critics sometimes took to her impersonation of the pert chambermaid—a stock character in nearly all the comedies of the day—was

243

that she was inclined to be too ladylike. She was wanting in the abandon and knowledge of low life which other noted actresses, her inferiors in many respects, threw into such parts. One cannot imagine her guilty of the mistake which Mrs. Abington made in playing Scrub in *The Beaux' Stratagem*. She was never otherwise than womanly even when she put on masculine garb, and she was essentially womanly in that she delighted to give pleasure to others.

It was a source of continual unhappiness that episodes in her life made her vulnerable to the attacks of the vicious-minded. As has been shown, the Olympic régime was embittered by the despicable pin-pricks of Westmacott. With the end of the Olympic and the culmination of her mistakes outside the theatre in bankruptcy came also the end of her persecution. This cessation may have owed something to her new departure in life and something to her marriage. In many aspects of her conduct it may be said that she was more sinned against than sinning.

Whether Westmacott had any remorse or that particular sources of her income having dried up she was not worth pursuing further does not matter very much. Certain it is that after her bankruptcy the *Age* let her alone, and it is to be noted that when she became manageress of Covent Garden Theatre its petty persecution ceased. It may be that Molloy Westmacott had parted with his interest in the paper ; but whether this was so or not, throughout the Covent Garden campaign the *Age* gave forth nothing but a song of laudation over everything that Vestris did. At times when occasion called for it faults were pointed out, but such strictures were confined to the play or to performers other than Vestris. For her there was nothing but praise. It is but fair to say that the theatrical criticisms of the *Age*, for which notorious journal not many people—certainly not the "fashionables"—had a good word, were in later years honest and outspoken, whether praise or blame, and afford better reading than those in the daily journals.

Despite Vestris's indifference to what is called the " value " of money she had the strong business instinct which is at the bottom of most successful enterprises. There was evidence of this in her nine seasons at the Olympic. She established a disregarded and not particularly flourishing theatre on a solid basis and made it the most-sought-after place of amusement in the metropolis. To-day, when gorgeous spectacle after spectacle has brought about a sense of satiation and even boredom, we cannot imagine the effect which Vestris's innovations had upon the public and upon stage-craft. Whether principally due to her or to Planché, the fact remains that many of the so-called novelties of recent times were anticipated at the Olympic, even to revues, two of which Planché prepared.

Covent Garden Theatre possessed an immense advantage over the Olympic. The Olympic was " cribbed, cabined, and confined." Drury Lane and Covent Garden, by virtue of their patents, had the privilege of being open all the year round and any sort of dramatic entertainment could be produced. The Haymarket could only be opened for the drama during the summer. No other than these could perform anything but burlettas. The Lyceum was specially licensed for English opera and musical operas (there seems to have been no objection to boxing entertainments, and the theatre was so used for this purpose more than once) ; and at the Adelphi and Olympic burlettas alone could be performed. At Astley's, the Savoy, Sadler's Wells, no one had a legal right to open his mouth on the stage unaccompanied by music. Sometimes prosecutions for evasion of these restrictions were instituted, but magistrates were loth to commit and the managers of the patent theatres gradually dropped their opposition ; but it was still open to the common informers to proceed if it paid them to do so. As already mentioned, the manager of the Fitzroy in Tottenham Street was prosecuted and fined. The Strand Theatre, however, openly defied the law for nearly two years.

The absurdity of the restrictions became still more absurd in the time of Lent, and, as Planché points out, during the Lenten season the theatres in the parish of St. Paul's, Covent Garden, were rigorously restricted from the performance of a moral or poetical play on Wednesdays or Fridays during that period; but a theatre that happened to be on the other side of Oxford Street or of Waterloo Bridge was unaffected. The performers at Drury Lane and Covent Garden lost two nights' salary every week, but they could go to Greenwich or Richmond and act what they pleased there. Passion Week was unknown in the theatres two or three miles from St. James's Palace.

In entering upon possession of Covent Garden, Vestris's shrewdness and experience must have convinced her that the size of the building, its connection with the higher walks of the drama, and the character of the audiences accustomed to assemble within its walls had to be seriously considered. The kind of entertainment suitable for the " Olympic parlour " would not do for the arena of Covent Garden, if only on the score of expense. The cost of producing an Olympic fairy extravaganza would be doubled. Even were such a production deemed expedient, it was doubtful whether the larger theatre would draw sufficient of the Olympic crowd to pay for the experiment.

Apart from this, it is pretty clear that Madame had an eye for a programme which would attract the serious as well as the frivolous playgoer. Shakespeare, she conceived, was the safest line to take. The old comedies were more or less in the nature of revivals, but Shakespeare was ever fresh, provided an adequate cast could be found. Playgoers then would crowd to see a new Hamlet, a new Macbeth, and this was

Madame's difficulty. Edmund Kean was dead, and the only man of eminence to succeed him was Macready. But Macready was unavailable, and had he not been it is doubtful whether Vestris would have offered him an engagement. Moreover, his stilted style was not attractive, and, what was worse, certain mannerisms were obvious, and, as generally happens with imitation, the mannerisms were reproduced by others, who could not see that they were defects and not excellences.

The chief obstacle, however, lay in the fact that Vestris and Macready were in a sense rivals. Macready's management of Covent Garden was a failure; a woman's might be a success. In comparing the two the *Satirist* wrote on June 12th, 1840: " The pretensions of Vestris are of a much higher order, in whatever way we may look at them, than those foisted upon us by Macready; he is a mere pretender—a charlatan in art; she is clever, a thinking, a very superior woman. . . . . What Vestris has done for the dramas she has brought out at this theatre has been in the way of embellishment—she could do no more; she could give the form, but it was impossible to impart the soul. Now Macready attempted both; he, good easy man, not only embellished the plays he brought forward at Covent Garden, but attempted the spirit also—that is he resorted to unusual diligence to teach the performers about him to talk on the stage in the same way that he is wont to do himself, and those who visited the theatre under his management saw not *one* Macready but a dozen—or rather some dozen men and women *ape*-ing the ' disjointed chat ' of the King Raven who had only to flutter his wings to set on the whole flight to ' win exclamations from the few and laughs from the many.' "

A Shakespearean " star " being beyond her reach, Madame had to do the best with the material at her disposal. She hardly made a happy choice in selecting *Love's Labour's Lost*. The comedy had the doubtful advantage of not having been acted for a generation, and maybe she thought people would come out of curiosity, or perhaps she chose it because it gave her a chance of continuing her Olympic programme of elaborate scenery and appointments. She had an eye, however, to her own particular patrons, and advertised that she " intended to devote one evening each week to the performance of those entertainments which for so many years have constituted the attraction of the Olympic Theatre." She also made an announcement which reads curiously nowadays. " The gas," it runs, " has been entirely removed and replaced by wax candles "—an expensive process which no doubt found its place in the heavy bills which gradually accumulated during the next two years. Be this as it may, it can hardly be doubted that wax candles, provided there were enough of them, were preferable to the bad gas and imperfect appliances of those days.

September 30th, 1839, was fixed for the opening night. The theatre was densely crowded, but the gods were outraged because the shilling gallery had been made into an eighteen-penny one and their wrath marred the success of the evening. They " filled the lower gallery to suffocation," says Mr. James Anderson, who was the Biron of the play, " and the demonstrations of indignation were terrific. The comedy was interrupted, often stopped, and all but ' damned ' by the tremendous noise and uproar. At length, after many fruitless attempts to be heard and apologise, a man carrying a placard on a pole gave the malcontents to understand that the shilling gallery should be opened the following night. After three hearty cheers from the conquerors, the play was allowed to proceed and finish. This came too late, for the poor play had received its quietus in the very first act."

This was a disheartening beginning, but the initial mistake was in selecting *Love's Labour's Lost*, a play as unfamiliar to the audience as it was to the actors and in itself possessing no opportunity for individuality—and individuality to the Shakespearean public of that day was everything. The eighteenth and early-nineteenth-century playgoers knew their favourite Shakespearean tragedies and comedies by heart, and they were more concerned with John Kemble, George Frederick Cooke, Edmund Kean, Mrs. Siddons, Miss O'Neill, and other "stars" than with the play itself. They had the established traditional "business" at their fingers' ends. They watched keenly for new readings and new interpretations of famous lines, and found a pleasure in comparing them with the old ones and in discussing their merits.

In *Love's Labour's Lost* they were without this pleasure. The comedy is comparatively colourless. Interest is not concentrated in any particular character. The company was full of talent, represented as it was by Anderson, Keeley, Bartley, Meadows, Cooper, Vining, Mrs. Nisbett, Mrs. Humby, Miss Rainforth, Madame herself, and others; but it was not a company identified with Shakespeare, while the shortcomings of the play itself were scarcely compensated by Grieve's beautiful scenery, Planché's accurate and picturesque costumes, and the gorgeous colouring and general effect due to Vestris's artistic conception.

Love's Labour's Lost was a failure and was withdrawn after a few nights, and Madame Vestris and her husband found that the receipts from the plays put on as stop-gaps "were," writes Charles Mathews, "not only insufficient to meet the great expenses of the theatre, but utterly destructive of all hopes of repaying the previous losses and liabilities." A solicitor friend advised the winding-up of the enterprise, and Mathews was seriously considering this policy, while Madame occupied herself with the preparation of a novelty which she saw was the only thing—if successful—to save them. Sheridan Knowles was the dramatic poet of the day. His *Hunchback* and *Virginius* had brought him into prominence, and he was at that moment engaged on a play in blank verse. This play—*Love*, as it was called—was selected, and was produced on November 10th, 1839.

Vestris had a part in the drama suited to her powers and enabling her to display herself in male habiliments. Perhaps it was this which attracted her and which she hoped would also attract the public, otherwise the play had no special merit. "Mrs. Mathews," one critic writes, "as Katherine had the only part which gave relief to the play and her assumption of the knight was excellent. She looked in her male attire as young and as handsome as ever she was."

Westland Marston gives an analysis of her acting which brings the character before us : "Madame Vestris," he says, "was quite in her element. She had to stimulate, often in male disguise, a sincere but slow and taciturn lover ; to send him on her errands, and jest at his delay or non-attention ; to reflect on his courage, challenge him to fight, and then cleverly evade the meeting. In her disguise of a young gallant, to affect to him that she (Katherine) had broken her ankle and limped, that her wrist went ' zig-zag,' that her complexion was ruined, that she had squandered her wealth ; to exult, with a roguish smile, that his honest heart was still faithful to her, then once more to quarrel and order him to his knees, and, when the incensed knight at last rebelled, to throw off her page-ship's cloak, and reveal his tormenting but loving Katherine—this was comedy, not very brilliant, and at last, rather tiresome, but quite suited to Madame Vestris—comedy in which she delighted." The press notices were rather inclined to damn the play with faint praise, and, truth to tell, it is somewhat dull reading. But Sheridan Knowles was looked upon by many as running nearer to Shakespeare than any of his contemporary dramatists, and the reception of *Love* was uproarious and loud cries of "Author !" were raised at the fall of the curtain—" a vulgar custom," wrote the *Age*, in disgust, " first encouraged by Mr. Dickens and last by Sir E. Bulwer."

Sheridan Knowles, it must be confessed, was much more amusing as a personality with his pure and unadultered Irishisms than in anything he ever wrote. His " bulls " were delightful. Planché records how one day he said to Abbott (an actor long connected with Covent Garden and afterwards manager of a Dublin theatre), with whom he had been acting in the country, " My dear fellow, I'm off to-morrow. Can I take any letters for you ? " " You're very kind," said Abbott, " but where are you going ? " " I *haven't made up my mind.*" Another time, meeting O. Smith, the famous actor of lurid parts in the Adelphi melodramatic days and so called from his impersonation of " Obi " in *Three-fingered Jack*, in the Strand, he seized him by the hand, shook it heartily and inquired affectionately after his health. Smith knew Knowles only by sight and had never spoken to him, and remarked, " I think, Mr. Knowles, you're mistaking me for somebody else. I am O. Smith." " My dear fellow," cried Knowles, " I beg you ten thousands pardons—I took you for your namesake T. P. Cooke ! "

Despite the languid praise of the press, *Love* proved fairly acceptable to the public, but the treasury did not overflow and things began to look black when Vestris by a happy thought put on as an afterpiece to *Love* that ever-present refuge in the time of trouble —*The Beggar's Opera.* The opera was no novelty. It had been presented in divers forms from time to time since 1728. The various Macheaths and Pollies were innumerable. As the rollicking highwayman, Vestris had made her name. It would seem to her the last thing to revive the fortunes of an embarrassed management. Yet it had done this not once but many times, and probably Madame thought it might do so once more.

Vestris had seen *The Beggar's Opera* put on the stage often and often, and it must have been repugnant to her artistic sense when a dull-witted or cheeseparing

manager treated the early eighteenth-century play
as though it had been written the day before yesterday
and dressed it accordingly. This kind of thing had
been tolerated by audiences because they knew no
better and had seen nothing different. Vestris thought
for herself and now had a chance of putting her
thoughts into action. She produced the opera with
the costumes of the day when Lavinia Fenton as Polly
Peachum captured all hearts. The experiment was
an instant success. At last the public had a complete
picture not only of the opera but of the times. " In
an instant," writes Charles Mathews, " to the surprise
of everyone, ourselves included, up went the receipts,
the houses were crammed, and a long and successful
career was the consequence. The corner was turned,
the public responded to our efforts, and we sailed
once more before the wind."

The cast of this revival was a notable one. Mr. W.
Harrison, afterwards of the Pine and Harrison English
Operatic Company, was Macheath, Miss Rainforth,
destined to sing in the same opera years later with Sims
Reeves, was Polly, Mr. W. Farren, Peachum, Mr.
Bartley, Locket, Mr. Harley, Filch, and Lucy, Madame
Vestris. Perhaps the best tribute to Vestris's success was
the fact that the Drury Lane management should in
rivalry put on the opera also with costumes of the
proper date and with Mrs. Keeley as Macheath. Mrs.
Keeley had made a huge success in a " breeches part "
as Jack Sheppard and was in every respect a capable
actress, but she could not drive from the public's
mind its recollection of Vestris in the same character,
and the popularity of the Covent Garden version of
the opera was not in any way impaired. It is interesting to read in the *Age*, considering its insults
in times gone by, that Vestris " only escaped playing
Lucy to perfection because she could not appear
but as a gentlewoman even when she tries."

The failure of *Love's Labour's Lost* did not turn
Vestris from her designs on Shakespeare. *The Merry*

Wives of Windsor was her next venture, and herein she was successful. Mrs. Page she had played many times before, and she was admirably supported by Mrs. Nisbett as Mrs. Ford. Mathews was Slender, Bartley, Falstaff, and Miss Rainforth, as Anne Page, sang charmingly. The pantomime produced proving popular, continued the prosperity. This prosperity, however, was only on the surface. Charles Mathews says pathetically : " The greater the success the worse I found my position. As soon as the money began to flow in my sufferings became almost intolerable. At the first sniff of blood the tigers were let loose. While I paid no one, no one seemed to care, but the moment Jenkins got his money, Jones became rampant. ' Why pay Jenkins ? Why not pay me ? You've used me shamefully and you must take the consequences.' Multiply the Jenkinses by ten and the Joneses by hundreds, and the sum-total of persecution may be conceived. Writs and executions showered upon me, and the whole proceeds of our country engagements were swallowed up by the ravenous Jenkinses and Joneses without in any way appeasing their cravings." One is almost tempted to think, remembering Charles Mathews's reputation in money matters in later life, that he took this lesson to heart and carried it out practically. He did his best to live in an ideal world where creditors ceased from troubling and debtors were at rest !

CHAPTER XXII

VESTRIS REVOLUTIONISES THEATRICAL ART

Production of Leigh Hunt's *Legend of Florence*. State visits of Royalty. A bad time for Shakespeare. Vestris's disputes with Sheridan Knowles and Samuel Lover. Madame carries her point. *A Midsummer-Night's Dream*—Vestris's wonderful triumph. A Shakespearean revelation. Madame's liberality. Her excellent management behind the curtain. Vandenhoff's tribute. Madame not to be dictated to. Horace Walpole's *Castle of Otranto* as a pantomime. Production of Boucicault's *London Assurance*. An enormous success. Its curious inner history.

MATHEWS's whimsical account of the worries which prosperity brought in its train may be taken with the proverbial grain of salt. Neither he nor Madame was addicted to prudence when Fortune smiled, and they failed to free themselves from the burden of debt as others more level-headed might have done. The pantomime of 1839–40, *Harlequin and the Merrie Devil of Edmonton*, brought money into the treasury, and the run of *Love* continuing, there was no necessity to incur further expense in the production of novelties. Meanwhile an actor of " serious " parts from whom much was expected presented himself in a Mr. Moore. To give him a chance, *Hamlet*, *The School for Scandal*, *The Hunchback*, and *John Bull* were put on during January and February 1840. Moore failed to realise the hopes entertained and nothing further was heard of him.

The marriage of Queen Victoria on February 10th, 1840, was an event of the utmost interest, and Vestris took advantage of the occasion to produce *The Fortunate Isles*, a pageant for which Bishop provided

254

the music. A number of historic notabilities in the
nation's records ranging from Edward III to Nelson
were put on the stage to a musical accompaniment, the
chief singers being Miss Rainforth, W. Harrison,
and Madame herself. On the Queen's return to
London the management received a " royal command,"
and Her Majesty, accompanied by Prince Albert, paid
the theatre a state visit.

With March 1840 came Leigh Hunt's *A Legend of
Florence*. It was not an unqualified success. The
great poets of the early nineteenth century—Byron,
Shelley, Coleridge—had tried their hands at writing
for the stage, but apparently they were not of the
stuff of which dramatists are made and Leigh Hunt
was no better. But he was satisfied with its reception
and also with the £200 he received, which he found
" a great refreshment to my sorry purse." He was
also much gratified by Queen Victoria and Prince
Albert witnessing the performance twice and by the
Queen expressing her satisfaction with it.

Hunt owed the introduction of the play to Madame
Vestris to his friend Mrs. Orger, and in his *Autobiography* he expressed his indebtedness " to the zealous
interest taken in it by those two cordial persons "
(Mr. and Mrs. Mathews), and " to the talents and
sympathy of Miss Ellen Tree, the tears down whose
glowing cheeks encouraged me while it was read and
who has since told me that she regarded the heroine
as her best performance." He remarks incidentally :
" Not that it did for me what I was told it might
have done had I let the husband retain his wife,
or had less money perhaps been laid out on its
getting up."

A Legend of Florence kept the bills during March,
interspersed with revivals of old favourites reminiscent
of the Olympic days, and the season was brought to
an end with Planché's fairy extravaganza, *The Sleeping
Beauty of the Wood*, to give the piece its full title,
which continued the theatre's prosperity. Vestris

played Princess Is-a-belle (the humour of the day ran in the direction of puns more or less inane) and she was the life and soul of the piece. The air was full of " interesting " rumours apropos of Queen Victoria's marriage, of which the author availed himself.

" The burlesque," wrote the *Satirist*, " was one of the best-conceived satires and certainly one of the most brilliantly appointed spectacles ever brought upon the boards. The Royal usages on occasions of royal christenings were scrupulously adhered to, and midst the bellowings of trombones, the agonies of violoncellos, and the epilepsy of fiddles appropriately thrown into convulsions by the roar of the bass drum, which did duty for the Park guns, the theatrical world was made aware of the awful fact of the solemnisation of the rite at the same moment that ' Lord-High-Everything ' exclaimed ' Thanks, ye slaves, the Royal babby's got a name.' " Topical allusions, if apt, are always keenly appreciated, and as *The Sleeping Beauty* was full of them and as the lines were peppered with jokes, more or less bad, the extravaganza caught on.

But there were people who expected from Madame something more in keeping with one of the national theatres—something more solid than comedy, *The Beggar's Opera*, and extravaganzas. The critic of the *Satirist* was one of these punctilious persons, and others may have thought with him. At the end of the first season he solemnly admonished her in these terms :

" The times are against her. There is a lack of dramatic impulse though perhaps not of dramatic feeling in the country. The public want something better than second- and third-rate actors placed in first-rate parts. . . . They want something to provoke an appetite for Shakespeare. They want to see him represented properly, and their own ideas of the great bard, formed in the study, realised on the stage. Bring

MADAME VESTRIS'S HANDWRITING.
(First draught of a letter to Montagu Gore.)

back the days of the elder Kean or of Siddons, and you restore a wholesome taste for theatrical representation. . . . Madame Vestris must seek for an O'Neill, a Cooke, or a Kean ere she can command success in her future management. . . . People are sick of the fustian of Macready and the mechanical imitation and croaking imbecility of Charles Kean. . . . The state of the drama is lamentable, and why it is that we have no prominent actors or actresses on the stage at the present time is to be traced to there being perhaps no school open as in all other branches of art for teaching on recognised principles the rudiment of acting."

Possibly : but Madame had her own ideas and her own plans. She meant to have Shakespeare adequately represented, but not by tragedians—who were not to be secured.

The season 1840–1 opened in September, a month earlier than was customary, with *The Sleeping Beauty*, which continued to attract for fifteen nights, and together with its thirty-eight nights of the first season constituted a record for this class of entertainment. Then followed on September 20th a new play by Sheridan Knowles, in connection with which Madame Vestris showed her shrewdness and experience. Sheridan Knowles called his drama *John of Procida*, which Madame altered to *The Bride of Messina*, greatly to the dramatist's dissatisfaction, so much so that, according to report, he took the manuscript away. Another rumour had it that Vestris expected Knowles was writing her a comedy, and when a tragedy was presented to her instead she waxed warm and behaved rather rudely to the author, who walked out of the theatre and went to the Haymarket to offer it to Webster ; but that gentleman being out of the way, Mr. Knowles returned home, where he found a message couched in friendly terms from Madame Vestris begging him to bring his play back to Covent Garden.

Commenting on this, the *Age* remarked : " Madame was right. The choice of a title, one that the public would readily understand, is a very important matter, and in both cases Vestris was a better judge than Lover and Knowles." Probably no one was more deficient in judgment in everything that concerned himself than Sheridan Knowles. He seemed to be unable to discriminate between his good and his bad efforts. Gerald Griffin, the author of *The Collegian*, upon which Boucicault founded his *Colleen Bawn*, writing to his brother, said, " Have you read *Virginius* ? It will be worth your while to get it ; but if you would retain the good opinion it will give you of Knowles, don't read his *Caius Gracchus*. It is a poor piece of folly."

The Bride of Messina had but a languid reception, and Lover's *Greek Boy* met with no better fate. On October 13th Planché's version of Beaumont and Fletcher's *Spanish Curate* was produced and ran for twenty-one nights. Meanwhile Vestris, undeterred by the failure of *Love's Labour's Lost*, was making preparations for another Shakespearean revival of a far more arduous character, but one completely to her taste. She threw her whole heart into the production of *A Midsummer-Night's Dream*, and achieved a superb triumph. The care and study bestowed upon the scenery and accessories, the sense of art and delicate fancy which pervaded the play from beginning to end, impressed the critics and delighted the public. Mr. Dutton Cook has pointed out that for the first time in this play Shakespeare was treated with respect, and text and spirit preserved, and this opinion has been endorsed by every manager who afterwards ventured upon the play. The version of Madame Vestris was the model they followed.

The press was unanimous in its praise. One critic wrote : " A just, generous, and graceful homage has been paid to Shakespeare, and the management is entitled to our high approval of almost to invent a

fairyland for the stage—to invest it with a dreamy spirit
—to produce beautiful contrasts of scenery—to people
it with an elfin world costumed with the fantastic
splendour which tells a tale of power, riches, and
romance." Other notices were equally laudatory.
The play was introduced by Mendelssohn's overture,
probably the first occasion on which this masterpiece
of youthful genius was performed amid appropriate
surroundings. Beethoven was also called upon, and
in the incantation, given by Vestris as Puck, one musical
critic " recognised the two-four movement in A minor
from one of that composer's symphonies so often
encored by the Philharmonic Society." Weber's
Preciosa was utilised for the ballet scenes, but—to our
advanced taste it sounds like bathos—" the only
musical encore of the evening was C. E. Horn's duet
' I know a bank where the wild thyme grows ' " !

On the first night, November 17th, 1840, the enthusiasm of the audience mounted higher and higher
as the play proceeded, and the climax was reached
with the final scene which by Planché's happy thought
embodied the spirit of the lines :

> Though the house give glimmering light,
>   By the dead and drowsy fire,
> Every elf and fairy sprite
>   Hop as light as bird from brier ;
> And this ditty, after me,
> Sing, and dance it trippingly.

The back of the stage by Grieve, the famous scene-
painter, Planché says, was so arranged that " at the
command of Oberon it was-filled with fairies bearing
twinkling coloured lights dancing and flitting about
and altogether illustrating the text." The delight
of the audience knew no bounds, and Vestris at the
fall of the curtain was vociferously shouted for. It
is not too much to say that *A Midsummer-Night's
Dream* established Vestris's reputation as a theatrical
manager.

The year 1841 commenced with a recurrence of monetary troubles. It was characteristic of both Vestris and Charles Mathews not to let expense stand in the way of completeness. Had they been less lavish in the way of luxuries they might not have been landed in difficulties. A weekly paper remarked at the beginning of 1841 : "Mrs. Mathews is a very liberal lady. She pays in advance, and many of our modern authors are too happy to meet with such a generous creature." Dramatists, company, artists, furniture-dealers, were treated in the same open-handed manner. The enormous rent charged by the lease-holders, among whom was Charles Kemble, was the stumbling-block. But even here, as will be seen when the circumstances attending the collapse of her enterprise are recounted, Vestris acted up to her word. She had extraordinary energy, and besides being a born organiser, she saw to everything with her own eye. Vandenhoff, who played the "lead" in 1841–2, says :

"Let it be recorded, to Vestris's honour, that she was not only scrupulously careful not to offend propriety by word or action, but she knew very well how to repress any attempt at *double-entendre* or doubtful insinuation in others. The green-room in Covent Garden Theatre was a most agreeable lounging-place, a divan adorned with beauties, where one could pass a pleasant hour in the society of charming women and men of gentlemanly manners, and from which was banished every word or allusion that would not be tolerated in a drawing-room. A man must be hard to please who was not agreeably entertained, with such gratification to ear and eye, as could be found in the elegant society and ladylike conversation of Ellen Tree, the sprightliness of Mrs. Nisbett, the quaint humour of Mrs. Humby, besides the attractions of a bevy of lesser beauties, the 'jesting spirit' of Harley, the amusing egotism of Farren, and the jokes, repartees, anecdotes, and reminiscences of others;

and this with the addition of a popular artist, or of
one or more dramatic author. . . .

"The first green-room in Covent Garden Theatre
was a withdrawing-room, carpeted and papered elegantly; with a handsome chandelier in the centre,
several globe lights at the sides, a comfortable divan,
covered in figured damask, running round the whole
room, large pier ornamental glasses on the walls,
and a full-length movable swing-glass; so that, on
entering from his dressing-room, an actor could see
himself from head to foot at one view, and get back,
front, and side views by reflection, all round. . . .

"The green-room was exceedingly comfortable
during the Mathews and Vestris management. Indeed
I must pay them the compliment of saying that their
arrangements generally for the convenience of their
company, the courtesy of their behaviour to the
actors, and consideration for their comforts, formed
an example well worthy to be followed by managers
in general, who are not, I am sorry to say, usually
remarkable for those qualities. In fact, the reign
of Vestris and her husband might be distinguished
as the *drawing-room management*. On special occasions—the opening night of the season, for example,
or a 'Queen's' visit—tea and coffee were served in
the green-room; and frequently between the acts,
some of the officers of the guard, or gentlemen in
attendance on the royal party, would be introduced,
which led, of course, to agreeable and sometimes advan-
tageous acquaintances."

Westland Marston writes much to the same effect.

It is not to be denied that Vestris had a temper—
how could she have had her own way without one?
And when she was put out everyone knew it. Westland
Marston tells how one night he entered late and found
that some accidental circumstance had provoked the
house. The whole audience had discovered that
Vestris was in an ill-humour. She passed through
her comic scenes "with a sullen brow and with a

haste and negligence so marked that unless she had been the *enfant gâtée* of the house her almost contemptuous indifference might well have brought on her an emphatic rebuke." She was not to be dictated to by anyone.

The story goes that she once had occasion to find fault with Zerbini, the leader of the Olympic orchestra, who put on airs and declared that he would not be led by Madame Vestris or any other directrice who had chosen to place upon him the musical responsibility of her establishment. To give emphasis to his words, the leader flourished his fiddle-stick at Madame in defiance, upon which the lady called in the police, and finally Zerbini found himself *en route* for Bow Street!

On the other hand, when she was in the mood no one could be more adroit in making the retort courteous. It is related that when she was playing at the Norwich theatre, and there was a general disposition to encore her favourite song, "Pray, Goody," opposition to the popular call was offered in a rudely strenuous manner from a private box, the sole occupant, who was a person of local importance, giving himself some very magisterial airs. However, the house was too strong for him, and the song was repeated. As soon as the singer came to the couplet—

> Remember when the judgment's weak,
> The prejudice is strong,

she dwelt with retarded emphasis on the words, and, turning to the side-box, dropped a charming little curtsy. The consequence was that she had to sing the song a third time.

The so-called pantomime of that year—little more than a harlequinade—was based on Horace Walpole's fustian romance *The Castle of Otranto*, and of the production it was said that it could hardly be more absurd than the original. Melodrama had come into being, and *The Mysteries of Udolpho*, *The Castle of Otranto*, and M. G. Lewis's *Monk* formed favourite reading, while lurid plays after the fashion of " Monk " Lewis's *Rugantio* drew crowded audiences. The subject of the Christmas entertainment at Covent Garden was consequently familiar enough and the burlesque did very well. The pantomime, it should be noted, was simply a panorama followed by a harlequinade. The time for elaborated " openings " of perverted nursery-tales with gorgeous transformation scenes and attenuated harlequinades had not arrived.

The most important event of the season 1840–1 was the production on March 4th, 1841, of Boucicault's *London Assurance*, a comedy which even now has not wholly lost its attraction, though it does not appeal to the Londoner of to-day as it did to the Londoner of 1841. *London Assurance* was announced as having been written by Mr. Lee Moreton, but it was soon known that Moreton was a *nom de théâtre* for Bourcicault, afterwards spelt Boucicault. His real name was Lardner.

By one of the misunderstandings peculiar to the stage, in which everybody is right and everybody wrong, an impression gained ground that Mr. John Brougham was author or part author of the play. John Coleman, in his *Players and Playwrights*, says : " When *London Assurance* was sent in, it was a crude, inchoate, invertebrate sketch. The author was young, and at that time docile, and glad to accept any hint from the eminent artists who supplied the unrivalled cast. He was also ready to cut, slash, alter, or turn the work inside out, if it were necessary. In point of fact, although the play was written by Boucicault, it was edited by Charles Mathews & Co. Apropos, one of the *canards* which obtained years ago was that John Brougham had collaborated with D. B. in the production. During the run of that delightful play, *Arrah-na-Pogue*, at the Princess's, I asked

Brougham if there was any truth in the rumour ; his reply was, 'Not the slightest.' "

Anderson (*Life of an Actor*) gives a different version of the story. " When the comedy," he writes, " was first put into rehearsal, John Brougham and Dion Boucicault appeared as the joint-authors. But soon ' a change came o'er the spirit of their dream '— there was a hitch somewhere. The original Dazzle was written for an Irishman, and John Brougham was to have played the part. Then it was discovered there would be nothing for Charles Mathews to do in the comedy. The consequence was, the part had to be rewritten for the manager. This produced *un désa-grément* betwixt the authors. At length an arrange-ment was made that Brougham, ' for a consideration,' should relinquish his share in the authorship to Bouci-cault, and resign the part of Dazzle to Mathews. What the real nature of the arrangement was I never could make out. I have a distinct recollection, however, that on the first night the comedy was acted there were calls for the author."

The reports in the newspapers confirm this to the effect that " Vestris got into a towering passion when John Brougham presented himself at the wing to go on with Boucicault. This she would not permit, and indignantly ordered him to go away, giving instructions to the ' green-coats ' (stage-keepers) to prevent him appearing on the stage." On the twentieth night the comedy was announced in the bills as having been written by D. L. *Bourcicault*, as he at that time spelt his name.

The cast—an excellent one—of *London Assurance* was as follows : Sir Hartley Courtley, W. Farren ; Charles Courtley, Anderson ; Max Harkaway, Bartley ; Dolly Spanker, Keeley ; Dazzle, Mathews ; Mark Meddle, Harley ; Grace Harkaway, Vestris ; Lady Gay Spanker, Mrs. Nisbett ; Pert, Mrs. Humby.

Of these Charles Mathews was the best. The part of Dazzle fitted him like a glove, and few actors who have impersonated the character have approached him. Vestris was also well suited in Grace Harkaway. The piece ran fifty-nine nights, the number also of the run of *A Midsummer-Night's Dream*.

The Easter extravaganza was *Beauty and the Beast*, Vestris, of course, personating the first, and Bland, who excelled in the mock-heroic, the second.

CHAPTER XXIII

VESTRIS *VERSUS* MACREADY

Managerial difficulties. Vestris dependent upon old successes. The debut of Adelaide Kemble. Her instant triumph in *Norma*. Great success of Douglas Jerrold's *Bubbles of the Day*. Jules Benedict —Adelaide Kemble's protégé. Vestris projects the presentation of *Comus* and Purcell's *King Arthur*. Macready, alarmed, issues a counterblast. Madame joins battle. An angry controversy. *Comus* produced at Covent Garden. A wonderful spectacle. Leffler the bass singer. How Balfe let him down. Vestris as Cherubino in *The Marriage of Figaro*. The first performance of the opera on the English stage in a complete state. A bomb-shell from Charles Kemble. Mathews and Vestris receive notice to give up possession of Covent Garden. Allegations of arrears of rent due. The lease forfeited. The farewell performance. The *Morning Post* a champion of Vestris.

SEPTEMBER 1841 found the management without any novelty in view. Had there been one the impoverished exchequer would hardly have warranted expenditure of the money which Vestris loved to lavish on a new production. She played her trump cards, *A Midsummer-Night's Dream* and *London Assurance*, during the first month of the season; and having nothing to supplant them she was compelled to continue until Christmas, when the pantomime-extravaganza *Guy Earl of Warwick, or Harlequin and the Dun Cow* was in readiness. This was highly successful, and Payne as clown and a legitimate successor of Grimaldi made a hit. The writer of the notice in one paper declared it to be " the best we have seen since the days of *Harlequin Gulliver* now turned twenty-four years ago." Another notice pays a warm tribute to the care and completeness of the stage management. " Covent Garden," it ran, " is the very nursery of a playhouse—

there is not a joint in its boards, a flap in its scenery, a twinkle in its lights, which is not replete with mechanism, and effects follow each other with a rapidity and a precision that defy calculation in the proportion they excite astonishment."

The pantomime could be relied upon to last until February, but what was to follow gave much ground for anxiety. New operas were talked about, but nothing materialised. Then came the advent of an operatic star which put a new complexion upon things. Miss Adelaide Kemble came and sang and conquered. Her appearance was no doubt due to the influence of her father, Charles Kemble, who was one of the proprietors of the theatre. *Norma* was the opera selected for her debut (January 16th, 1842) on the English stage, and she won an instant triumph. The treasury recovered, and Charles Mathews calculated he would, to use his own words, " at length emancipate myself from debt and have solid hope for the future." But, he adds, little did Miss Kemble " imagine that her triumph would be my ruin, but so it turned out."

However, for the time being Vestris and her husband basked once more in the sunshine of prosperity and put on a new comedy, *The Irish Heiress*, by Boucicault. The play was not received with favour. It was pronounced " vulgar " and the part Vestris undertook was declared to be unsuitable. But there was nothing but praise for the mounting. " Unless the spectator," said one newspaper, " goes and beholds and judges for himself he would be loth to believe such a perfect identity with the salons, boudoirs, dressing-rooms, dining-rooms of our very best houses could be contrived. . . . Not a toilet or a *tapis* is incomplete."

Mere furniture and accurate appointments never yet saved a play, and *The Irish Heiress* soon met its fate, to be followed by a new comedy which had quite a different fortune. This was Douglas Jerrold's *Bubbles of the Day*. Jerrold had found a subject which lent itself admirably to his mordant wit and he made the most of it. Vestris was not in the cast, but she had an excellent substitute in Mrs. Orger. Charles Mathews also was in his element in a part which displayed his airiness perfectly. All the critics were full of praise.

Meanwhile Adelaide Kemble was drawing the crowd. The theatrical public in those days wanted plenty for their money. The evening's entertainment generally lasted four hours at the very least. The " half-pricers " had to be considered. A fair sample bill was *Elena Uberti*, a mediocre opera by Mercadante with Adelaide Kemble, *The Critic*, and Charles Mathews in an afterpiece *Charles the Twelfth*. Sometimes the *pièce de résistance* alone was mentioned and the evening was filled up with " other entertainments." Apropos of *Elena Uberti*, the fashion of the times in dragging in other composers' music to suit the prima donna or for other reasons was adhered to. In this case a scena by Pacini was introduced, while a new finale was written by Jules Benedict, the first time probably that the future popular composer, who made his home in England, had any of his music performed in this country. Benedict was a protégé of Adelaide Kemble's. In a letter dated July 23rd, 1841, to Charles Mathews relative to her engagement at Covent Garden she writes : " Do tell me if you would be willing to engage a most able friend of mine as director of the music at your theatre ? Benedict was a pupil of Weber's, is himself an excellent composer and a most conscientious artist and gentlemanlike person. I think it would be a great thing to have him. Will you let me know what you think of this suggestion ? " Apparently Charles Mathews adopted it.

If Vestris were disposed to be irritable at this time, she had ample justification. Her anxieties were increasing and the production of a novelty of the spectacular kind was a vital necessity. She could only shine amid brilliant surroundings, and comedies did not suffice. The public were thoroughly familiar with her old triumphs in this direction. Spectacle combined with her personality must be the two principal factors in any fresh venture. She had formed this combination in *A Midsummer-Night's Dream*, and *The Masque of Comus* suggested another. She had in her mind a third—Purcell's *King Arthur*, but *Comus* was decided upon and preparations made. When the matter was first talked over, Tom Cooke was her musical director and she was bound to consult him. Shortly after he transferred his services from Covent Garden to Drury Lane, then under the management of Macready, who had opened it with a magniloquent programme of drama and English opera which he failed to carry out. It is more than likely that Cooke, without any intention of forestalling Vestris's plans, may have mentioned to Macready what was in the air at the rival house, and to Madame's annoyance Macready announced for future production not only *Comus* but *King Arthur*!

Upon this the lady gave battle and issued an address through the newspaper " to the Public." She pointed out " that a new arrangement was commenced during the recess with the view of being brought forward at the beginning of the present season. Unforeseen circumstances occasioned its postponement until the Christmas pantomime necessarily superseded it, and meanwhile not only *Comus* was advertised as forthcoming at Drury Lane, but by a singular coincidence Dryden's opera of *King Arthur*, which had been brought under the consideration of this management by another person. It is not the practice at this theatre," she went on, " to advertise dramas till the time positively fixed for their production, as circumstances continually occur which might compel the management to break faith with the public ; at the same time it is not thought necessary to relinquish preconceived ideas or change determinations (formed without reference to any other establishment) in consequence of the announcement of revivals of

the regular and popular dramas of the British stage—
as much the property of one theatre as the
other."

The allusion to Macready not by name but as
a " person " was a feminine thrust which showed the
intensity of Madame's anger, and she hurried on the
production of *Comus*. It appeared on March 8th, and
was mounted with the usual lavishness and received
with delight. Vestris aimed at a spectacular effect
which she knew well enough was beyond Macready's
capacity, and, perhaps in order to mortify her rival,
she spent more money on the piece than the result
warranted. Vestris herself was the " cynosure of all
eyes." The *Post* wrote : " The entry of the Baccha-
nalian subjects in the beginning of the piece is gorgeous
and characteristic in the extreme, heightened to the
utmost degree by the perfect abandonment thrown
into the first Bacchante by Madame Vestris, who in
manner, dress, joyous yet graceful action seemed the
very perfection of joyous revelry."

Leffler, a powerful bass singer, who was a great
favourite, especially in boisterous ditties, was an ideal
leader of " tipsy dance and jollity "—and he gave forth
the well-known " Now Phœbus sinketh in the west "
with immense gusto. The audience probably knew
his taste for the flowing bowl. If they did not, it
was hardly the fault of Balfe, who on one occasion
gave him away completely. Balfe had put on an
English opera called *Scaramaccia*, and Leffler was to
take the leading part. He failed to turn up, but wrote
to Balfe, who, on the audience expressing in their
customary emphatic way their disapprobation at the
long " wait," came down to the footlights to give an
explanation which was couched in these terms :

" Ladies and gentlemen,—I hardly know what to
say, but perhaps the best thing I can do is to read
the letter of Mr. Leffler, who was to have sustained
the part of Scaramaccia but who did not attend rehearsal and who has thus excused himself to-night :

> Dear Balfe, I'm very sorry to declare it,
> But I have drunk so much claret
> That I can't play to-night, d——n it.
>   Yours faithfully, Adrian Leffler."

It was not a very nice thing for Balfe to do, as the letter was a private one, but consideration for others was never the outstanding virtue of the theatrical profession.

Macready certainly showed a grasping, selfish spirit towards Vestris in trying, as a showman would say, to " queer her pitch." He did not produce *Comus* until some time after, and in no way did Vestris's version, which was almost entirely musical, clash with Macready's. The tragedian as *Comus* was all in all, or believed himself to be so, and the production was mainly histrionic. In respect to *King Arthur*, the case was different. Cooke packed as much music as he could find in Purcell's operas other than *Bonduca*, the original of *King Arthur*, but it was not put on the stage until November 16th, 1842. Macready's announcement a year and a half before of what he was going to do and making it appear that an immediate production was contemplated can only be considered as a piece of sharp practice. However, one must be grateful that sooner or later he *did* bring out the opera, as it gave to Sims Reeves in " Come if you dare " his first chance of displaying his glorious voice and furnished the stepping-stone to his subsequent wonderful career as the finest tenor of his or any other age.

On March 16th came a notable revival of *The Marriage of Figaro*, Adelaide Kemble playing Susanna and Vestris, Cherubino. This was the first time that the opera had been put on the English stage in a complete state. This was much to Madame's credit, for in past times, influenced by the debased taste of the day, she had, as already recorded, played sad tricks with the opera. But even in this excellent performance poor Mozart was not allowed to have his own way. Why was Susanna permitted to sing " *Voi che sapete*,"

the exclusive property of Cherubino ? The cast was
hardly perfect. Susanna did not suit Miss Kemble
as well as Norma ; Vestris, while otherwise charming
as Cherubino, was too pert for the realisation of the
character ; Leffler was a too boisterous and joyous
Figaro, and Russell (a new bass singer—could it have
been Henry Russell ?) was too staid. Shortcomings
notwithstanding the opera was continued until Easter,
when the last of the Covent Garden extravaganzas,
The White Cat, was produced.

Despite the various successes of 1841–2, the burden
of debt had never been lightened. There was a deficit
of some £600 in the payment of the rent of several
thousands, " and," writes Planché, " with the usual
liberality and good policy of the proprietors of theatres
in general, Madame Vestris, who had raised Covent
Garden once more to the rank it had held in the days
of the Kembles, and paid her heavy rent to the shilling
during two brilliant seasons, was denied the opportunity of recouping herself from losses caused by a
most exceptional circumstance, and coolly bowed out
of the building." In a word, the proprietors of
the theatre demanded their pound of flesh and took
legal proceedings to recover it. This meant the
ruination of Vestris's enterprise.

It was characteristic of feminine intuition that
before disaster arrived Vestris had a foreboding as to
what was going to happen and why. Planché recounts
how " when dining with her and Charles Mathews
Madame Vestris said abruptly after a short silence,
' Charles, we shall not have the theatre next year.'
' What do you mean ? ' he and I exclaimed simultane-
ously. ' Simply what I say.' ' But what reason,'
inquired Mathews, ' can you possibly have for thinking
so ? ' ' No particular reason ; but you'll see.' ' Have
you heard any rumour to that effect ? ' I asked. ' No ;
but we shall not have the theatre.' ' But who on
earth will have it, then ? ' we said, laughing at the
idea ; for we could imagine no possible competitor

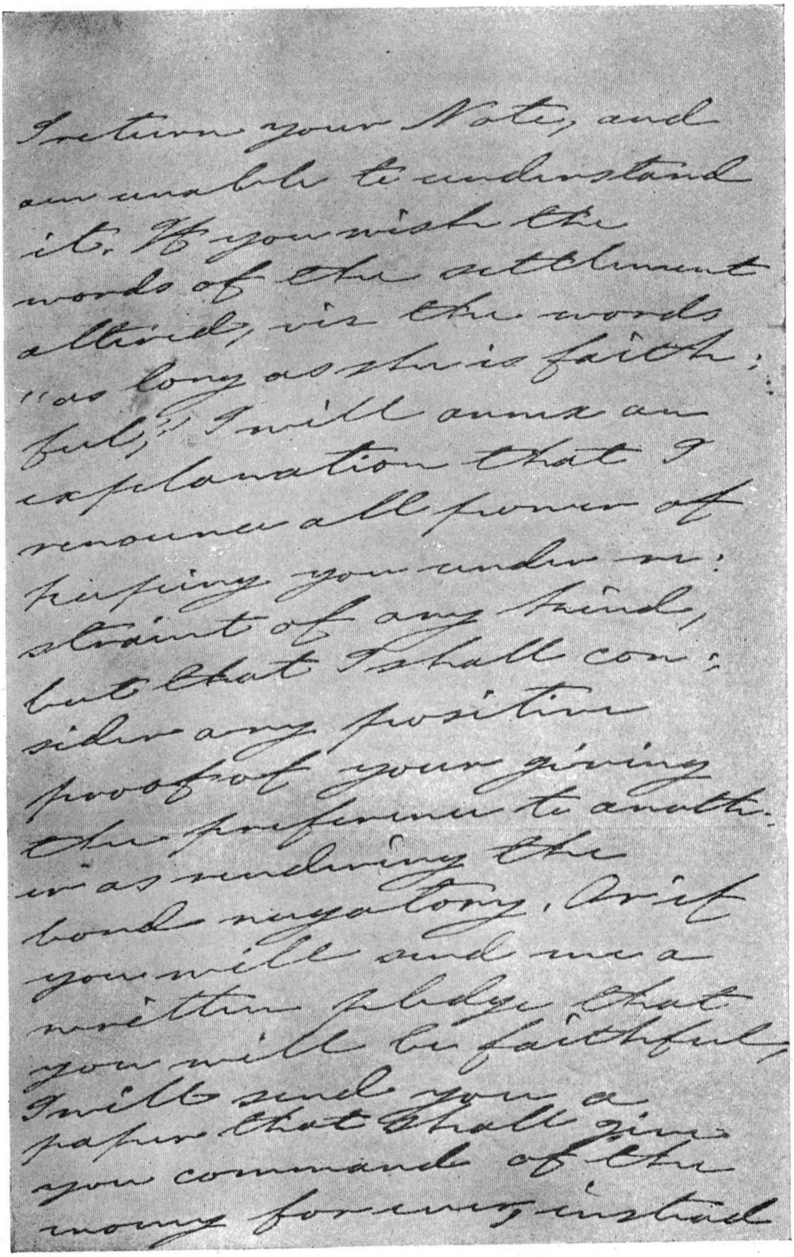
I return your Note, and
am unable to understand
it. If you wish the
words of the settlement
altered, viz the words
"as long as she is faith:
ful," I will annex an
explanation that I
renounce all power of
keeping you under re:
straint of any kind,
but that I shall con:
sider any positive
proof of your giving
the preference to anoth-
er as rendering the
bond nugatory. Or if
you will send me a
written pledge that
you will be faithful,
I will send you a
paper that shall give
you command of the
money for ever, instead

MADAME VESTRIS'S HANDWRITING.
(From a letter to Montagu Gore.)

likely to pay so high a rent. ' Charles Kemble,' was her answer. ' He will think that his daughter's talent and popularity will be quite sufficient, and we shall be turned out of the theatre. But,' she continued, seeing us still incredulous, ' three things may happen. Miss Kemble may be ill ; Miss Kemble may not get another opera like *Norma* ; and Miss Kemble may marry.' Every one of these predictions was fulfilled. The rent not being fully paid up according to the conditions of her lease, it was declared forfeited ; and Mr. Charles Kemble took the theatre himself upon his own shoulders."

The final performance took place on April 30th, when *La Sonnambula, Patter* v. *Clatter,* and *The White Cat* were given. On Charles Mathews appearing on the stage in *Patter* v. *Clatter,* of which piece he was the author, the greeting was incessant and protracted, and the applause was renewed after he had delivered a farewell address, in the course of which he said in reference to the theatre :

" My partner and I have been its directors for three years, during which time we have endeavoured, at much personal and pecuniary sacrifice, to sow the seeds of that solid prosperity which would, we hoped, one day, manifest itself in permanent satisfaction to you, and in a golden harvest to ourselves ; but alas for the mutability of human affairs ! Our first season was merely sowing—our second little more than hoeing —and, though the third has been growing, we must leave to other hands the fourth, which might have been our mowing. *Why* we have felt it our duty to quit these premises, I will not intrude upon you to explain. Suffice it to say, that in quitting them, we leave not only our business, but our good-will to our successor ; and if, ladies and gentlemen, that successor should prove to be a gentleman—the admired representative of that thrice-honoured theatrical family, another gifted daughter of whose gifted house it is our pride to have brought so triumphantly under your notice—

in that case, ladies and gentlemen, I can only say that, as far as one manager *can* forgive another, it will afford us much consolation should the change prove to be for his and your gain."

After Mr. Mathews had retired, calls for Madame Vestris were heard in every part of the house, and " she appeared, led on by her husband, in the dress of the character she sustained in the after-piece, whereupon the whole audience rose *en masse* and vehemently cheered her. In a few minutes the stage was covered with chaplets of flowers, directed towards her from the boxes nearest the proscenium. Several of these she picked up, and pressed to her lips with an emotion that she could not conceal."

The attitude of playgoers towards Eliza Vestris was one of affection as much as admiration. For twenty years she had been their darling, and whatever may have been her foibles and weaknesses privately, she had ever been staunch to her public. Her claims to their regard rested on her sincerity and on her freedom from ostentatious pretension. No theatrical management had ever equalled hers for complete-ness and conscientious fulfilment of promises. The *farceur* spirit which Elliston could never resist was not hers. She was without the arrogance, the mean-ness, and the overweening vanity of Macready. She had not a particle of the impudent charlatanism of Alfred Bunn. Charles Kemble was an ignoramus—certainly as regarded matters operatic—and Stephen Kemble a blunderer. Drury Lane under Price sank to mediocrity and reached its lowest depth with Captain Polhill, a debauchee, and his servile assistant Alexander Lee. Vestris purified and elevated the English stage, and to think that after her unceasing efforts in the direction of art she should be ousted from her position through a piece of sharp practice dictated by rapacity must have been galling in the extreme. No wonder the heartfelt sympathy of the last audience she was fated to delight at Covent Garden Theatre affected her deeply.

This sympathy was not her only solace. She could not have been otherwise than intensely gratified at the tribute to her talents and her personality paid to her by the *Morning Post* the day before her farewell performance. Only of a histrionic artist of exceptional merit would one speak in such glowing terms, and it is but right to reproduce the article in full as a matter of justice to Madame Vestris, about whom the average playgoer of to-day knows very little and probably still less of the great services she rendered in the advancement of the English stage.

The article, it will be noted, is more than a tribute. It gives the circumstances under which Mr. and Mrs. Mathews were compelled to quit the theatre, and as such deserves to be placed on record :

" To-morrow night Madame Vestris takes (with a benefit) her farewell of the Covent Garden stage—a stage she has both refined and adorned—and we will not suffer the occasion to pass without paying a valedictory tribute to her claims as a lady and an actress upon a public she has more delighted than any individual of her time.

" Preliminarily, however, let us state what we have heard as to the pecuniary disputes which have ended in this most-to-be-regretted result. The rent conditioned to be annually paid for the theatre was £7,500, with (we are informed) a verbal understanding that if the sum of £5,000 were actually paid in each year, Mr. Mathews was not to be molested for the difference. More than £15,000 have positively been paid during the three years' lesseeship for rent, and in addition a sum little if any short of £14,000 for properties, the value of which, however much it may benefit the theatre itself, cannot in any way be converted to the advantage of Madame Vestris or her husband. Independently of these facts, we are given to understand that neither of them have drawn their own salaries, although everybody else in the establishment has been paid in full. We make this statement upon authority we deem to be conclusive of its truth, and we are sorry to be obliged to add that from the same source we hear that in violation of the fulfilled verbal agreement one of the proprietors of Covent Garden Theatre has sued Mr. Charles Mathews upon the legal document, a step which has compelled both himself and Madame Vestris to vacate their theatrical home and seek in a rival establishment the protection and support they ought to have found in their own.

" We will not anticipate the judgment of the public in this affair, but this we will state, that we know enough of its sympathies with justly established favourites to feel assured that a hearty and enthusiastic welcome awaits the appearance of Mr. and Mrs. Charles Mathews within the walls of Drury Lane Theatre, whither their new fortunes will shortly conduct them.

" What has not Madame Vestris done for the English stage ? Let those who are close watchers of its phases answer. She has banished vulgarity, coarse manners, *double-entendre*, and impertinence from the boards over which she presided, and in their place has evoked the benefits that flow from a dramatic interpretation of polished manners, refinement, and politeness. Her green-room was the resort of the learned, the witty, and the wise, a miniature picture of polite and well-bred society whence a wholesome example spread itself on all within its influence. Once communicated to the stage, it became communicable to the public, and sure we are that a desirable tone of refinement both in manners and conversation has been extensively spread in private life by the lady-like deportment and acting of Madame Vestris.

" To art she gave an impulse of no mean importance. Witness the magnificent scenery, as appropriate as it was beautiful, which her fine taste caused to be continually brought before the public. The *mise en scène* was never perfect until Madame Vestris taught her

painters how to execute and the public how to appreciate her own pictorial conceptions, and to her judgment in this way the playgoing world has been indebted
for much of its theatrical enjoyment."

The unfortunate end of Vestris's strenuous efforts
at Covent Garden may be summed up in Charles
Mathews's words. " The theatre," he writes, " was
taken out of our hands, after three years of labour
and outlay to establish it, in order that others might
reap the expected harvest ; our property was all
confiscated to meet the alleged arrears of rent amount-
ing to £14,000—the scenery, wardrobe, and properties
we had brought from the Olympic included—and
we found ourselves adrift with nothing left but a
piece of plate (presented by the company) and the
debts of the concern."

CHAPTER XXIV

A STORMY TIME AT DRURY LANE

Mathews in the Queen's Bench Prison. Charles Kemble shows no mercy. Mathew's bankruptcy annulled. An engagement offered by Macready. Macready's grasping nature. His jealousy of Vestris. Why he engaged Madame and her husband. Vestris at Drury Lane. She is systematically kept in the background. Macready's manners. Vestris shows fight. Her biting sarcasm. A stormy scene. Vestris throws up her part in *King Arthur* and quits the theatre. Macready's disingenuous version of the dispute. His ignorance of and contempt for music. Vestris and Mathews engaged at the Haymarket. Owing to Mathews's blunder financial difficulties pursue them. Mathews again a bankrupt. Termination of the Haymarket engagement. The Lyceum enterprise entered upon.

For some weeks after the eviction from Covent Garden Charles Mathews was occupied in straightening out his affairs for his examination in bankruptcy. Part of this time was spent in the Queen's Bench Prison, thanks to the oppressive law which then regarded a debtor as a criminal. When a statement of accounts was published it showed that his debts from December 1837 amounted to £27,499 17s. 11d., of which he received consideration for £26,200 2s. 11d., and the remainder related to Madame Vestris.

The theatre, according to the statement, was taken with an agreement to pay a rental of £5,000 to £7,000 a year, after deducting £60 a week for Mathews and Madame Vestris. The theatre was rented three seasons. For the first season £5,000 was paid for rent, the second season £6,150, and the third £2,384, independent of £700 to be received from private boxes and £1,400 from the conductors of the German Opera. During the first season there was a nightly loss of £22, the second season showed a loss of £10 a night, and this loss in the third season amounted to £41 14s. The total loss on the three seasons was £13,286 16s. 2d.

No allusion was made to the verbal agreement by which if fulfilled by the tenants they were not to be molested. A verbal agreement is, of course, open to more than one interpretation. Mathews's assertion that £15,000 had been paid was correct if the rent of the boxes and the amount due from the German Opera Company to whom the theatre was let be added, the total sum being £15,634. But apparently the third year's rent was due before these two items could be included, and if the proprietors of the theatre were inclined to be lenient (which they were not) they would have appreciated the situation. But Kemble was anxious to dominate the theatre once more. He ignored the fact that Madame Vestris had restored its fortunes, which under his management had fallen very low, and he wanted to share in his daughter's success. His fatherly feeling can be excused, but not the grasping spirit which accompanied it.

The sympathy shown on all sides for Vestris and her husband was very genuine. The consideration extended towards Mathews was evidenced by his treatment while in the Queen's Bench Prison. As a matter of fact he was saved from an actual experience of the sordid life within the walls. He was given a room over the porter's lodge fitted up into " a really elegant boudoir " by a former occupant, a wealthy, reckless young nobleman, and here he spent a week. Subsequently he stayed for a month in the country until, as he writes, " the day of emancipation arrived, and without a word of reproach or opposition the burthen of debt was removed from my shoulders and I walked the earth a new-born babe."

Before the crash came Vestris was making arrangements for the future. Of their provincial engagements they were sure, but what of the winter season in London ? Covent Garden Theatre, after what had

happened, was unthinkable. There remained Drury
Lane and the Haymarket. Macready had entered
upon the management of the first-named during the
previous year and he had discovered in Madame Vestris
a formidable rival. Their feelings towards each other
were made fairly plain in the little passage of arms over
Comus and *King Arthur*. Vestris's attitude was one
slightly approaching contempt. Macready regarded
Madame with the jealousy of a narrow mind. One has
not to read much of his *Diary* to discover that he was
mean, vain, and intolerant of opinions other than
his own. The audience which did not admire his
presentation of the tragic art was a collection of
ignorant brutes. There was but one kind of dramatic
entertainment, and that was tragedy. There was
only one tragedian in the world, and he was William
Charles Macready.

Of music Macready was wholly ignorant and he
had no taste for it. Musicians and singers were
beneath his notice. When Bishop was made Sir Henry,
he wrote bitterly of the composer's elevation, and over
Sims Reeves he tried to dominate and received a
defiance which must have astonished him considerably.
Henry Phillips, the popular baritone, he treated
slightingly ; he was rude to Clara Novello ; and Tom
Cooke, his musical conductor, did not have a very
easy time of it. When Madame Vestris announced
in her bills that seats could be reserved at a charge of
a guinea each, he recorded (February 21st, 1842) :
" No newspaper takes notice of this ; no newspaper
notices the difference in my arrangements. Had I
done half as much, how they would have swept upon
me ! What is there more vile and worthless than a
newspaper writer—perhaps nothing."

He loved flattery. Under May 21st, 1840, his
Diary contains this item : " Acted Halbert Macdonald
with much feeling. . . . I heard Vestris was in the
house and saw her applauding vehemently. Has she
discovered that a theatre cannot be conducted without

actors ? Or does all this mean anything ? " Actors
or no actors, Macready saw in Vestris the only manager
able to compete with him. In February 1840 she
was only at the commencement of her Covent Garden
campaign, but he feared her, and his prejudice prevented him giving her credit for sincerity. Vestris
was no hypocrite, and she would not have applauded
Macready had she not felt like it.

Throughout Vestris's occupation of Covent Garden,
Macready was nervously anxious about her proceedings
and eagerly swallowed every piece of theatrical gossip
which told to her detriment. " It is not a fitting
spectacle—the National Drama in the hands of
Madame Vestris and Charles Mathews," is one carping
item (September 13th, 1840). On October 1st of
the same year he records : " Talk with Brydone about
state of Covent Garden, and learned that all were
wishing me to be there except Vestris." This was
not at all likely to be true and is emphatically contra-
dicted by Macready himself in the following entry
four days later : " Covent Garden actors had signed
a declaration of allegiance and support to Madame
Vestris."

His vanity peeps out in the entry of October 6th,
in which he records his visit to Covent Garden to
see Knowles's play and thus comments : " I paid for
entrance, a slight reproach, I think, to the manners,
taste, and feeling of the present management. . . .
I was, or seemed to be, quite unknown in the theatre
where not a year ago I was the observed of all observers.
Such is the world ! "

After the production and success of *London Assurance*
there was much talk concerning its authorship and
also concerning other works of Lee Moreton (Dion
Boucicault's pseudonym), and Macready on February
6th, 1841, writes in reference to a rumour brought
to him by Miss Helen Faucit " that this Mr. Lee Moreton, on the rejection of the play called *Woman* by
Vestris, sent it to me ; that I said I would act the

play if he would take the good speeches out of the
woman's part and put them into mine, . . . I tried
vainly to recollect in years back any circumstances
respecting such a play . . . I could think of
none."

Considering that Macready was unfavourably disposed towards Mr. and Mrs. Mathews and was not
one to help anyone out of pure sympathy, it is at
first sight puzzling to understand his reasons for making
overtures to them when their days at Covent Garden
were numbered. It may be regarded as a certainty
that negotiations were not started by the Mathewses.
Charles Mathews in his *Autobiography* is silent on
the matter. He has not a word to say concerning
either Macready or his and Vestris's engagement at
Drury Lane. Doubtless he had good reason for
reticence. Their association with Macready was
an exceedingly unpleasant one. Macready exhibited
himself in an odious light, and, writing years after,
Mathews probably saw the futility of raking up con-
troversial matters which must have left a bitterness
in his mind quite foreign to his nature.

The motive which prompted Macready's offer to
Vestris and her husband was soon suspected, and
these suspicions found utterance in the press and
were confirmed by Macready himself. In the *Diary*
he shows plainly enough that his object was entirely
selfish and for his own protection. Under April 9th,
1842, appears the following : " I agreed to give Mr.
and Mrs. C. Mathews the terms for which they stood
out, viz. £60 per week. It is a very great salary, but
it is paid in consideration of enfeebling a position as
well as adding to my own strength. . . . Called at
Beasley's and found there Mr. Charles Mathews and
Madame Vestris. I met them very frankly and good-
humouredly, heard much that was irrelevant and
some things that amused me ; at last concluded an
engagement with them for two years at a salary of
£60 per week for Drury Lane. Parted with them,

they started off in their carriage, I in my shabby old hackney cab."

Macready's frankness, interpreted by the light of what followed, may be doubted ; hardly his envy, of which the concluding words of the entry are evidence. Neither can much dependence be placed on his good-humour. There was certainly not a trace of good-humour in what he wrote on May 1st of the same year : " Read Mr. Charles Mathews's speech on the closing of Covent Garden. It was worthy of Mr. C. M. and ' the management of Madame Vestris.' Players, poor players ! " If this record expresses anything at all, it is grim satisfaction at the misfortunes and downfall of his rivals.

Macready opened the winter season of 1842–3 with *As You Like It*. Vestris and Mathews made their first appearance in *The Follies of a Night*. Vestris's performance throughout was delightful and that of her husband equally so, wrote the *Age* (now the *Age and Argus* and minus Molloy Westmacott, really quite a model of decorum), but Mathews's acting as Roderigo in *Othello*, which followed, was declared to be " execrable." Possibly, but no discredit is to be attached to the actor. The blame belonged to Macready, who, either through ill-judgment or, what was more likely, malevolence, thrust Mathews into a part for which he was wholly unsuited.

As the season advanced Macready soured. His overweening vanity was ruffled by unfavourable criticisms in many newspapers which the fulsome flattery of the *Morning Chronicle* failed to soothe. He had an old grievance against the critics. During his first season at Drury Lane the *Weekly Dispatch* unmercifully attacked him and the outraged tragedian sued the offending paper. He was further infuriated when an unsympathetic jury considered that £5 was a sufficient solatium for his wounded feelings. This disappointing verdict biased his mind towards the press and probably increased his irascibility and arrogance

where his company was concerned. He was soon at
loggerheads with Vestris, to whom he gave little
chance for distinction. It was gall and wormwood
to see her rapturously applauded, and he, *the* tragedian,
receive but a moderate show of hands.

An outburst in the *Age and Argus* brought matters
to a crisis. It ran : " Drury Lane will shortly be in
a state of revolt if Mr. Macready does not relax from
his habitual routine of tyranny. . . . When Mr. Macready engaged Madame Vestris, he ought to have had
no other object in view than turning her great talents
and popularity to account ; but in the palpable spirit
of wishing to crush her fame and wound her feelings
she has become a comparative cypher. . . . Mr.
Charles Mathews has been thrust into Fag, and the
name of his wife, that for some years has blazoned
conspicuously in the *affiches* of all theatres, can only
now be discovered in them by virtue of a magnifying
glass." The troublous state of things was further
accentuated by a charge of meanness brought against
the manager, he having arbitrarily closed the theatre
on more than one occasion to benefit his pocket by
docking the salaries of his company.

Meanwhile the indignation of Vestris was simmering
and it rose to boiling-point. She threw up her engagement in the second week of November. The
story is given thus in a journal of the day :

" In the morning preceding the performance of
the *Duenna*, Madame Vestris had an interview with
Mr. Macready, and, drawing his attention to a
playbill she held in her hand, pointed out to him the
glaring manner by which through the extinctic
support he gave to the plays he himself performed in,
he rendered the effect of all others negative, and how
seriously this proceeding was contrary to the spirit
of her engagement ; and after pointing out a series
of indignities heaped upon her, proceeded to state
that she had often heard of the devil being painted
blacker than he was, but she never knew his *exact*

colour until she met with Mr. Macready! That he had altogether violated their contract and that no consideration on earth should induce her again to act under his management. The immediate cause of this outbreak—which a day or two must under any circumstances have brought to bear—was the non-payment of the salaries for the evenings he so wantonly and unnecessarily closed the theatre—together with the prospect, since realised, of two similar stoppages occurring in the week now expired.

"This, as we have observed, was the immediate cause; the *latent* one was the series of indignities which Mr. Macready has heaped upon this lady from the moment she entered the theatre. . . . A few months ago this lady was in the management of the rival theatre and the most powerful antagonist the lessee of Drury Lane had to contend against; but circumstances . . . led to her dethronement, and to prevent her remounting that throne, Mr. Macready with great prudence offered herself and her husband a good salary for the season. . . . With a full knowledge of the power she had wielded and the calamities she had undergone, Mr. Macready should have done all he could to prevent her feeling her situation. . . .

"In addition . . . there are professional reasons why it was his policy to do all this, for Madame Vestris is one of the most celebrated performers ever known to the London stage and stands at this moment before her audience as one of the most accomplished ladies and popular actresses who have ever been admitted to their favour. . . . But he acted altogether on an *opposite* principle, studied to degrade her to the lowest pitch, and—but for her own proper spirit—he *would* have done so."

Macready was, as the Rugby boy described Dr. Temple, "a beast," but he was not, as the boy admitted, "a just beast." He could not be honest even to himself. His version of the passage of arms as set down in the *Diary* runs: "About to begin rehearsal

. . . when Mr. C. Mathews wished to speak to me.
Madame Vestris followed him into my room and began
a *scene* which lasted two or three hours—on the lady's
part much Billingsgate and false assertion, on his much
weakness and equivocation. I would not relinquish
their engagement, but offered to defer the pecuniary
point. She threw down her part in *King Arthur* and
left the room, stating she would not act after next
week if the full salary were not paid." Macready here
was both disingenuous and evasive. He avoided the
main issue—that of continually slighting the two most
accomplished members of his company. The offer
to " defer the pecuniary point " was a shuffle to escape
liability, and Vestris's flat refusal to have no more
to do with a man who was as shifty as he was vain and
arrogant was only what was to be expected from the
high-spirited woman.

The part in *King Arthur* which Vestris contemptuously rejected was an insignificant one, that of
Venus, little short, as one critic described it, of " a
pantomime character." The principal woman in
the opera, Philodel, was given to Macready's pet
protégée, Miss P. Horton. Priscilla Horton was a
clever girl, but in those days an immature singer.
Previous to committing the egregious blunder of
casting her as Acis in Handel's serenata, we find Macready writing : " Must speak to Miss P. Horton about
taking lessons in singing "—a sufficient proof of his
ignorance and indifference where music was concerned. The assignment of the parts in *King Arthur*
was a gross insult to Madame Vestris, whether inten-
tional or not.

Macready, blinded by his inflated opinion of himself,
threw away a golden opportunity. The audience
wanted to see Vestris, but her few appearances were
confined to Lady Teazle and Lydia Languish, neither
of which was suited to her, and Don Carlos in *The
Duenna*. Here she was seen to much more advantage.

The renewal of Dryden's opera deserves especial

notice, as in it sang one who afterwards established himself as an idol of the British public—Sims Reeves. But as to Vestris, it is clear that she was purposely kept in the background, and she must have felt an intense relief when she defied and escaped from the autocratic rule of a self-appointed oracle.

Two more references to Vestris occur in the *Diary* and with these Macready may be dismissed. " Had some little conversation with Maddox," he records (with almost a chuckle one can imagine), while Vestris was touring, " who told me that Vestris's and Mathews's engagement at Dublin was a failure owing to the potatoe disease—a black look-out ! " The last entry in 1840 describes a lucky escape from an embarrassing situation. " Left home for Manchester," it runs. " At the station asked for a coupé and was told it was engaged, and whilst I was arranging my seat in a carriage a person of the station came and told me that there was one seat in the coupé unoccupied, but that ' Mr. Mathews and Madame Vestris had the others, and perhaps I might not like it.' I laughed and said, ' Certainly not,' and that I was much obliged."

Vestris and Mathews were not long without an engagement, and the end of November 1842 saw them installed at the Haymarket, then under the management of Benjamin Webster. The productions in which Vestris and her husband were concerned during the winter do not call for special mention. They were pieces thoroughly familiar and acceptable to the audience.

Provincial engagements followed, and then came financial disaster, the shadow of which had been projected for some time and in the summer of 1843 completely darkened the prospects of the embarrassed couple, in spite of strenuous efforts on the part of both to emerge from it. Their fresh misfortunes may be said to be due to Mathews's irresponsible habit which led him to take a self-imposed burden for which there was no necessity. Excess of zeal is mischievous enough, but it may be questioned whether excess of conscientiousness be not worse. The new disaster came about in this way. Directly his bankruptcy arising out of the Covent Garden failure was annulled Mathews expressed his intention of discharging his obligations, outside the protection given by law. Nothing could be more admirable, and had he been contented with endeavouring to carry out this intention by force of will all would have been well. But instead he entered into fresh legal arrangements concerning his old debts, gave bills that were negotiable, and within a twelvemonth he was saddled with a burden which from some £4,000 had become " ten or twelve by the magic of law and accumulated interest."

The position in which Charles Mathews found himself was doubtless harassing enough to him personally, but it must have been doubly so to Madame Vestris. Her indomitable and energetic spirit could not but have chafed under this fresh misfortune. She had gone through the wretched experience of sustaining a burden of debt too often not to dread it. The galling part of the present situation was that it was an insurmountable barrier to further enterprise. To serve where she had ruled was too humiliating to contemplate. She and Mathews fell back upon provincial engagements, and they worked their hardest to free themselves from financial liabilities, but to no purpose.

Whether the difficulties into which Charles Mathews had voluntarily plunged were incurred after consultation with Madame and how far she advised him for or against it is impossible to say. It is hardly likely that she had no voice in the matter. His next step, he himself says, was taken on the advice that he could better bring his creditors to reason by withdrawing himself out of their jurisdiction, and " in a fit of despair " he relinquished his engagement at the Haymarket Theatre and fled to France. This

MADAME VESTRIS.
(From the collection of the late A. M. Broadley.)

proved a blunder. The law pursued him and with
greater severity, and finding, as he says, " that all
legal documents could be passed to foreign holders
and be enforced more rigidly on that side of the water
than on this," he addressed a letter to his creditors,
putting forward his position, and once more sought
the protection of the Bankruptcy Court.

It is not necessary to go into the details of this
unhappy state of affairs. Those who wish to do so
will find them fully dealt with in the *Life of Charles J.
Mathews*. The upshot was that Mathews entered
into an arrangement under which he agreed to set
aside £1,300 a year in discharge of his debts, and once
more he and Vestris made a fresh start and returned
to the Haymarket.

It was not until the beginning of 1845 that matters
settled down to anything like tranquillity. In February *The Merry Wives of Windsor* was produced at
the Haymarket. Vestris was Mrs. Page—a character
which she had played now and again for something
like twenty years—and Mrs. Nisbett was Mrs. Ford.
Farren essayed Falstaff; Charles Mathews, Slender;
and Mrs. Glover, Dame Quickly. The performance,
according to contemporary criticism, was a very
delightful one. In February came one of Charles
Mathews's inimitable impersonations in *Used up*. He
played the part with perennial spontaneity almost to
the end of his days.

At a performance some time in April a few un-
mannerly and unfeeling people attempted to create
a demonstration hostile to Vestris—" low fellows,"
we are told, who considered themselves aggrieved
by the arrangement under the bankruptcy. The
attempt failed, and the majority of the audience
burst into hearty applause.

Vestris bravely surmounted her troubles and on
the stage she was as brilliant as ever. One of her
triumphs was Flipante in Farquhar's *Confederacy*,
" admirable in conception," said the *Age and Argus*,

" perfect in execution—the best thing she has done for years."

In October was produced Boucicault's *Old Heads and Young Hearts*, which was preceded by an altercation between Vestris and the dramatist, who, with his Irish temperament, was always ready to be combative. The cause of difference was Vestris's complaint that her part required strengthening. Boucicault refused to make any alteration and the critics supported him. " Madame looks remarkably well and her acting is worthy her appearance," wrote one. " Why on earth should we want the part made stronger ? Boucicault was quite right in refusing to comply—she has exactly what she should have—or makes us think so."

At the termination of these Haymarket engagements they played for some weeks at the Princess's, and then, the Lyceum being vacant, the enterprising couple determined to make another bid for the laurels of management.

CHAPTER XXV

THE END OF A GREAT CAREER

The Lyceum campaign. Vestris's enormous responsibilities. The house splendidly redecorated. Abolition of the " half-price " system. Vestris's dramatic reforms. A magnificent reception. Production of *Box and Cox*, with Buckstone and Harley. Walter Watts and the beautiful Mrs. Mowatt. A tragic romance. Planché's gorgeous extravaganzas. The scenic artist super-eminent. The evolution of the modern pantomime transformation scene. A string of successful pieces. The search for novelties. Melodrama in eight acts! Frequent illnesses of Madame Vestris. The management shows signs of decay. The final flicker of the candle. Madame Vestris's last appearance. Charles Mathews's bankruptcy and arrest. Vestris's death. The pathetic end of a great career and a great artist.

AFTER going through the ordeal of three bankruptcies —one attached to Vestris and two to Charles Mathews —to resume the responsibility of management was a bold venture. The difficulties facing the enterprising couple were enormous. They had no capital ; they had only just emerged from a heavy burden of debt and a long spell of intense anxiety, yet this bitter experience did not deter them. Both Madame and Charles believed in themselves, and they had good reason for that belief.

What was to be their programme ? They had no place in the legitimate drama. Vestris's essays in that direction were open to criticism, and in Shakespeare she dared not go beyond *The Merry Wives of Windsor*, *As You Like It*, and *A Midsummer-Night's Dream*. Charles Mathews was impossible in any Shakespearean part. The charm of their acting was in their individuality, and they could only display this charm in pieces written to suit them, and mounted with the good taste and completeness with which they were identified. It was too much to expect them to produce the spectacular dramas which had yielded triumphs at the Olympic and Covent Garden. Since the collapse of the Covent Garden management, due not to any shortcomings of their own, but to circumstances outside their control, they had fretted the days away. They pined to plunge once more into gay comediettas and fairy extravaganzas set in gorgeous surroundings, untrammelled by hard-and-fast stage traditions. The end of it was, the two sanguine spirits took their courage in both hands, secured the Lyceum, and hoped for the best.

Considering what they had to encounter, the marvel is that they should have maintained their position at the Lyceum for so long. Mathews writes : " For seven years we worked day and night, and with unvarying success ; but the want of capital to fall back upon was for ever the drawback upon our efforts. Every piece had to be got up upon credit, and the outlay had always to be repaid before a profit could be realised ; and all the large receipts accruing from the brilliant houses from Christmas to Easter were more than swallowed up by the utter blank that followed from Easter to Michaelmas."

But they had no thought of fresh misfortunes when on October 18th, 1847, they opened the theatre with *The Light Dragoons*, by Dance, in which Mathews, Harley, Charles Selby, and Mrs. Stirling, the latter charming in her youthful exuberance, appeared ; and with Planché's *The Pride of the Market*, wherein Vestris displayed all her old vivacity and elegance. She was supported by Leigh Murray and Buckstone. Ever on the side of the public's comfort and convenience, Madame Vestris instituted the " no fees " system—an example which no other contemporary manager dared to follow ; and she abolished " half prices," always a source of annoyance to those who had paid for an entire evening's entertainment. The "half prices" were mostly shop assistants who came in more merry than wise and made themselves objectionable in various ways.

Nothing could be more encouraging than the auspices under which the season commenced. The public were delighted to see Vestris back in her rôle as Queen of the Stage. She did not disappoint their expectations—indeed she exceeded them. The *Times* wrote :

" For beauty of decoration this house will not lose by comparison with any in London. It is no longer the same edifice it was three weeks ago. The ugly balcony, which always made it look empty, however crowded it might be, has been pulled down, and the front of the dress circle is bowed out like that of Covent Garden, and the central chandelier is also removed and a beautifully painted ceiling is laid open to the view. . . . The problem of combining a massive splendour with a general appearance of lightness has been most happily solved. . . . The new drop-scene representing a crimson curtain falling over a light background is by Mr. Beverley, who is engaged as scene painter to the establishment and who promises to be one of the finest artists in his line. . . . The house will no doubt be conducted on the plan which made the Olympic under Madame Vestris one of the most celebrated theatres in London. If so, it would supply a gap which has been felt for the last eight years."

Other papers were equally enthusiastic over the novel attractions and the general brightness. The *Era* took a broader view. Its words are pertinent to the tribute paid more than once in these pages to the influence exercised by Vestris in the advancement of the stage :

" Madame Vestris," it declared, " is the champion *par excellence* of the Living Drama. It was Madame Vestris who years ago set the bold example of discarding the hackneyed and worn-out plays which cant still calls ' standard,' of clearing the mirror of

nature from ' legitimate ' cobwebs and dust, and of
making it represent the manners, habits, and follies
of the age *we* live in. Shelving the conventional in
comedy and in sentiment, banishing the patriotic,
the mawkish pathos, the dreary soliloquy, the skin-deep
virtue, . . . Madame Vestris suddenly brought out
a sparkling series of pictures of good society, painted
up as dramatic necessity required, but only heightened
for the sake of ' art,' *not* distorted for the sake of
effect. . . .

" To Madame Vestris appertains the honour of
having smashed the cant preached by ignorant managers who really knew no better ; lazy actors, who having
by long study mastered a part prefer repeating it
usque ad nauseam to attempting a new one ; bigoted
critics, who having been told in childhood that Shakespeare was ' for all time ' believe that all time is to
be spent on seeing his noble plays parodied or made
spectacles; and the mass of folk of one idea, who because
they have but that one claim to dictate what ideas
shall be presented to other people. Honour to the
good revolutionist *citoyenne* Vestris ! "

The last words were apt enough. Revolutions
were smouldering in Europe and broke into flame in
1848.

Used as Vestris was to enthusiastic and warm-
hearted receptions, she never had one so genuinely
emotional as that which greeted her when she stepped
upon the stage. The packed house, to use Edmund
Kean's words, " rose " at her. She was overwhelmed,
and it was some minutes before *The Pride of the Market*
could begin. Charles Mathews was received with
equal heartiness if not with demonstrations so pronounced. Night after night the house was crowded,
and the hall-mark of success was set when the names
of a whole string of aristocratic patrons who had
attended the performance appeared in the newspapers
from time to time. London in the winter of 1847
was plagued by a severe visitation of influenza, but

despite this it was noted that there was no falling-off in the Lyceum audiences, while all the other theatres were half empty. Maybe the brightness of the Lyceum and the magnetic influence of Vestris were regarded as wholesome tonics.

No dramatic novelty deserving special notice was produced during the first three months of the season save one—the perennial *Box and Cox*. It was produced on November 1st, 1847, Buckstone playing Box, and Harley, Cox. It was hailed with shouts of laughter, the peculiar humour of Buckstone being exactly suitable to the farcical character he impersonated.

The author of *Box and Cox* was Maddison Morton, who unintentionally was connected with as tragic and as curious a story as is to be found in the history of the English stage. Morton made a good deal of money out of *Box and Cox* and invested some of it in the purchase of two £50 shares in the Globe Insurance Company. Some time after, being pressed for money, he determined to sell these shares, and chancing to meet in the street Walter Watts, a dandified, dressy little man with theatrical tastes, who, Morton knew, was a clerk in the Globe, he suggested that Watts should purchase the shares, which Watts did. Whatever may have been in Watts's mind at the time, it is very clear that Morton had not the slightest idea of the extraordinary legal issue to which the sale of these two shares led.

Watts at that time was lessee of the Marylebone Theatre, and fired by the example of Madame Vestris, or by some personal ambition, was transforming this dingy and inconvenient theatre into a luxurious home of the drama. It was a rash undertaking, for Marylebone as a locality for theatrical enterprises was, as it is to-day, out of the beaten track. But Watts was smitten by the charms of the "beautiful Mrs. Mowatt," an American actress who came here with a reputation for talent which she hardly sustained. Watts's ambitious schemes knew no bounds. He

went one better than Vestris in providing sumptuous
saloons for the refreshment of the audience and equally
sumptuous dressing-rooms for the company, numbering
some forty actors and actresses, all leading members
of the profession.

Neither the campaign nor the " beautiful Mrs.
Mowatt " was a success. Watts relinquished the
Marylebone and took the Olympic, in which he spent
a small fortune. Suddenly the sword of Damocles
which had been hanging over the dressy and genial
little man fell. He was arrested on a charge of having
robbed the Insurance Company with which he was
connected of £80,000 ! How he contrived to make
use of his position to do this does not here matter.
What is of consequence is the two shares he bought
of Maddison Morton. He contended that as he was
a shareholder he was also a partner, and therefore he
could not be proceeded against, and this contention
was upheld. But the intricacies of the law are mani-
fold. Watts had misappropriated cheques, and he
was indicted on a charge of stealing a piece of paper
(i.e. a cheque). This cheque was a blank one, which he
had filled up and cashed, and his conviction was based
on the theft of the paper. The trumpery nature of
the legal offence made no difference in the sentence
passed, which was ten years' penal servitude.

Tragedy lay in the sequel. That night he hanged
himself in his cell in Newgate, and it was said that
when his clothing was removed round his neck was
found a miniature portrait—that of the beautiful
Mrs. Mowatt.

Christmas entertainments were always eagerly looked
forward to by the theatrical public. Managers vied
with each other in the production of pantomimes,
but not the conglomerate shows such as we have to-day
grown accustomed to—and of which, maybe, are tired.
They were comparatively simple affairs—a comic plot,
the characters in which afterwards figured as clown,
pantaloon, harlequin, etc., in the harlequin. Gradually,

however, the gorgeous Christmas pieces introduced by Vestris with Planché's help were influencing the old-fashioned pantomimes, and though the transformation scene had not in the late forties come into its own, Planché seemed to have some foreboding that the "things of beauty" of which he was the author would at no distant date run riot and refuse to be curbed by good taste.

At first Planché was able to keep the scenic artists within bounds. *The Golden Branch* (Christmas 1847), *Theseus and Ariadne* (Easter 1848), *The King of the Peacocks* (Christmas 1848), and *The Seven Champions* (Easter 1849) were all excellent specimens of a delicate fancy, humour combined with bright and artistic surroundings and novel effects. The scenery, costumes, and mounting were subordinate to the human interest, the chief burden of which rested upon Vestris, from whom the rest of the characters seemed to draw inspiration.

Planché found an able coadjutor in Beverley, the scene-painter, then at the outset of his career. Beverley revelled in the scope which Planché's fairy extravaganzas gave him. He saw possibilities in his imaginative faculties and in his brush which he longed to fulfil, as Planché was destined to discover.

On Boxing Day 1849 Planché produced *The Island of Jewels*. He writes of this : " The novel yet exceedingly simple falling of the leaves of a palm tree, which discovered six fairies supporting a coronet of jewels, produced such an effect as I scarcely remember having witnessed on any similar occasion up to that period. But alas ! ' this effect defective came by cause.' Year after year Mr. Beverley's powers were tasked to out-do his former out-doings. The last scene became the first in the estimation of the management. The most complicated machinery, the most costly materials, were annually put into requisition, until their bacon was so buttered that it was impossible to save it. As to me, I was positively painted

out. Nothing was considered brilliant but the last
scene. Dutch metal was in the ascendant. It was
no longer even painting, it was upholstery. Mrs.
Charles Mathews herself informed me that she had
paid between £60 and £70 for gold tissue for dresses
of the supernumeraries alone, who were discovered
in attitudes in the last scene of *Once upon a Time there
were Two Kings.*"

During the seven years of Vestris's management
of the Lyceum many comedies and farces were produced which became established favourites until
fashion and a new school of acting rendered them
obsolete. *A Wonderful Woman, A Game of Speculation,
Cool as a Cucumber, A Phenomenon in a Smock Frock,
A Day of Reckoning, Done on Both Sides, Not a Bad
Judge, Delicate Ground, Poor Pillicoddy, Little Toddle-
kins*, among others possibly survive in the memories
of very old playgoers, but to the present generation
they represent nothing.

Vestris was always in quest of novelty, and her efforts
to be ever up to date must have entailed a great
strain on her nervous system. Maybe she could see
that fairy extravaganzas, though enormously successful, must eventually pall. Each one was pronounced
by the critics to be better than its predecessor, but
there was bound to come a time when the force of
invention could no further go.

Moreover, there was the heavy outlay to be considered, and—but very few people knew this—she
and her husband were clogged by debts. Charles
Mathews had learned little by experience. His opti-
mism led him to believe what he wished to believe.
At the outset of the Lyceum enterprise a friend who
had the reputation of being very wealthy promised to
finance him. Mathews, after he had embarked in the
new venture, discovered that the reputed millionaire
was a man of straw, and he had to go on single-handed
as best he could. For years he and Vestris bravely
faced the struggle, but gradually their resources

dwindled.   Circumstances were too strong for them, and worst of all was the precarious health of Vestris. She may not at first have suspected it but what proved to be a mortal disease was gradually undermining her constitution.   Yet outwardly she was as gay and as energetic as ever.   The reputation of the Lyceum was her first thought, and well or ill she must keep faith with the public.

However, the time came when the production of expensive novelties of the kind with which she was identified was beyond her reach.   Another kind of entertainment was sought for, and, always in advance of her time, for the Easter attraction of 1852 she put on a piece of stupendous length, in some of the scenes in which she anticipated the realistic melodramatic efforts associated with Drury Lane and Sir Augustus Harris.   This piece (from the French) was entitled *A Chain of Events*, and was in eight acts!   Under the title of *Les Dames de la Halle* it had made a great hit in Paris, and its adaptator to an English dress was George Henry Lewes.   The plot was exceedingly complicated and some of the scenes highly sensational, one indeed, that of a ship sinking with all hands, John Coleman was of opinion has never since been equalled. The house of fairyland and of laughter hardly seemed to fit in with lurid melodrama, but it ran for fifty nights, probably because no adequate substitute was in readiness.

The winter season of 1852 began to show the poverty of the land, and old successes were revived one after the other until Christmas, when Planché came to the rescue with a characteristic extravaganza, *The Good Woman in the Wood*, Vestris enacting the Good Woman.   The extravaganza ran till Easter, Vestris acting with all her old vivacity and receiving congratulations all round upon her improved health.   The melodramatic experiment of the year before was repeated in what was termed *A dramatic tale in* 9 *chapters, entitled A Strange History*.   It was a cumbrous, complicated affair and was deservedly damned with faint praise. Its life was but a short one, and in desperation *The Good Woman in the Wood* was put on again together with old pieces such as *Used up*, of which Charles Mathews bore the burden. No announcement concerning the few appearances of Vestris was made, but it was pretty obvious that her absence was owing to illness. Charles Mathews did his best to "carry on," but he was not Madame, and it is not surprising to read that the house was but "thinly attended."

The summer passed on, and when the winter season of 1853 commenced on October 31st, all that the management could do in the way of novelty was a farce with the ill-omened and clumsy title of *The Commencement of a Bad Farce which it is hoped will turn out Wright at Last*. The piece introduced Wright the comedian, so long associated with Paul Bedford at the Adelphi, and no introduction could have been more unfortunate. The farce throughout was heartily hissed, and subsequently the first half of the title and of the piece was cut out and *Wright at Last* alone remained. But the mutilated version was not much of an improvement and was soon withdrawn. Old pieces were revived, and an effort was made to produce at Christmas a worthy successor to former triumphs. *Once upon a Time there were Two Kings* was the result.

This proved to be Planché's last fairy extravaganza and was pronounced to be in no way inferior to its predecessors, but it was shorn of its brightness by the frequent non-appearance of the one attractive personality who was the life and soul of every piece in which she took a part. An indifference, a sort of disposition to let things take care of themselves, a weakening of intuitive power, began to creep over the management. The guiding hand, the alert, versatile brain were wanting.

It is sad to find, apropos of the 1854 Easter "novelty," *Give a Dog an Ill Name*, which was announced but was not produced without any apology being forthcoming, the *Era* writing : " The house was very poorly attended.   Everything in front looked half dead and languid—boxes, box-keepers, decorations, audience, house and curtains alike—all seemed dingy, faded, and unreal.   We heard no explanation offered for the non-production of the new piece and no dis-satisfaction expressed at its non-appearance.   Indeed, no one seemed to know that one had been promised or to care about it or to have energy or spirit enough to express their feelings on the subject."

On the following evening the piece was put on, but it failed to attract.   It was too evident that decay had set in.   Mathews was harassed by clamorous creditors.   Poor Vestris on a sick-bed could do nothing. The end was approaching and salvation was im-possible.

Indomitable to the last, Madame roused herself to assist at her husband's benefit on July 26th, 1854. Remembering the unhappy state of affairs, the title of the play, *Sunshine through the Clouds*, savoured of irony.   There was to be no more sunshine for the gifted woman who for over thirty years had been at once the idol and the pet of the public.   Those who saw her on this occasion as sprightly and as great a mistress of her art as ever could not believe that they were gazing upon Vestris—who seemed to possess the secret of eternal youth—for the last time, but it was so. The occasion does not appear to have been marked by any particular demonstration, but this is easily accounted for.   That Vestris would never again appear on the boards she had graced for so long was a probability which entered into no one's head.

The summer season of 1854 closed, the winter season crept on apace.   Charles Mathews had to face the situation alone.   The enforced retirement of Vestris meant a loss which could not be made good.   Nobody could enter the Lyceum without thinking of the bright, airy spirit whose smile would never again delight them, whose sweet, luscious voice had thrilled them for the last time. Charles battled with the situation as best he could, but his helpmate, his support, was gone. The climax came at the end of 1854. The winter—it was the first year of the Crimean War—was intensely severe. A heavy and prolonged fall of snow blocked the streets. For days traffic was exceedingly difficult. The theatres were inaccessible. The treasury of the Lyceum was empty, and one impatient creditor selected the moment to descend upon the manager with all the hardness of the law.

Once more Mathews found himself a bankrupt, but he was not without friends, and it was intimated that should he pass honourably through the bankruptcy ordeal a fund would be awaiting to start him afresh. These hopes were only in a measure fulfilled. The Court granted the bankrupt a full discharge with all honour ; a lease of the Lyceum was secured, a brilliant benefit for Mathews and Madame was got up, and once more the theatre was in their possession. But fortune was still perverse. Disputes arose out of the disposal of the subscription fund. Some of the subscribers refused to join in the dispute and handed over their subscriptions, but many availed themselves of the opportunity to back out, and Mathews, made desperate by impending responsibilities and continual pinpricks, " took a bold resolve," to use his own words, " and, defying consequences, abruptly brought the season to a close, shut the doors, and cut management for ever." This announcement was made on March 24th, 1855.

Meanwhile Vestris, fighting, as one may be sure she did, against the fell disease which was gradually consuming her, had her last days embittered by the vanishing of everything that she valued. Never more would she exercise that art which had always been part of her life; all her brilliant managerial triumphs had ended in disaster; the stimulus of applause, the indescribable thrill at the sounds of approbation of which she had been conscious on thousands of occasions, she had experienced for the last time. Everything that had once been pleasant was now but a memory tinged with sadness.

Then came the final crash. Charles Mathews was arrested for debt while fulfilling an engagement at Preston and was thrown into gaol. This was on July 5th, 1856. In Mathews's *Life* will be found the letters he wrote to his wife during this tragic time, and pathetic indeed they are. Vestris's letters are not given, and it is as well. That she did her best to cheer him one may be certain. In one letter it would appear she proposed, ill as she was, to journey to Lancaster where he was imprisoned, but he implored her to dismiss the idea. He obtained his release on August 1st, and hastened to London. He was in time to soothe the last hours of his wife, but no more. She died on August 8th.

The news of her death came as a shock both to the public and to her friends, for with her optimistic spirit she believed she would recover, though the terrible pain she was suffering must have told her a different tale. The press was full of eulogistic notices, but only that of the *Era* need be quoted, as it epitomises sympathetically her genius as an artist and her versatility and charm of character, its strength and its weakness, as a woman.

"Those," said the writer, "who have only seen this gifted actress within the last ten or fifteen years know nothing of that indescribable spell of fascination which she threw around the spectator and which she carried with her into private life. . . . Possessed of the most refined taste, utterly divested of affectation, and generous by impulse to an extent of which without touching upon private matters we cannot definitely allude to, the gay, the gifted Vestris has been as enthusiastically admired in some circles as she has been as ruthlessly condemned and even calumniated in others.

" It would be an easy task to rake the tales of scandal from oblivion that have been freely uttered of her days gone by, but she has expiated all her faults, even if much that were said against her were true, and much that has been said of a detracting kind is not true. . . . But when the temptations of her early career are remembered, when the coarse and lavish flattery to which she was subjected as a child is considered, and when the example of her first husband, who should have guided her conduct and not have ridiculed all the highest principles of morality before her eyes, is called to mind, there will be a sufficient explanation of, if not an excuse for, the errors into which she fell.

" Of the good she did, of the refined influences that were shed over dramatic art at her instigation, and of the benefit the public and profession have derived in consequence, too little unfortunately will be remembered. But among those who during the last half-century have contributed to the amusement of the metropolis there is not a name that stands more prominently forth or will be more missed than that of Madame Vestris."

Vestris was fifty-nine when she died. She had since she was eighteen been prominently before the public until she was fifty-seven, and during those thirty-nine years she had led a life of continual excitement, of conflicting emotions, and of passionate energy which would have worn out a dozen ordinary women before their prime. Vestris, on the contrary, never appeared to be growing old ; she never showed signs of weariness in her art ; she rarely failed to give an audience of her best, no matter what the characters —and their variety was amazing—she was playing might be. In one respect she was fortunate. She did not outlive her reputation. She did not " lag superfluous on the stage." She did not become unwieldy

MADAME VESTRIS AS CAPTAIN MACHEATH.
(From the collection of the late A. M. Broadley.)

like Siddons; happier than Dora Jordan, she was never unable to *look* the parts with which she had been identified early in her career; she was spared the terrible collapse in the sight of the audience which befell Woffington. She did not have to suffer the bitter pang of being relegated to play an old woman and of seeing a new youthful " star " in the character which once was hers. When past fifty her figure was as symmetrical, her smile as bewitching, her voice as fascinating as in her younger days.

Her personal charms and her subtle dramatic art belonged to her life and died with her. What has *not* died is the influence she brought to bear on theatrical reform and progress. The debt which the dramatic profession and the playgoing public owe to Eliza Vestris has never been adequately acknowledged. Perhaps neither the one nor the other is conscious of that debt. It remains all the same, and one has but to study the record of her five-and-twenty years of theatrical management to be convinced of this outstanding fact.

At the present day Madame Vestris is to most people but a name, yet when the list of remarkable women of the first half of the nineteenth century is scanned there is not to be found one who can be placed anywhere near the plane which she occupied. Madame Vestris stands by herself. She made the best of her genius; throughout her life she devoted her gifts to the enjoyment of others. She entered the stage at a time when the drama had sunk to a state of lethargic artificiality; she left it imbued with her own vitality, freed from the fetters of conventionality, and moved by an impetus the influence of which, despite the changes in taste and fashion, it still retains. Madame Vestris's management of the Olympic, of Covent Garden, of the Lyceum tells the same story of consummate art, of a devotion to the beautiful; of a passion for accuracy and completeness, an abhorrence of all that was stilted, of bad taste crusted by tradition, of the unforgivable sin—dullness.

If any member of the dramatic profession can be singled out for honour as one who, when she had the directing hand, never ceased to work for the advancement of the stage in its best aspects, that honour unquestionably belongs to Eliza Vestris.

APPENDIX

MADAME VESTRIS'S OLYMPIC MANAGEMENT

RECORD OF PIECES PRESENTED IN WHICH SHE APPEARED AND OF THE SONGS INTRODUCED. COMPILED BY MR. GUY TRACEY WATTS FROM OLYMPIC PLAYBILLS AND ANNOUNCEMENTS IN "MORNING CHRONICLE"

A list of the plays produced at Covent Garden and Lyceum will be found at the end of the *Life of Charles J. Mathews* (edited by Charles Dickens).

1831 (*First Season*)

January 3. *Mary Queen of Scots* (historical burletta). Miss Foote. *Olympic Revels.* Vestris. *Little Tochey* (comic burletta). Mrs. Glover.

January 24. *The Grenadier* added to the above. Vestris with songs : "Oh, they march'd through the town "; "A Savoyard's Song "; "Listen, dear Fanny." Liston.

February 28. *Duke for a Day!* Vestris as a page. Season ended March 26 with *My Great Aunt ; The Grenadier ; Chaste Salute ; Olympic Revels.*

1831–2 (*Second Season*)

October 1 (1831). *Olympic Revels.* Continued in the bill for some weeks.

October 27. *The Love Spell.* Vestris.

November 21. *The Widow, or My Uncle's Will.* Vestris with songs : "Under the Rose," and "Too soon I never can forget."

December 14. *Dumb Belle.* Vestris.

December 27. *Olympic Devils, or Orpheus and Eurydice.* Vestris.

February 28 (1832). *My Eleventh Day.* Vestris, Liston.

March 15. *The Young Hopeful.*

1832–3 (*Third Season*)

October 1 (1832). *Olympic Devils.*

October 22. *The Court of Queen's Bench* (music by John Barnett). Vestris.

November 28. *The Conquering Game !* Vestris.

December 26. *The Paphian Bower, or Venus and Adonis* (music by John Barnett). Vestris.

February 21 (1833). *A Match in the Dark.* Vestris.

1833–4 (*Fourth Season*)

September 30 (1833). *A Match in the Dark.* Vestris with song, " Why did I love ? "

October 1. *High, Low, Jack, and the Game* (music by Blewitt). Vestris with song, " The Gavotte de Vestris."

November 13. *Beulah Spa.* Vestris. Songs : " I'll make her speak out " ; " By the margin of Zurich's fair waters."

December 16. *The Welch Girl.* Vestris.

December 26. *Deep, Deep Sea, or Perseus and Andromeda.* Vestris.

1834–5 (*Fifth Season*)

September 29 (1834). *Loan of a Lover.* Vestris.

October 28. *The Retort Courteous.* Vestris. Songs : " Nothing new," and " They don't propose."

November 27. *How to Get Off.* Vestris.

December 26. *Telemachus, or the Island of Calypso* (music by Tully). Vestris.

January 5 (1835). *A New Farce.* Vestris as manageress of the Olympic. Liston.

February 9. *Why Don't She Marry ?* Vestris.

February 24. *Hearts and Diamonds.* Vestris.

March 14. *The Court Beauties.* Vestris.

1835–6 (*Sixth Season*)

September 28 (1835). *Love in a Cottage.* Vestris. Songs : " Love in a Cottage " ; " I'll be no submissive wife " ; " Rory O'More."

October 8. *The Two Queens, or Politics in Petticoats.* Vestris, Liston.

November 16. *The Beau Ideal.* Vestris. Songs: "Can't you guess ?"; "The poor blind boy"; "Beauty and Time."

December 26. *Olympic Picnic.* Vestris.

Jan. 11 (1836). *One Hour, or A Carnival Ball.* Vestris. Songs: "Love is the theme of the minstrel," and a Neapolitan Air. (First occasion on which Vestris and Charles Mathews appeared together.)

February 15. *A Handsome Husband.* Vestris. Song, "What can Beauty give one more ?" Charles Mathews.

1836–7 (*Seventh Season*)

September 29 (1836). *Court Favour, or Private and Confidential.* Vestris, Mathews.

October 31. *Olympic Devils.* Vestris. *He would be an Actor.* Mathews.

November 7. *Barrack Room.* Vestris.

November 30. *The Two Figaros.* Vestris, Liston.

December 26. *Riquet with the Tuft.* Vestris.

February 23 (1837). *The Sentinel.* Vestris, Mathews.

March 27. *The Rape of the Lock.* Vestris, Mathews.

1837–8 (*Eighth Season*)

September 29 (1837). *Country Squire.* Vestris. Song, "You will not surely love me less." W. Farren.

October 23. *Hugo Bambino.* Vestris. Songs: "Nina dear," and "The chiming of the vesper bell."

November 6. *A Dream of the Future.* Vestris, Mathews.

December 16. *The Ladder of Love.* Vestris. Song, "There never was so fine a show." Mathews.

December 26. *Puss in Boots.* Vestris.

January 18 (1838). *The Black Domino* (Auber). Vestris, Mathews.

March 1. *You Can't Marry your Grandmother.* Vestris, Mathews, Farren.

April 16. *The Drama's Levee, or a Peep at the Past.* Vestris, Mathews.

April 19. *A Hasty Conclusion.* Vestris, Mathews.

May 3. *Naval Engagements.* Vestris, Mathews, Farren.

May 31. Last night of season, and Vestris and Mathews depart for America.

1838–9 (Ninth Season)

January 19 (1839).   *Blue Beard.*   Vestris.

February 22.   *Our Cousin German, or I did it for the Best.*

February 28.   *Faint Heart Never Won Fair Lady.*   Vestris, Mathews.

March.   *Petticoat Government.*

April 1.   *Izaac Walton.*   Vestris.   Songs : " Come, live with me and be my love " (Bishop), and " Here's a health unto his Majesty."

May 2.   Revival of *High, Low, Jack, and the Game* and *One Hour.*   Vestris and Mathews.

May 31.   *Meet Me by Moonlight ; A Dream of the Future ;* and *One Hour.*   Vestris and Mathews.

(End of season and termination of Vestris's lesseeship.)

[Owing to the absence of American journals in this country so far back as 1838, the tour of Mr. and Mrs. Mathews in the United States is difficult to follow.   To the details given in Chapter XIX, an extract from a *Theatrical Biography* (1849) compiled by Mr. F. C. Wemyss, a well-known American theatrical manager, may, however, be added.   Mr. Wemyss says of Vestris : " The absurd cry that she was no actress and unworthy of the reputation she enjoyed was raised by prejudice and was anything but creditable to the judgment (which was never used) of the American public.   The manner in which she resented the mortification she experienced was ill-judged ; and her attack upon Jim Crow Rice, although not intended as ill-nature, was so construed, and gave him an opportunity to lampoon her with effect, in what he termed his own lyric style turning all her efforts into ridicule."   Of this passage of arms we can find no record elsewhere.]

INDEX

Aldborough, Countess, her freedom of speech, 64

Anderson, Joseph, squabble of with Madame Vestris, 154; 155; marriage of to Josephine Bartolozzi, 172; bankruptcy of, 215

Appendix, 307

Ayrton, musical director at the King's Theatre, 98; 116

Barnett, John, unjust accusation against, 138

Bartolozzi, Francisco, family history of, 27; 28

Bartolozzi, Gaetano, career of, 28

Bartolozzi, Josephine, description of, 82; debut of at Covent Garden, 28; marriage of, 172

Bartolozzi, Lucia Elizabetta (see Madame Vestris)

Benelli, King's Theatre, manager of, 91

Best, Capt., association of with Madame Vestris, 61; fatal duel of with Lord Camelford, 31; name of coupled with Josephine Bartolozzi, 82; 83; "Peagreen" Hayne a friend of, 106

Beverley, wonderful scene painting of, 297

Billington, Mrs., 23

Bishop, H. R., 91; 129

Boucicault, Dion, the *London Assurance* of, 263

Braham, John, popularity of, 42; ornamental singing of condemned, 49; singing of described, 50; acting of in *Oberon*, 126

Buckstone, acting of in *Box and Cox*, 295

Bunn, Alfred, incompetent as a manager, 207

Camporese, Madame, 65; a passage of arms of, with Madame Ronzi di Begnis, 85

Cargill, Mrs., as Captain Macheath, 52

Catalini, Madame, 23; first singer to receive a "call," 36; rapacity of, 63

Charlotte of Wales, Princess, 42

Chester, Miss, beauty of, 88; appointed reader to George IV, 89

Chorley, H. F., his opinion of Madame Vestris's singing, 23

Colbran, Madame, prima donna at the King's Theatre, 92

Colman, George, alleged to be "Griffinhoofe," 25; joke against, 114

Coveney, Harriet, as Macheath, 149

Dance, Charles, collaboration of with Planché, 167

Drury Lane Theatre and the "Theatre Royal Elliston," 45; Elliston's pageant of the *Coronation*, 67; an unruly audience at, 68

Duncombe, T. S., a man of fashion, 75; fracas of with Westmacott, 183; generosity of, 185

Ebers, relations of with Taylor, 20; engages Madame Vestris, 65; troubles over operatic stars, 86; transfers the King's Theatre to Benelli, 90; opens with opera at the Haymarket Theatre, 110

Elliston, Robert, engages Madame Vestris, 48; his style of advertising, 58; personates George IV in the *Coronation*, 67; produces *Giovanni in Ireland* at Dublin, 69

311